GOVERNED THROUGH CHOICE

I0112764

Governed through Choice

*Autonomy, Technology, and the
Politics of Reproduction*

Jennifer M. Denbow

NEW YORK UNIVERSITY PRESS

New York and London

NEW YORK UNIVERSITY PRESS
New York and London
www.nyupress.org

© 2015 by New York University
All rights reserved

References to Internet websites (URLs) were accurate at the time of writing. Neither the author nor New York University Press is responsible for URLs that may have expired or changed since the manuscript was prepared.

Library of Congress Cataloging-in-Publication Data
Denbow, Jennifer M., author.
Governed through choice : autonomy, technology, and the politics of reproduction / Jennifer M. Denbow.
pages cm   Includes bibliographical references and index.
ISBN 978-1-4798-2883-8 (cl : alk. paper) — ISBN 978-1-4798-4391-6 (pb : alk. paper)
1. Reproductive rights—United States. 2. Human reproduction—Law and legislation—United States. 3. Women—Legal status, laws, etc.—United States. I. Title.
KF3760.D46   2015
342.7308'5—dc23   2015005769

New York University Press books are printed on acid-free paper, and their binding materials are chosen for strength and durability. We strive to use environmentally responsible suppliers and materials to the greatest extent possible in publishing our books.

Manufactured in the United States of America

10 9 8 7 6 5 4 3 2 1

Also available as an ebook

CONTENTS

ACKNOWLEDGMENTS

Many people supported the writing of this book. My mentors at the University of California, Berkeley—Wendy Brown, Chris Kutz, Kristin Luker, and Sarah Song—deserve credit for motivating me early on to think more deeply and clearly. Each in her or his own way pushed me to go further, challenged me at crucial junctures, and supported the project. I am indebted to them for their guidance and support.

Fellow graduate students provided needed community and feedback at various stages. I'd like to thank especially Alexander Rosas and Justin Reinheimer for knowing when to talk academics and when not to. The project also benefitted from Barrie Thorne's spirited and generous workshop in the Department of Gender and Women's Studies. Members of the "accountability club" that grew out of that workshop—Katie Hasson, Hedda Høgåsen-Hallesby, Anastasia Kayiatos, and Preetha Mani—kept my thinking fresh and showed me the potential of intellectual community at a pivotal moment.

I'm also grateful to my law school friends—Carol Garvan, Madeline Howard, Kathryn Miller, Teresa Panepinto, Harini Raghupathi, Misti Schmidt, Sarah Spiegel, and Scott Zimmerman—who tolerated my theoretical perspective, helped me to understand the law more deeply, and always kept my focus on justice. In addition, the community of the *Berkeley Journal of Gender, Law and Justice* taught me a lot about feminist practice and the importance of intersectional analysis. Also, thanks to honorary Boaltie Rebecca Braun, who makes sure I never lose sight of the women whose lives and health are at stake in the passage of the laws I study. I'd also like to thank an anonymous friend for prompting me to write about sterilization and always keeping my thinking critical.

The project was transformed into a book at the University of New England, where my new colleagues read parts of the manuscript and helped me compose a proposal. I would like to thank Ali Ahmida, Rob Alegre, Michael Burman, Brian Duff, Amanda Hare, Alicia Peters, and

Julie Peterson for their help in this regard. I would also like to thank my students for their curiosity and engagement and for reminding me why I do what I do. The book has also benefitted from feedback at a number of conferences and from the careful attention of anonymous reviewers. I appreciate all of their work and commentary. I would like to thank Claire Rasmussen for her insightful and thorough reading of the entire manuscript.

In addition, a number of friends and family members have supported the writing of this book in myriad ways. Throughout I've benefitted from the love and generosity of people who believed in me and the project. Apart from those already mentioned, I thank Kallista Bley, Nick Lally, Molly McIntyre, and Nisha Swinton. My parents and siblings— Hannah, Carl, Bill, and Heather Denbow—encouraged me from a young age to think deeply and from different perspectives. Although they may not all like where it has led, each of them has been key to my intellectual growth, and I thank them for always believing in me. Michael Huggins deserves special recognition for his really careful reading of that one page, and for everything else.

***

Portions of this book have been previously published in modified form. Parts of chapters 1 and 2 were published as "Reproductive Autonomy, Counter-Conduct, and the Juridical," *Constellations: An International Journal of Critical and Democratic Theory* 21, no. 3 (2014). A shortened and modified version of chapter 4 was published as "Sterilization as Cyborg Performance: Reproductive Freedom and the Regulation of Sterilization," *Frontiers: A Journal of Women's Studies* 35, no. 1 (2014).

Introduction

The Possibility of Reproductive Autonomy

At the very moment when long-standing norms regarding gender, sexuality, and reproduction seem to be breaking down, women in the United States are facing increasingly severe restrictions on and scrutiny of their reproductive decisions. In state after state, legislatures are passing ever more restrictive requirements on abortion and more generally curbing access to reproductive health services. In 2011, states enacted an unprecedented 92 provisions restricting abortions, which overwhelmingly surpassed the previous record of 34 in 2005. From 2011 through 2013, states adopted a total of 205 restrictions. In the previous decade (2001–2010), states passed a total of only 189 restrictions.[1] One recent trend is to require women to undergo ultrasounds and listen to the fetal heartbeat before an abortion. Women also experience heavy surveillance of their decisions in the context of sterilization access. Physicians often turn away childfree women who seek sterilization and question such women's ability to make reasonable decisions about their futures. At the same time, states have subjected many women in prisons to sterilization procedures without full information or consent.

State actors often appeal to women's autonomy and rights to justify these restrictive laws and practices, even though the desire to control women's reproduction seems to motivate them. The ultrasound mandates, for example, purport to provide women with relevant information about abortion and thereby enable informed consent and personal autonomy. However, these mandates also increase surveillance of women and require the use of their bodies to garner the information that will supposedly encourage a more autonomous decision.

One way of understanding recent restrictions is to claim that they disingenuously employ concepts like autonomy and rights in a relatively straightforward effort to control women's decisions and bodies. I commonly receive this reaction when I discuss recent laws and explain their rhetoric. When I mention, for example, the names of laws like Texas's Woman's Right to Know Act, which includes a pre-abortion ultrasound mandate, people are usually dismissive of the legislative language and skeptical of its significance. They see such names simply as part of a trend to give laws titles that express the opposite of their intended effect. Dismissing the significance of language implies that the way these laws are framed and the logic behind them are not all that important to consider. They are simply and clearly attempts to restrict women's rights and intervene in their decision making. Yet if we assume that language is merely being manipulated, the underlying logic and arguments go unexamined, resulting in impoverished assessments of and reactions to reproductive rights discourse.

As I argue in this book, another way of thinking about the framing of recent reproductive restrictions is to see them as employing an understanding of autonomy that has a long and rich tradition. Understanding this helps us understand both the appeal and implications of recent interventions in women's reproduction. Examining how ideas like autonomy are employed in recent proposals and laws reveals that these restrictions resonate with the tradition of understanding autonomy as *proper* self-governance. In other words, the capacity for autonomy has often been understood in terms of the ability to reflect on one's situation and make rational decisions.[2] For Immanuel Kant, for example, autonomy involved analytically separating oneself from one's desires and impulses in order to legislate rationally for oneself. Such a rational being is free of external determinants of his or her actions and engages in self-reflection to ascertain the rational law. Autonomy involves submitting oneself to this law. While Kant was primarily concerned with moral autonomy, this view has been translated politically to mean that only those who are rational and have the capacity for autonomy are to be granted the right to autonomy. When this idea is used to evaluate individuals, what constitutes rationality tends to depend on prevailing norms and power relations. That is, the rational decision is that which conforms to prevailing norms and consolidates power relations. As Claire Rasmussen demonstrates in her careful study of how autonomy operates in various contemporary contexts, "the way that our perception of autonomy, who or what constitutes autonomy, is profoundly shaped by context-specific power relationships" (2011, xv).

Employed in contemporary notions of reproductive rights, autonomy as proper or rational self-governance serves a crucial function: it allows for the appearance of respect for women's rights and self-determination, while justifying increased surveillance and management of women's bodies and reproductive decisions. Crucially, race, class, and ability all affect how an individual's conduct is managed. Thus, while the use of ideas like autonomy, choice, and empowerment in recent reproductive regulations seemingly calls on a feminist tradition, those concepts are stripped of their transformative and critical potential. Instead, since autonomy is understood as proper self-governance, existing norms are reinforced.

This phenomenon is part of the rise of, in Rosalind Gill's words, a postfeminist sensibility "in which notions of autonomy, choice and self-improvement sit side-by-side with surveillance, discipline and the vilification of those who make the 'wrong' 'choices'" (2008, 442). As I argue, a particular understanding of autonomy has been crucial to how this sensibility has operated in reproductive law and politics. I argue that the logic behind many current reproductive policies rests on the idea that making certain choices demonstrates that one is not deciding rationally. Choosing to have an abortion, choosing to have children if you are on welfare, or choosing to get sterilized if you are young, middle-class, and female are all decisions that others, especially experts, often deem irrational and view as indicative of a failure to self-manage properly. Ultrasound mandates, for example, rest on the notion that women who choose to abort cannot be acting autonomously because abortion is never a proper choice. As such, intervention in a woman's decision making can actually promote autonomy.

This book, then, traces the simultaneous rise of the discourse of autonomy and surveillance in recent reproductive regulation. This rise has resulted in increased paternalism. This book's focus on how autonomy as *proper* self-governance operates in reproductive law and politics enables us to understand more fully the kind of paternalism at work. The paternalism invoked here is presented as a way to promote autonomy by encouraging or mandating a certain decision. Furthermore, as the book

argues, the idea that women have choice and control over their reproductive capacity enables others, such as the state and experts, to judge
whether women are making proper or improper reproductive decisions.
As Michel Foucault argued in his writing and lectures on governmentality, we can be governed through choice. The possibility of acting in a
variety of ways creates the conditions for power, and power presupposes
the subject who is free. I show how governmentality operates in contemporary reproductive law and politics in conjunction with autonomy
and surveillance.

This book makes three main arguments. The first argument is that recent reproductive regulations often present the capacity for autonomy in
terms of proper self-governance or self-management. This book examines the tradition of autonomy as proper self-governance and explores
how power dynamics affect judicial and social understandings of what
constitutes reproductive autonomy. As I argue with regard to recent legal
treatments of reproduction—including the jurisprudence of abortion,
ultrasound mandates, and the regulation of sterilization—women are
often thought of as improperly self-governing. This judgment then justifies the intervention of medical experts and the state. The way autonomy
is used in reproductive discourse in many ways reflects the limitations
of understanding autonomy as proper self-governance, which can be
traced to Rousseau's idea that freedom inheres in "obedience to a law
one prescribes to oneself" (1968, 65).

This book's second primary argument is that developments in reproductive technology have altered how reproductive autonomy is
conceived and thus how reproduction is regulated. For example, as the
ultrasound mandates show, states are using sonograms to surveil women
in new ways and to impose the state's understanding of pregnancy on
them. Furthermore, changes in reproductive technology have increased
individuals' ability to control and manage their reproduction, and thus
would seem to promote self-governance. However, these changes have
also led to increased scrutiny of decisions regarding procreation. Because such decisions are now framed and presumed to be "choices," it
is possible to criticize individuals for not making "better" or "more rational" choices. In this way, and as Foucault explained with the concept
of governmentality, we can be governed through choice and not simply
emancipated by it.

Third, this book argues that there is another understanding of autonomy that, if taken up in the context of reproductive regulations, would promote resistance to discriminatory and oppressive norms. Although the notion of autonomy is often employed in ways that further marginalize the marginalized, there is an alternative tradition of understanding autonomy in terms of critique and transformation. This tradition offers a promising perspective on reproduction and is found to varying degrees in the work of Foucault, Judith Butler, and John Stuart Mill. Furthermore, some of the very technologies that the state and medical experts often force on women and that enable increased scrutiny of reproductive decisions can also be used as practices of critique and transformation. I argue that childfree and sterilized women, for example, present a radical challenge to understandings of the female body and identity. Voluntary female sterilization can be understood as an autonomous practice that prompts cultural critique and transformation.

In making these arguments, the book makes contributions to the study of both autonomy and reproduction. It also uncovers how ideas like autonomy and motherhood function in American law and politics today. By examining reproductive politics through the lens of autonomy, I illuminate important aspects of how autonomy is often understood and implemented as well as how reproduction is currently regulated. The book thus provides critical feminist insights into the function of reproductive restrictions in the contemporary United States. It carefully examines the legal status of several reproductive practices. In providing an analysis of how autonomy is employed in current reproductive politics, as well as an account of a more transformative version of autonomy, the book also serves as a call to political theorists to consider the critical tradition of autonomy.

***

Many feminists and critical theorists have critiqued the notion of autonomy, which would suggest that autonomy should be abandoned for emancipatory projects, especially feminist ones. However, the other tradition of autonomy in which it is understood in terms of critique and transformation may be useful for feminist efforts for reproductive justice. Both Amy Allen (2008) and Rasmussen (2011) have explored this tradition of autonomy as transformation (or, in Rasmussen's terms, creativity) and uncovered it in the work of Foucault. This understanding of autonomy does not assume that the self is pre-political. Instead, in many of its forms, it relies on a notion of the self as constituted by social forces. Autonomy in this tradition involves reflecting on and calling into question the very norms and power relations that form us. Questioning and pushing back against such norms creates more possibilities for self-creation. This book explores both the tradition of autonomy as proper self-governance or self-management and the view of autonomy as critique and transformation. I argue both that autonomy as self-management is used in reproductive legal discourse to reinforce existing power relations and that emphasizing autonomy as transformation in current reproductive politics could challenge existing norms and relations of power.

Western political theory has a long tradition of viewing women as unable to govern themselves properly. In much of that tradition, women have been ignored in theories of the origin of the state. As a result, women's situation outside the political and inside the private, familial realm has been naturalized (Okin 1989). Many political theorists assumed that women lack the requisite natural autonomy to participate in the process of instituting a legitimate state. As Carole Pateman has argued, since freedom in political society originates with the social contract and because women have been excluded from participation in that social contract, women are decidedly unfree in this tradition. Moreover, by being left out of the process and the resulting social contract, women are subordinated to the men who institute the political society (1988). This analysis calls attention to the traditional binding of autonomy to the masculine: political theory has historically produced the autonomous individual as male. Correspondingly, this tradition understands women as lacking self-governance. Women thereby seem to require the rule of men to ensure their proper governance.

The traditional intertwining of autonomy and masculinity has led many feminists not only to critique the concept but also to turn away from it as a useful or emancipatory notion for feminist politics. Such critics argue that Western liberal theorists most often employ a view of autonomy that conceptualizes persons as individuals first. Any view of people as participants in a community or as connected to one another is secondary such that what separates us and what makes us autonomous are epistemologically prior to what connects us.[3] Robin West, for example, argues that autonomy relies on an atomistic view of the self that ignores the perspectives of women whose experiences often demonstrate the inherent interconnectedness of individuals (1988). West points in particular to some women's intimate bodily connections with fetuses to argue that a philosophy that views individuals as inherently separate does not speak to women's experiences or even to a range of men's experiences. After all, both men and women are born and often die in a state of dependence on others. An atomistic view of the self results in a derogation of relations of dependency and a masking of social relations. Alison Jaggar says of liberalism generally that it assumes that "individuals could exist outside a social context" (1988, 29). The worry is that this atomistic conceptualization of individuals leads to an assumption that self-sufficiency and independence are bound up with or even constitutive of autonomy in a way that denies social context and relations. Furthermore, since independence connotes maleness, whiteness, affluence, and able-bodiedness, we should be wary of invocations of an autonomy linked with independence.[4]

This strand of feminist thinking signals an academic turn away from the concept of autonomy, which the turn to poststructuralist thought has also fueled. According to common critiques of autonomy emanating from poststructuralism, which emphasizes the deep political and social construction of the subject, autonomy relies on a strict division between self and society. On this view, the autonomous self appears to be self-constituting and outside politics. Butler, for example, often eschews the concept of autonomy and instead employs the notion of agency. She describes agency as "directly counter to any notion of a voluntarist subject who exists quite apart from the regulatory norms which she/he opposes" (1993, 15). Butler's characterization of autonomy comports with Mark Bevir's understandings of autonomy and agency. Bevir defines autonomous subjects as those who "would be able, at least in principle, to have experiences, to reason, to adopt beliefs, and to act, outside all social contexts" (1999, 67). Agents are distinct from autonomous subjects in that they "exist only in specific social contexts, but these contexts never determine how they try to construct themselves" (67). In contrast, Carisa Showden acknowledges that autonomy can account for social relations and context, but nonetheless prefers agency. She argues that "agency is in fact distinct from and broader than autonomy" in that "[a]gency is autonomy plus options" (2011, 1). Showden, then, views autonomy as a less useful tool than agency for analyzing and transforming a social context that limits options.[5] Although the theorists surveyed here have varying understandings of autonomy and agency, they provide examples of the turn toward agency in some feminist thought. Perceived problems with the notion of autonomy, including its tendency toward hyper-individualism and obfuscation of social context, have prompted this turn.

I follow another set of feminist theorists who tend to see accounts of agency as limited in their usefulness. Lois McNay, for example, argues that agency is often conceptualized in a negative way that fails to account for the "subject's capability to deal with difference or otherness in terms other than exclusion or denial" (2000, 3). She argues further that agency often assumes the "essential passivity of the subject" (3). She calls for turning toward accounts of agency that theorize and allow room for creativity and autonomous action.[6] Although McNay prefers to reconceptualize agency, many feminist thinkers have sought to save and resignify autonomy rather than focus on agency in part because of the potential limitations of agency.[7] One prominent trend is to theorize autonomy in a relational way in order to respond to the critique that autonomy invokes an independent and atomistic individual (Nedelsky 1989, 2011; Mackenzie and Stoljar 2000; Friedman 2003; Ben-Ishai 2012). This work on relational autonomy contends that autonomy is fostered and developed in a social context. Jennifer Nedelsky, for example, argues that autonomy involves "finding our own law," where that law is "shaped by the society in which one lives and the relationships that are a part of one's life" (1989, 10).

The conceptualization of autonomy offered in this book both builds on and is distinct from work on relational autonomy. Like these theorists, I retain autonomy, and I agree with their assessment that autonomy is necessarily developed and expressed in a social context. However, in contrast to the trends in relational autonomy theory, I draw on poststructural thinking in providing an account of autonomy as critique and transformation. In doing so, the account I provide is more focused on political and social transformation than most relational accounts, which tend to focus on the development of individual capacities.

My preference for autonomy does not constitute a complete rejection of the concept of agency. In fact, as I conceptualize it, autonomy as critique and transformation incorporates important aspects of Butler's theorization of agency. Nonetheless, there are good reasons to prefer autonomy to agency. One reason is that agency is often understood broadly such that a wide range of activities are agentic. Agency is often employed precisely in order to show that women are not merely passive victims even when mired in oppressive circumstances. For example, according to how the concept is commonly understood, a woman who goes limp during a beating by her intimate partner in order to mitigate her injuries is exercising agency.[8] While it is important to bring attention to this kind of exercise of agency, this example illustrates that agency is not necessarily transformative or concerned with critiques of social forces.

Another reason I prefer autonomy is that, while its individualistic aspect can indeed operate in a negative way and has been rightly critiqued, it is precisely the focus on the individual in autonomy that is also important to its liberatory potential. Autonomy in its transformative register emphasizes the political and social importance of individual action. As I argue in chapter 1, in the tradition of autonomy as critique and transformation, the individual is valued and stressed precisely because of the potentially dangerous effects of custom and dominant norms. I retain autonomy rather than turn toward agency largely because autonomy brings more attention to the individual and the positive potential of individual conduct and eccentricity. In bringing more attention to the individual *in society*, autonomy can actually bring awareness to the construction of the self, as well as to the social context in which the individual resides.

Retaining the concept of autonomy rather than turning to a different concept also makes it easier to draw on the anti-paternalistic aspect of earlier autonomy theory. As Dorothy Roberts says in defense of liberty, it "stresses the value of self-definition, and it protects against the totalitarian abuses of government power" (1998, 302). Yet, as commonly employed, autonomy simultaneously operates in a paternalistic and anti-paternalistic way: it justifies both protection from external interference for those who "properly" self-regulate and interference for those who would make "improper" decisions. The autonomy as transformation tradition looks to those anti-paternalistic aspects of earlier autonomy theories while eschewing the exclusionary function that often accompanies them. Employing the notion of autonomy allows me to make recourse to the aspects of the concept that have given it enduring appeal. I simultaneously draw attention to and question its traditional presuppositions and implications.

Moreover, I am not, strictly speaking, offering a *reconceptualization* of autonomy. Rather, I show that autonomy as critique and transformation itself has a substantial heritage that is worth engaging. I show, for example, that both Foucault and Butler offer such readings of autonomy. While the concept of autonomy that I defend is clearly related to the concepts of liberty and freedom, I choose to employ and focus on the concept of autonomy in part because a number of thinkers upon whom I draw use this term. I argue that even Butler at times employs the notion of autonomy in a positive manner. Mill, however, favors the notion of liberty. In my discussion of Mill I explain why his understanding of liberty can also be understood as a conceptualization of autonomy. Nonetheless, his use of liberty supports the point that there is conceptual overlap between liberty and autonomy. Despite this, I focus on autonomy, not just because it is employed by a number of thinkers on which I draw, but also because its concern with self-governance can be easily used to draw attention to the context in which the self exists.[9]

***

One of the book's central theoretical arguments is that bringing post-structuralist thinking on the social production of the self to bear on the concept of autonomy necessitates thinking of it in terms of critique and transformation. On this reading, the notion of autonomy becomes about the possibility of what Foucault calls counter-conduct and what Mill calls eccentricity. Through personal actions that challenge dominant, normal ways of thinking, being, and knowing, one creates new possibilities for action for oneself and others. The autonomy as proper self-governance tradition sees autonomy as inhering primarily in a personal realm that should be devoid of improper interference. The alternative version of autonomy recognizes that the personal and political are intertwined. Because the self is constructed and embedded in social relations, society shapes the self at the same time that individual actions shift force relations that construct the self. Autonomy thus involves the shifting of force relations that themselves constitute the subject. To take part in the creation of alternative cultural conceptions and new ways of life is at once an expression of autonomy and a political act that may prompt reflection and affect the possibilities for others' conduct.

In this way, this version of autonomy transcends the traditional division between public and private. Individual conduct should be protected, but not because it is conceived of as private. Rather, individual conduct is never divorced from the public and political contexts in which it operates. In other words, individual "private" decisions have political significance, but that does not mean that such decisions should be understood as "public" in a way that would open actors up to coercive paternalism. This understanding of autonomy also complicates the relation between personal and political autonomy. Personal autonomy is thought of as one's capacity to govern oneself, whereas political autonomy often refers to the use of autonomy to ground and provide limits on political institutions. Full political standing often rests on one's ability to be autonomous. While the autonomy as proper self-governance tradition, as I will argue, often slips from the personal to the political so that those who are not viewed as personally autonomous are denied full political subjectivity, the critical tradition is not concerned with the ascription of autonomy. Moreover, personal autonomy is political in the critical autonomy tradition in that autonomous acts have ramifications for shared public life.

Theorizing autonomy in a way that accounts for the socially constitutive character of individuals and desires dislodges autonomy from an atomistic or pre-social account of the self. It is precisely this ability for concepts like autonomy—as Butler says in general of "the key terms of modernity"—"to acquire non-ordinary meanings [that] constitutes their continuing political promise" (1997, 145). The use of autonomy in this context creates dissonance precisely because it is often presumed that autonomy is linked with ideas of authenticity and independence of the self. As I argue in chapter 1, this dissonance means that the very reworking of the term can both disturb its common associations and be a way toward "configur[ing] a different future" (Butler 1997, 160). Since the state has often regulated women's reproduction for the sake of the "social good" and in ways that reinforce discriminatory norms, configuring a different future in which autonomy as transformation is emphasized is especially important in the context of reproductive regulation. An emphasis on self-governance as critique and transformation may be a means toward a different configuration of gender and reproduction.

On this view of autonomy as critique and transformation, regulatory apparatuses that constitute some individuals as inappropriate or unfit reproducers restrict autonomy, although actions that challenge the ascription of unfit reproducer can prompt critical reflection and transformation. Additionally, cultural, legal, and medical understandings that align female identity with motherhood play a role in producing and reinforcing ideas about the female body and the naturalness and inevitability of procreation. The range of acceptable bodily configurations, as well as reproductive behaviors and desires, is thus delimited. Opening up new cultural understandings of gender and reproduction is important for reproductive autonomy when it is understood in terms of transformation. On the view of autonomy as proper self-governance, the creation of cultural forms is not a concern for autonomy. Instead, acting in nonnormative ways may justify paternalistic intervention. Although autonomy is often understood in this narrow sense of control of oneself, on the interpretation of autonomy as critique and transformation, autonomy is bound to the shifting of force relations.

As this book argues, transgression of cultural norms is an important way of constructing alternative cultural forms. Moreover, transgression is possible not only at the level of discourse, but also at the level of materiality, especially to the extent that the female body is conflated with the maternal body. In the context of reproduction, bodily mutability often happens at the hands of technology. Technological transformations of the body, such as the cutting of the fallopian tubes, can themselves be important sites for the transgression of reproductive norms. This is the case even though reproductive technology is frequently used in a way that reinforces existing power relations, such as when physicians in prisons perform sterilizations on women who have not given their consent. Thus, the context in which technologies are used and how they are understood is of paramount importance in evaluating them. In joining an engagement in theoretical debates and arguments about autonomy with a critical examination of female reproductive autonomy, this book makes a much-needed intervention into contemporary reproductive politics in the United States. Focusing on autonomy as transformation can help anchor a feminist approach to the politics and law of reproduction and provide some grounds for the evaluation of legal and political interventions.

This book offers a critique of current understandings of autonomy in reproductive rights and regulations as well as an alternative understanding of autonomy that may have promise for critical reproductive politics. The critical autonomy tradition I identify, however, cannot be molded strictly into a law reform strategy, nor does it have an easily identified basis in existing legal doctrine. I do offer some modest recommendations regarding promising legal approaches. I argue that law and legal frameworks could be reoriented such that they stop enforcing the autonomy as proper self-governance tradition and thus open up room for nonnormative practices. However, the promise of autonomy as critique and transformation cannot be subsumed into a law reform strategy, which is one reason why this book is primarily focused on the discourse of autonomy and not rights. As a number of critical legal scholars have shown, an overemphasis on rights and law reform often limits and undermines critical political projects.[10] As Dean Spade explains, "rights mediate emergent social groups, and rights claims often serve as the resistance framework of such groups, yet declarations of universal rights often actually mask and perpetuate the structured conditions of harm and disparity faced by those groups" (2011, 30).

***

This book considers how autonomy operates in American reproductive law and also looks at how changes in reproductive technology have altered how the female subject, female physiology, and reproductive autonomy are conceived. The book examines the ways technologies are used to promote or hinder autonomy, as well as the ways they redefine what it means to exercise autonomy. While this book takes up the specific issues of abortion, ultrasound, and sterilization, everything from the birth control pill to fetal testing to in vitro fertilization has changed how procreation is now approached.[11] Consequently, one important aspect of the following exploration is a consideration of how technoscientific changes have affected reproduction and reproductive law in the contemporary United States.

Current technology is both continuous with and distinct from earlier birth control methods. A wide variety of birth control methods, ranging from sterilization to intrauterine devices, were used in the preindustrial world. Historical evidence demonstrates that birth control practices were widespread and varied, even dating back to antiquity (Gordon 2007). Linda Gordon argues that, historically, "the burden of involuntary child-bearing was not the result of *lack* of technology but of the *suppression* of technology" (2007, 21). Nevertheless, contemporary developments are distinct in that they have increased the effectiveness and safety of birth control. Sexually active heterosexual women can now have the expectation that childbirth be almost completely voluntary. Gordon notes that this expectation "was itself produced by its historic possibility. Lacking that kind of effective contraception, women in preindustrial societies did not form such high expectations" (2007, 14).

Technology, therefore, has rendered procreation a voluntary choice in a way that has profound implications for how reproductive outcomes are evaluated. For example, technology informs the discourse of "responsible" procreation, which plays an important role in contemporary reproductive politics and is explored throughout this book. Using the idea of governmentality, I argue that judgments regarding who is and is not making proper reproductive decisions converge with the notion of autonomy as proper self-management to justify interference in procreative decisions that experts deem to result from poor or irrational decision making. Thus, this book examines the ways heightened concerns about and regulation of reproductive decisions have coincided with the increased ability to manage reproduction.

Although technology has opened up possibilities for bodily transformation, the challenge, as Donna Haraway notes, is to understand the technological, especially in its union with the biological, as a potential source of both dominations and fruitful disruptions. In the history of reproductive technology and its regulation, both potentials have been realized. For example, state actors continue to coerce women in prisons, who are disproportionately women of color, into sterilization, while experts often deny sterilization to women they consider fit for reproduction and who do not have children. However, as I argue in chapter 4, voluntary sterilization may usefully disrupt the common link between woman and mother. One of my goals in this book is to keep the possibilities of both domination and emancipation in view as I consider how attention to autonomy as critique and transformation might be able to counter domination and provide potent grounds for challenging discriminatory practices.

Although reproduction has long been a site in which the state (as well as medical and social science experts) has intervened to control bodies and the population, the intensity and character of current reproductive regulations suggest that they are distinctive. One way of understanding the severity of current restrictions on reproductive rights and health services is to view them as reactions to broad transformations in the gender system. Feminism and queer activism have played a crucial role in transforming how gender, sex, and sexuality are socially understood. The increased visibility of lesbian, gay, bisexual, trans, intersex, and gender-queer individuals challenges normative understandings of gender and sexuality. Sexual intercourse has become increasingly decoupled from reproduction. The use of technology to facilitate the reproduction of single cisgender[12] women, gay and lesbian couples, and the infertile may call into question the presumed "naturalness" of reproduction. Thomas Beatie, a transgender man who was pregnant in 2008, became one of the starkest and most visible examples of recent cultural changes regarding gender and reproduction (Halberstam 2012, 31–33).

Anxiety about these transformations in social understandings and practices of gender, sexuality, and reproduction, which extend beyond changes in the relationship between heterosexual sex and procreation, may be fueling the recent rise in reproductive restrictions. However, given this book's focus on the avoidance of procreation through abortion and sterilization, it is primarily concerned with the construction and regulation of the bodies of women who engage in heterosexual sex. Such sex is generally what necessitates the interventions in question. However, the regulation of abortion and sterilization intimately affects people other than just cisgender women. Although heterosexuality is often taken for granted in discussions of abortion and sterilization, trans men and genderqueers access reproductive health services like abortion and contraception and face serious stigma and obstacles in doing so. Throughout the book, I maintain awareness of this reality while grappling with the rationales behind legal regulations, which often reflect and reinforce normative understandings of cisgender women.

***

This book focuses on technologies that foreclose reproduction and considers their potential to serve as forms of resistance. While a similar dynamic of governance through choice may mark many assisted reproductive technologies like surrogacy and in vitro fertilization, this book's emphasis on nonreproductive practices distinguishes this project and fills a gap in existing scholarship on technology and reproduction. Paying attention to nonreproductive technologies is important in part because technologies that enable reproduction often fit more easily within the paradigm of "natural" reproduction. In contrast to much of the existing literature on technology and reproduction,[13] this book brings attention to technology and nonmotherhood. This focus on nonreproductive technologies allows for a more radical questioning of the naturalness of maternity and shows how technology can disrupt ideas of maternal essence and nature. Procreative technologies are often used in contexts in which the nonreproductive female body is presented as dysfunctional. These technologies, then, tend to reinforce the idea of women's inherent maternal nature. A premise of this book is that we ought to question the identification of woman with mother. Moreover, because this identification is bound up with heteronormativity, calling into question that identity constitutes an important queer project.

Despite this book's focus on practices primarily used by heterosexual women to disrupt or disable the reproductive function, it builds on and contributes to scholarship in queer theory regarding reproductive norms, futurity, and citizenship. Lee Edelman analyzes how the queer, as a figure of sterile narcissism, stands against the politics of reproductive futurism. Reproductive futurity refers to the inability to conceive of politics without a notion of the future brought about through reproduction and symbolized by the figure of the Child. By "queer," Edelman means all those who are "stigmatized for failing to comply with heteronormative mandates" (2004, 17) such that we can understand nonreproductive female bodies as queer. In fact, Edelman links abortion politics to the association of the queer with death and the lack of a future. He asks, "Who *would*, after all, come out *for* abortion or stand *against* reproduction, *against* futurity, and so against *life*?" (2004, 16). This book considers what it means for women to refuse reproduction, and thus stand against one of the mandates of heteronormativity.

Noting the importance of futurity and reproduction to politics allows for a better understanding of the current intensity of debates over reproduction. As Lauren Berlant writes in *The Queen of America Goes to Washington City*, intimate issues such as "pornography, abortion, sexuality, and reproduction; marriage, personal morality, and family values" have become "key to debates about what 'America' stands for, and are deemed vital to defining how citizens should act" (1997, 1). Berlant refers to this new domain of politics as the "intimate public sphere," in which the survival of the nation is thought to depend on "personal acts and identities performed in the intimate domains of the quotidian" (4). This public intimacy is especially invested in reproduction. As Edelman explains, that which seemingly stands against reproduction appears as a danger to the social order.[14]

While Edelman's work provides a helpful context for understanding the intensity of debates over reproduction, he leaves underexplored the ways race and class complicate the expectations to conform to reproductive norms. This book responds to that lack by examining the complexities of the way reproductive futurism, although functioning as a pervasive political ideal, is also consistently denied to those who are disenfranchised. Some questions with which this book grapples are, What does it mean for those whose reproduction is stigmatized to take a nonprocreative stance? Does it undermine the identification of woman with mother on which the intensive regulation and heightened pressure not to reproduce implicitly rely? Could it be understood as a strategy of resistance, even though the result would seem to conform to a neo-eugenic logic that calls for the nonreproduction of women of color and women in poverty? In investigating these questions, the book combines a critical analysis of reproductive futurity with a hope that a future can be brought about that might escape the pragmatic politics of today that are mired in and thus unwittingly sustain dominant discourses and power relations. This book examines the subversive potential of nonreproductive female bodies and in doing so inquires into how a political future that does not invest female bodies with the compulsion to reproduce and that does not manage the population through the regulation of women's reproduction might be brought about.

Therefore, although this book examines nonprocreative practices, it does look toward the future. I follow José Esteban Muñoz in taking up a kind of queer utopian thinking to move beyond the pragmatic politics of today.[15] Utopian thinking enables envisioning something other than what is. In doing so, it stands against "a version of reality that naturalizes cultural logics such as capitalism and heteronormativity" (Muñoz 2009, 12), as well as the intertwined logics of patriarchy and racial oppression. Rather than focusing on a logic of autonomy that focuses on who has the proper capacity for autonomy for the purpose of ascribing political subjectivity in the present, autonomy as transformation is forward-looking. Autonomy is to be valued for its ability to show what is possible. By protecting individual conduct, especially when that conduct counters dominant norms and power relations, autonomy may prompt critical inquiry and social transformation. Showing what is possible is critical at this moment in which the logics of capitalism, heteronormativity, patriarchy, and racial oppression often seem unassailable.

The version of autonomy that this book advances, then, rests on the idea that, as Roberts puts it, "[t]he right to reproductive autonomy is . . . linked to the goal of racial equality and the broader pursuit of a just society" (1998, 311). In her influential book, *Killing the Black Body*, Roberts shows how the state degrades and manages black women's reproduction. She also shows how a narrow definition of liberty that is disconnected from equality and social context justifies this management. She argues that liberal theory ignores the discriminatory and unequal social context in which people make decisions. By examining the tradition of autonomy as proper self-legislation, this book adds to this critique of how ideas like liberty and autonomy function in reproductive discourse. I show how appealing to the idea of autonomy as proper self-governance justifies paternalistic interference in women's reproductive lives in a society that is ostensibly committed to autonomy. The book also shows how racial, class, and gender hierarchies inform judgments of what constitutes a proper reproductive decision. In addition, I argue that the critical tradition of autonomy can be used to combat those hierarchies and that the tradition assumes the equal intrinsic value of individuals.

***

The book begins in chapter 1 with an investigation of different theoretical understandings of autonomy. Western political thought has often appealed to autonomy in separating rational self-governing agents who should be afforded protection against interference from irrational individuals who require guidance and intervention. Historically, women, slaves, and people of color were viewed as lacking the ability to govern themselves and thus not full rights-bearing political subjects. The first chapter traces the tension created by autonomy's simultaneously liberating and exclusionary potential, as well as the related puzzle of how the socially constituted self can be self-governing. This inquiry begins with an examination of the thinking of Rousseau and Kant, whose understandings of autonomy have been foundational to Western political thinking. I argue that each grapples with the effects of outside forces on autonomy and posits an understanding of autonomy as adherence to self-given law. I then briefly consider how these tensions manifest in contemporary philosophical accounts of autonomy. I argue that such accounts tend to downplay the political effects of being deemed nonautonomous.

After a consideration of these accounts of autonomy, the chapter turns to the poststructuralist thinking of Foucault and Butler, which has surprising implications for autonomy. Foucault and Butler argue that power and force relations constitute the subject, but they nonetheless demonstrate the possibility of the subject's agency or autonomy. In fact, as I argue, these thinkers show that the construction of the subject, rather than undermining any possibility for agency, actually serves as the condition of possibility for it. Butler's understanding of the relation between agency and the social constitution of the subject is important for understanding that autonomy and social construction are not necessarily contradictory ideas. The chapter shows that in some of his later work, Foucault articulates an understanding of autonomy as critique and transformation. I also argue that this view of autonomy resonates with the thinking of Mill on the concept of liberty. The chapter concludes with a discussion of why reproductive autonomy should be valued.

Chapter 2 is concerned with how the framing of the right to abortion affects autonomy. In this chapter, I examine legal arguments on the right and left that neglect the larger potential cultural significance of the right to abortion—which would involve the reconstruction of cultural forms—because of different but sometimes parallel understandings of abortion's relation to women and motherhood. I investigate, first, the 2007 U.S. Supreme Court case of *Gonzales v. Carhart*[16]—which upheld the congressional Partial Birth Abortion Ban Act—and the woman-protective argument it advances. That approach to abortion relies on an understanding of women as victims and as essentially maternal such that it reinforces the discursive mother-woman link and undermines efforts to reconstruct cultural conceptions of women and reproduction. Consistent with the tradition of autonomy as proper self-government, the woman-protective antiabortion argument purports to advance women's autonomy by encouraging women to make the proper choice.

After examining *Gonzales v. Carhart*, the chapter argues that the defense of the right to abortion based on an antisubordination interpretation of the Fourteenth Amendment of the U.S. Constitution circumscribes the significance of the right to abortion by premising it on a subordinating social structure. The right is presented merely as a necessary escape hatch. Crucially, both the framework in *Carhart* and the antisubordination approach depoliticize abortion by casting it as an act marked indelibly by injury. In focusing on the demonstration of injury, both legal approaches to abortion leave out important aspects of autonomy.

The chapter then examines how the right to abortion operates differently for different individuals. Using Foucault's notion of governmentality, I argue that the option to abort creates possibilities for governance and changes the way a woman's actions with regard to pregnancy are evaluated. Given that some women's reproduction is devalued and encoded as "irresponsible," this change in moral evaluation could lead to pressure to choose in a "responsible" manner. The chapter concludes with a discussion of an approach to the right to abortion that emphasizes autonomy as critique and transformation. On this account, the right is defended, not just because it protects an individual from interference or domination, but because that protection is crucial in part for the larger political significance that is captured in the Foucaultian notion of counter-conduct.

Chapter 2 thus introduces key developments in abortion jurisprudence that provide a foundation for understanding some of the newest forms of abortion restrictions that are examined in the following chapter. Chapter 3 examines recent state-level informed consent to abortion laws, with a focus on laws that mandate ultrasounds before abortion. In these laws and the legal decisions upholding them, the maternal nature of women is assumed and autonomy is presented in terms of a medicalized and legalized notion of informed consent rather than in a politicized or transformative way. Instead, consistent with the tradition of autonomy as proper self-management, autonomy is presented as a conservative and weak concept. This permits expert and ideologically driven understandings of risk and security to be used to curb autonomy while claiming to enable it. I argue that this legal discourse relies on and reinforces limiting understandings of gender and autonomy.

The chapter begins with an exploration of gender, neoliberalism, and biomedicalization. I argue that neoliberal and postfeminist perspectives, which emphasize the freedom and independence of agents and obscure power relations and social context, are entangled with current debates over reproductive health and services. Feminist ideas of rights and empowerment are thereby perverted and employed to justify calls for individual responsibility and heightened surveillance of women. The chapter argues that in recent reproductive law, neoliberal and postfeminist perspectives converge with the tradition of autonomy as proper self-governance to produce a new understanding of autonomy as risk avoidance. Moreover, the biomedicalization of reproduction, which frames reproductive health as a matter of individual moral responsibility, has facilitated and converged with these frameworks. The frameworks of postfeminism, neoliberalism, and biomedicalization provide context for the examination of recent state-level abortion restrictions and the role of ultrasound within them. I argue that sonograms play a key role in shaping and representing cultural and political understandings of pregnancy and fetuses.

Chapter 3 briefly considers the transformative possibilities of technology, but this discussion is elaborated in chapter 4's examination of the practice of sterilization. Chapter 4 builds on the discussion of the medicalization of reproduction, as well as the co-constitution of technology and politics, both of which are introduced in earlier chapters. Chapter 4 considers the potential destabilizing effects of voluntary sterilization. I offer an analysis of the practice that relies on a combination of Butler's notion of performativity and Haraway's cyborg theory. I consider sterilization as a performance that has the potential to disrupt associations of womanhood with motherhood. Moreover, I argue that the sterilized body might be read as a cyborg figure in which organism and machine are united and intertwined. In this way, the sterilized body subverts not just the idea of women as inevitably maternal, but also widespread binary notions of woman-man, nature-culture, and organism-machine. Relying on cyborg theory, which draws attention to the disruptive potential of contemporary entanglements of organisms and machines, allows for an examination of issues of the body and technology that are often left out of research on nonreproduction. These issues are crucial to consider if, in accordance with a critical view of autonomy, the identification of the female body with reproductive desire is to be challenged. The reading of sterilization offered here leads to an engagement with both the regulative and performative aspects of nonmotherhood, as well as with the materiality of the body. This focus on the body reveals the technological transformation of sterilization as a challenge to the prevailing production of female identity and maternal desire at the level of the body.

In taking up sterilization in chapter 4, this book examines legal regulation, technology, and medical expertise. As opposed to most scholarship on sterilization, the chapter deals with both coerced and voluntary sterilization. The chapter begins with an exploration of the history and contemporary context of voluntary and involuntary female sterilization. It shows how, historically and continuing into the present, women who are deemed unfit are in danger of involuntary sterilization while those who are deemed fit face barriers to accessing sterilization. In both instances, experts presume that the women whose conduct they would regulate lack the ability to govern themselves properly.

This chapter was motivated by a friend who, after some trouble, became one of the childfree and sterilized women who are one of the subjects of chapter 4. Time and again, people—even self-identified feminists and progressives—stood astonished, with mouth agape, at her decision. There seemed to be something deeply troubling to them about a young, white, female, soon-to-be attorney choosing to forgo the possibility of ever bearing children. People assumed that she would regret her decision and that she could not possibly really know her mind about the issue: there was an underlying sense that she was being irrational—that her decision could be understood as nothing else—even as she articulated sound arguments in her defense. As chapter 4 argues, the judgments my childfree friend encountered and the accompanying difficulty of attaining sterilization have much to do with gender and autonomy. Furthermore, the constructions of the ideal reproducer and of the overly fertile, irresponsible reproducer are deeply entwined. The ideal reproducer could not be imagined without its negation. Chapter 4, then, keeps both compulsory and voluntary sterilization in view as it traverses the medical production of the maternal woman, the legal regulation of sterilization, and the sterilized woman as a cyborg figure that might disrupt the very medical production of woman-mother that undergirds sterilization regulation. I argue that sterilization's techno-medical intervention in the body holds the potential to subvert dominant notions of maternal desire and its connection to women's presumed reproductive capacity. In doing so, it could enhance reproductive autonomy understood in terms of critique and transformation.

Chapter 5 revisits many of the themes of the book and investigates their broader import and applicability. This concluding chapter explores how notions of private and public are wielded in reproductive regulations. I argue that women's bodies are sometimes presented as public spaces and are at other times privatized. I show that these representations are connected to how autonomy is understood. Another topic that is explored in chapter 5 is how autonomy as critique and transformation could be used to promote reproductive justice projects. I argue that the alternative tradition of autonomy shows how a context that emphasizes individual self-direction enables resistance to existing relations of power. Chapter 5 also provides an overview of how each of the policy areas I investigate in the book would benefit from an approach anchored in the autonomy as critique and transformation tradition. I combine this overview with a consideration of the limitations and potential of legal change. Finally, the conclusion examines the links between cyborg theory and autonomy in its transformative register. I argue that cyborg theory has important resonances with the alternative autonomy tradition and also that it can push some of its insights further. In particular, cyborg theory draws needed attention to the critical and transformative possibilities of nonreproductive technologies that I show play a crucial role in the management of reproduction.

1

Autonomy

The Self and Society

At its most basic, autonomy means self-governance. The term comes from the Greek words for self (*autos*) and law (*nomos*) and originally referred to a group's governance of itself, but has since been used to refer to the individual's self-governance. In the context of state authority and individual entitlement, the notion of autonomy often plays a somewhat contradictory role in Western thought. Political theorists and state actors sometimes view rights as appropriately afforded to those who have the requisite capacity for autonomy. That is, proper political subjects who are fully endowed with rights are those who already display adequate capacities for self-governance. At the same time, thinkers often view rights as a means toward autonomy. They often appeal to autonomy as individual self-rule as a justification for limited state rule because individuals need to be protected from unjust interference to ensure their continued self-governance. Rights therefore enable us to be autonomous.

Historically, the politically enfranchised tended to view women, slaves, and people of color as lacking the ability to govern themselves and thus not rights-bearing political subjects. This historical constitution of the marginalized relied on and reinforced the aporia between the body and the mind. The socially disenfranchised were strongly associated with their bodies and bodily functions and therefore deemed irrational. The assumption was that they could not put aside their immediate bodily desires and, in the case of women, their reproductive capacity, in order to reflect dispassionately and rationally on circumstances in the way that was necessary for autonomy. The view that autonomy means proper or rational self-governance was thus used to deny the ascription of autonomy to those on the margins and also reflected and reinforced the idea that rationality inhered in the ability to transcend one's body or step outside oneself.

As a consequence, autonomy has tended to function as an exclusionary idea. At times thinkers and state actors appeal to autonomy in order to separate rational self-governing agents from irrational individuals who need guidance and intervention. Unsurprisingly, these determinations tend to reflect existing power relations in society. There is thus a tension between autonomy as a liberating idea and autonomy as an exclusionary idea in much Western political thought. On the one hand, the state should protect autonomous subjects from interference so they may direct their own lives. On the other hand, the state should afford that protection only to those who can properly exercise their reason and govern themselves appropriately. Those who are deemed incapable of proper self-governance are, as a result, often subject to interference or "guidance" in their decision making. In other words, this understanding of autonomy justifies paternalism. Many views of autonomy are thus characterized by the tension between wanting to uphold self-governance as a value and not trusting individuals' ability to govern themselves.

Another tension that arises in much Western thinking on autonomy concerns the related puzzle of how one can be self-governing if society shapes or deeply forms the self. The concern is that socialization—sometimes oppressive socialization—shapes or warps people's values and desires such that they cannot be understood as properly self-governing. Many autonomy theorists understand that society shapes the self and that we cannot uphold autonomy as a central political or moral value without accounting for this. Moreover, when individuals are understood as socially formed, it becomes possible to try to mold individuals into the kinds of people who can properly govern themselves. Rousseau, for example, puts forth a political system that would shape people into appropriate political subjects.

Despite this awareness of socialization in studies of autonomy, scholars have not given serious attention to the implications for autonomy of the Foucaultian notion that, more than being merely socialized, the subject is constructed or produced by force relations and regulatory apparatuses. Poststructuralists who take up this idea tend to dismiss the notion of autonomy as relying on a pre-social self, while autonomy theorists often dismiss poststructuralism and its implications. Nonetheless, Foucaultian thought contains a tradition of autonomy as critique and transformation. On this view, the social production of the self enables, rather than undermines, autonomy. In this tradition, autonomy involves calling into question norms and opening up the possibility for the transformation of cultural formations. Counter-conduct or eccentric action that challenges the customary or natural can help bring about transformative possibilities. Autonomy in this tradition is generally understood more as a practice than an attribute of individuals. Not engaging in the practice would not provide grounds for paternalism or political exclusion.

In this chapter I trace these various tensions—of autonomy operating as both an exclusionary and a liberatory concept, as well as the seeming tension between autonomy and the social formation of the self— within a number of treatments of autonomy. I begin by examining the thinking of Rousseau and Kant, whose understandings of autonomy as proper self-governance have been foundational to Western political thinking. Each grapples with the effects of outside forces on autonomy and posits an understanding of autonomy as adherence to self-given law. Each thinker is in some way concerned with distinguishing those who are properly self-governing from those who are not, and so they illustrate the exclusionary function of autonomy. I then briefly consider some contemporary accounts of autonomy. I argue that those accounts resonate with the proper self-governance tradition and its exclusionary function that would justify paternalism toward those who would make improper decisions.

This survey of different conceptions of autonomy provides a deeper look into the varied ways theorists have understood the concept, whether thinking of it primarily in terms of its personal, moral, or political value. I argue that thinkers in the proper self-governance tradition, while they might view personal autonomy as the grounds or justification for government, do not view protection of autonomy as important for its critical or transformative role. In contrast, in the thinking of Foucault, Butler, and Mill, autonomous conduct always has a political dimension tied to its critical and transformative potential. Furthermore, the discussion of Rousseau and Kant in particular provides some historical context for the later discussion of autonomy in contemporary reproductive politics. I illustrate that each thinker understands autonomy in terms of proper self-governance and views the socially marginalized as nonautonomous. In later chapters I show that the way autonomy manifests in current reproductive law and politics has important resonances with these exclusionary understandings of autonomy.

After a consideration of accounts of autonomy as proper self-governance, the chapter turns to the poststructuralist thinking of Foucault and Butler. Poststructuralism is often thought to have heralded the "death of the subject" because of its sustained critique of the idea that subjectivity is a pre-social, prediscursive phenomenon (Benhabib 1995; Friedman 2003). Far from proclaiming the death of the subject, however, poststructuralism reorients the subject. If there is any death, it is of the understanding of the subject as a pre-social, self-constituting entity who wields power but is not deeply constituted by power. In fact, these thinkers argue that the construction of the subject, rather than undermining any possibility for agency, actually serves as the condition of possibility for it. As Butler puts it, construction "is the necessary scene of agency, the very terms in which agency is articulated and becomes culturally intelligible" (1990, 147). The chapter shows how Foucault thinks about the autonomy of constructed selves in some of his later work in which he articulates an understanding of autonomy as critique and transformation. In addition, I discuss the ways this view of autonomy resonates with the thinking of John Stuart Mill on the concept of liberty. The chapter also examines the approach to knowledge that undergirds the various views of autonomy examined in the chapter.

These two views of autonomy—as proper self-governance and as critique and transformation—orient the coming discussion of reproductive practices and regulation. This chapter thus provides an in-depth theoretical account of these views. In doing so, I show the importance of examining the presuppositions and tensions of thought on autonomy and call on political theorists to examine the alternative tradition of autonomy. Furthermore, the chapter provides theoretical grounding and nuance for subsequent discussions. The first tradition of autonomy is evident in the state's historic and ongoing attempts to interfere with or shape individual decisions so that they comport with social norms and expectations. Applied to reproduction, the second tradition illustrates the importance of engaging in disruptive, nonnormative reproductive practices for the sake of reproductive autonomy. That is only an important consideration if reproductive autonomy should be valued, and so the chapter concludes with a discussion of the importance of reproductive autonomy.

Obedience to the Self-Prescribed Law: Rousseau and Kant

Jean-Jacques Rousseau's thought perhaps illustrates the difficulty and complexity of being autonomous within society better than any other thinker. In the *Second Discourse*, Rousseau observes that it is difficult, if not impossible, to know what is original or natural about man and what is artificial (1964, 92–93). In employing the device of the state of nature, he imagines what man would be like before society and before the state. In doing so, Rousseau highlights the extent of man's plasticity and acknowledges that society has profoundly altered man. In the *Second Discourse*, the vision of freedom that Rousseau offers is opposed to living in society and involves the unfettered ability to do what one pleases. He provides a vision of freedom in which living in society leads to dependence on others and thus an increased susceptibility to others' commands. Therefore, in the *Second Discourse*, Rousseau puts forth an asocial understanding of freedom.

The opposition between freedom and society provides the grounds for Rousseau's discussion of freedom in *The Social Contract*. In that work, he thinks through how one may be free in society, and in doing so attempts to resolve the tension between freedom and society. He sees in his ideal civil society the possibility for a new kind of freedom, which he characterizes as "obedience to a law one prescribes to oneself" (1968, 65). The only way for this form of freedom to be achieved is through the general will, which is the expression of the collective autonomy of the individuals who contract to institute civil society. It is an embodiment of the common or collective will and its content is determined by what is good not for the individual, but for the collective. Rousseau writes that the "general will alone can direct the forces of the state in accordance with that end which the state has been established to achieve—the common good" (1968, 69). The social contract stipulates that everyone must agree to the contract, that legislative rule must be participatory, and that economic inequalities among citizens must be limited. These conditions are meant to ensure that the governing will is general. Since each person plays a role in the legislation of the general will, obedience to it cannot be said to be contrary to autonomy. Acting in accord with the general will ensures obedience to self-legislated law. On the account in *The Social Contract*, then, autonomy involves submitting to self-imposed limitation.

Rousseau's recognition of human plasticity is fundamental to his account of freedom in *The Social Contract* since it suggests the possibility that people could be molded into beings who could be free. Rousseau's civil society depends for its success on the proper constitution of men, because only such men will submit to their own self-legislation. His civil society is set up to produce the sort of men who will ensure its continued existence, although it is unclear how, upon its founding, men will be oriented toward the institutions that sustain society. Rousseau introduces the lawgiver and civil religion to resolve this problem. Through civil religion, the lawgiver, whose office is extragovernmental, takes advantage of the contingent nature of humanity to shape and perhaps manipulate individuals into the sorts of beings who can transcend their individual wills and become "part of a much greater whole" (1968, 84).

In *Emile*, his treatise on education, Rousseau considers the same issue of molding men into the kinds of beings who will be autonomous by submitting to the law they prescribe to themselves. The figure of the tutor who educates Emile is in many respects similar to that of the lawgiver in that his job is to make his pupil's will accord with the general will. According to Rousseau, "good social institutions are those that best know how to denature man, to take his absolute existence from him in order to give him a relative one and transport the I into the common unity" (1979, 40). Once people enter civil society, the task for education is to instill virtue, to mold men into understanding that their individual interests are not at odds with the collectivity's. In making such a man of Emile, the tutor must relentlessly manipulate Emile's environment so that when he fails to act virtuously, he sees the "evils" that result "as coming from the very order of things and not from the vengeance of his governor" (1979, 102).

In Emile's education lies the possibility for the freedom that results from one's needs matching one's strength:

[T]he truly free man wants only what he can do and does what he pleases. . . . [S]ociety has made man weaker not only in taking from him the right he had over his own strength but, above all, in making his strength insufficient for him. That is why his desires are multiplied along with his weakness, and that is what constitutes the weakness of childhood compared to manhood. (1979, 84)

He goes on to say that, by multiplying needs and thus creating dependency, "laws and society have plunged us once more into childhood" (1979, 85). It is this sort of dependence on men that renders humanity unfree. The goal, then, of Emile's education is to free him from this sort of dependence and unfreedom. The only way to do this is to "substitute law for man and to arm the general will with a real strength superior to the action of every particular will," and this can be accomplished only through the shaping of virtuous citizens such as Emile is to become (1979, 85).

Significantly, Emile's future wife, Sophie, does not need to receive the same education as Emile because of her procreative capacity. As Brian Duff explains, "Sophie's destiny is guided by her potential to give birth one day" (2011, 39). Since women's "proper purpose is to produce [children]," Sophie's education need not prepare her for political life (Rousseau 1979, 362). Unlike Emile, she feels constraints so that she may become submissive and docile. This renders her ultimately dependent on Emile and incapable of the self-governance required of political subjects. Autonomy is afforded to and functions as a political ideal only for men.

Rousseau's account of the possibility for self-governance in both *The Social Contract* and *Emile*—in which he ultimately relies on the external, manipulative figures of, respectively, the legislator and tutor—illustrates the perceived need to protect men from themselves, even as they are granted authority over women. As he writes, "[T]here is no subjection so perfect as that which keeps the appearance of freedom. Thus the will itself is made captive" (1979, 120). Autonomy inheres in submitting to what appears to be one's own self-prescribed law. In the context of political society, this involves self-limitation. Moreover, for Rousseau self-governance is not an isolating ideal. It requires grappling with our attachment to others and to our existence as part of a collectivity. It is therefore not merely a matter of individual, unattached self-rule.

Like Rousseau, Kant understands autonomy in terms of obedience to a self-given law. However, Kant, whose philosophy was deeply influenced by Rousseau, is less concerned with preserving freedom given our social formation. He is more concerned with preserving freedom in the face of the determinist view of the physical world precipitated in part by Newtonian science. For Kant, we can only have a moral duty to act in ways we can actually act. If our actions are predetermined, then we could have a duty to do nothing but what we in fact do (Guyer 2000, 228). Kant is also more concerned with the significance of autonomy for morality than Rousseau, who thought about how autonomy can ground political society. Nonetheless, Kant does write about autonomy and politics as well and, as I argue, his understanding of moral autonomy can be connected to some of his more political thought.

The distinction between the noumenal and the phenomenal realms allows Kant to account for determinism but nonetheless preserve freedom and morality. The noumenal realm consists in the world of things in themselves, whereas the phenomenal realm consists in the world of appearances. The phenomenal realm is ruled by the law of causality and thus determinism. Although humans exist in both realms, when we interact with the world of sense objects, we are determined in that objects cause us to behave in certain ways and desire certain things. The noumenal realm, however, consists in "what reaches consciousness immediately and not through affection of the senses" (Kant 1998, 451). The noumenal realm holds out the possibility for nondeterminism and thus for freedom.[1]

Drawing on Rousseau's idea that freedom inheres in self-prescribed law, Kant argues that only self-given laws that originate in the exercise of reason can bind rational agents. We have access to moral principles through the faculty of reason. Moreover, the categorical imperative is the moral law. To act in accord with the categorical imperative, by acting on rational principles that can be valued for all rational agents rather than the contingent inclinations of the individual, is to act autonomously. Kant explains the categorical imperative in the following way: "Act upon a maxim that can also hold as a universal law" (1991a, 225). When a moral matter is at stake, one can act on the basis of either reason or inclination. To act autonomously, you must act on the basis of reason. Your inclinations may coincide with what reason demands, but they cannot be the basis of your action. Thus, in acting in accord with the rational will, and thereby autonomously, one is not swayed by the pushes and pulls of desire that mark the phenomenal world. Autonomy requires putting these externally determined things aside as the basis for action and instead acting on the basis of the rationally arrived at self-given law. In acting on the basis of desire or mere custom or habit, one acts heteronomously (Kant 1998).

Rasmussen has called the tradition of which Kant is a part "autonomy as law." She describes Kant's version of the autonomous individual as one who is free of external determination of one's actions and who also expresses "a willingness to engage in self-limitation based on reflection or the ability to make oneself the object of analysis. Autonomy is not anything goes, but rather it is constituted by the act of making the law" (2011, 7). To be clear, Kant would not have viewed his moral principles as requiring self-limitation. For Kant, acting on the basis of reason is what makes one the author of the laws under which one acts. Acting on the basis of one's contingent desires and inclinations means that one is not acting autonomously or in accord with the self's rational agency. Thus, in such situations, it is not that one is failing to limit oneself but that one is not acting in accord with the self. Autonomy, then, cannot be understood on his terms strictly as self-limitation.

However, if we reject Kant's beliefs about the meaning of the self, then we can view his version of autonomy as a kind of self-limitation because it requires that one control the nonrational self to act autonomously.[2] In offering such a vision of autonomy, Kant assumes that it makes sense to think of a self outside society and prior to its social embeddedness. The formation of desires and habits is not strictly a matter of concern for autonomy, since when we act on the basis of desire or habit, we are acting heteronomously. What is important for autonomy is that the individual can put aside desires, passions, and custom as the basis for moral action.

As a political matter, Kant argued that we must treat others as though they are autonomous because we cannot know anyone's true motives, including our own. We can thus legislate only on external actions, and any such legislation should be compatible with equal freedom for all (1991b). However, Kant's philosophical assertions about equality and treating others as though they are autonomous sit in uneasy tension with his writings on race. In fact, Kant wrote extensively on racial hierarchy, which he claimed was evidenced in the rational and moral superiority of Europeans over all other races (Eze 1997). His philosophico-anthropological writing contains statements like, "The Negroes of Africa have by nature no feeling that rises above the trifling" (1997, 55). In *Physical Geography*, Kant asserted, "Humanity is at its greatest perfection in the race of the whites" (1997, 63). In the same work, he wrote,

> The inhabitant of the temperate parts of the world, above all the central part, has a more beautiful body, works harder, is more jocular, more controlled in his passions, more intelligent than any other race of people in the world. That is why at all points in time these peoples have educated the others and controlled them with their weapons. (1997, 64)

Given that the capacity to reason grounded his moral and political philosophy, this hierarchy implied that only whites were proper moral and political agents. This claim would justify their domination of others. Kant's writings on race reveal that he does not in fact treat all others as if they were autonomous and of equal intrinsic value.

More generally, Kant viewed women and all individuals in a state of dependence as passive citizens who are not "fit to vote" (1991a, 126). As he wrote in *The Metaphysics of Morals*, "an apprentice in the services of a merchant or artisan; a domestic servant (as distinct from a civil servant); a minor . . . ; all women, and in general, anyone whose preservation in existence (his being fed and protected) depends not on his management of his own business but on arrangements made by another (except the state)" lack "civil personality" (1991a, 126). Their dependence on others renders them "mere underlings" who "have to be under the direction or protection of others" (126). On the rationality of women specifically, Kant equivocates. Nancy Hirschmann argues that "Kant is rather ambiguous on the question of women's rationality, in some places indicating that women are naturally rational, in others that women are naturally irrational, in yet others that they have the natural capacity for rationality but should not develop it" (2003, 58).

The example of Kant shows how autonomy has been understood to inhere in the exercise of reason. His thinking also illustrates how even a seemingly deep commitment to equality can coexist with political exclusion. That is, even as Kant appears to provide an inclusive and equal understanding of moral and political autonomy, in practice he excludes a range of people from political society because of judgments about their autonomy and rationality. We can see how believing in autonomy as proper self-governance—here, acting in accord with the categorical imperative—can coexist with an exclusionary political practice grounded in some people's supposed lack of intelligence, reason, or independence.

Both Rousseau and Kant view autonomy as inhering in proper self-governance achieved by legislating for and obeying oneself. Both thinkers also divide people into those who are capable of proper self-governance and those who are not. Rousseau and Kant also suggest that there is a disjuncture between autonomy and desire. Autonomy, or what I will for myself, cannot be understood strictly or unqualifiedly as that which I merely want. For Rousseau, individual preference must conform to the collective will. For Kant, desire cannot be the basis of rational self-legislation. Acting on the basis of reason is the only way to achieve autonomy.

Proper Self-Governance and Exclusion in Contemporary Accounts of Autonomy

Contemporary accounts of autonomy eschew Kantian metaphysics but are concerned with some of the same tensions and issues that Rousseau and Kant addressed. For example, contemporary theorists of autonomy continue to be concerned with the disjuncture between autonomy and desire. They are concerned with the process by which individuals might come to think of themselves as willing a particular end for themselves, rather than merely acting on or being controlled by what they desire. In debating the best conceptualization of autonomy, philosophers have developed two different ways of approaching it—as either procedural or substantive. While there is variation within both of these approaches, the procedural accounts are generally concerned with the process by which a person adopts a certain desire, value, preference, or plan (Dworkin 1988; Frankfurt 1971; Meyers 1989; Friedman 2003; Barvosa-Carter 2007). On most procedural accounts, true or unproblematic self-knowledge is that which is arrived at after a specific process. For Gerald Dworkin, for example, "autonomy is conceived of as a second-order capacity of persons to reflect critically upon their first-order preferences, desires, wishes, and so forth and the capacity to accept or

attempt to change these in light of higher-order preferences and values"
(1988, 20). Moreover, one's desires and values must be formed in such
a way that influences on one's reflective faculties advance those faculties rather than undermine them. While philosophers like Dworkin put
forth accounts of autonomy that would guard against unjust interference
in individual decision making, by offering limited accounts of proper
decision making, they leave room for paternalism toward those who
eschew such modes of reflection or such an understanding of the self.[3]

Substantive accounts such as Kant's require certain substantive commitments—in his case, to a particular moral law. Some substantive accounts are concerned with the processes by which a person arrives at
desires or preferences, but they also include substantive restrictions on
the content of an agent's values or desires. Often substantive accounts
require that one has to make decisions consistent with upholding autonomy as a value (Benson 1994; Stoljar 2000; Oshana 2006). These
accounts are meant to guard against the perceived problem with procedural accounts, which is that they would allow for the assignment of
autonomy to those who, although in oppressive circumstances, nonetheless reflect on their preferences and endorse their subservient role.
Natalie Stoljar, for example, argues that when women's decisions reflect
internalized sexist norms, they should not be deemed autonomous. Instead, there need to be "restrictions on the contents of agents' preferences" (2000, 95). Both procedural and substantive accounts assume
that an agent's mere representation of a value or desire as her or his own
is insufficient to ground autonomy. Consequently, they seek to separate
out preferences or commitments that are *really* one's own from those
that are not. As in Kant's formulation, contemporary philosophical accounts of autonomy assume a disjuncture between autonomy and mere
desire or preference. To say that I prefer or choose a particular outcome
is not to say that that outcome is expressive of autonomy. Certain procedural or substantive requirements must be imposed in order to assure
the congruence of choice and autonomy.

Although the strict division between process and substance is somewhat misleading,[4] theorists in both traditions tend not to consider the
political implications of being ascribed as autonomous (or not) and also
do not consider the political elements of autonomy itself. This is true
even though procedural and substantive theorists have turned toward

understanding the self relationally. Catriona Mackenzie and Stoljar note that relational autonomy refers not to any unified account of autonomy but to a series of attempts to bring the socially situated nature of the self to bear on autonomy. In their words, "the focus of relational approaches is to analyze the implications of the intersubjective and social dimensions of selfhood and identity for conceptions of individual autonomy and moral and political agency" (2000, 4). In accord with this idea, many contemporary philosophical accounts of autonomy are concerned with the social formation of the self and, in particular, the consequences of oppressive socialization for autonomy.

Although the autonomy as critique and transformation tradition that I discuss later in this chapter shares relational autonomy theorists' concerns with understanding the self in society, it is more focused on challenging and transforming oppressive social forces. Relational approaches, like the other approaches considered in this section, are primarily focused on determining what autonomy is for the purposes of ascribing personal autonomy. In contrast, autonomy as critique and transformation is focused on conceptualizing autonomy given the social construction of the self for the purpose of understanding and promoting social transformation. Stoljar, for example, offers a reading of autonomy that would render any woman whose actions reflect internalized sexist norms and thus violate the "feminist intuition" nonautonomous (2000), but her account is not primarily concerned with how sexist social forces can be transformed or with how transformation might arise from the practice of autonomy itself.

Thus, although aware of the effects of socialization on individuals' decisions and understandings of themselves, contemporary philosophical conceptualizations of autonomy often do not adequately consider the political effects of being deemed nonautonomous. As John Christman puts it, being marked as autonomous is to "enjoy the status marker of an independent citizen whose perspective and value orientation get a hearing in the democratic processes that constitute legitimate social policy" (2004, 157). Consequently, a lot rests on judgments of who is competent and how oppression and socialization affect competency. Although contemporary thinkers analytically separate personal autonomy from political autonomy, in practice the division between the two is slippery. The determination that an individual lacks personal autonomy often has political consequences, and in practice the project of figuring out who is autonomous cannot be easily separated from its political implications. The assignment of nonautonomy to individuals justifies paternalistic intervention, whereas the ascription of autonomy generally entails protection from paternalistic intervention (Christman 2004, 158).

Like Rousseau and Kant, contemporary philosophical accounts of autonomy assume that autonomy is not simply about doing what one wants. Instead, it involves acting in a particular, proper way. Defining autonomy in terms of *proper* self-governance necessitates separating people into proper and improper self-governors. Contemporary theorists, while not explicitly judging people's competency for self-governance on the grounds of race or gender as Rousseau and Kant do, are generally concerned with determining which ways of thinking or acting are truly autonomous. Such judgments of what is truly autonomous are likely to reflect power relations in society. Others judge individuals as autonomous or not depending on whether their thinking and actions comport with the accepted way of acting autonomously. In practice, as I demonstrate in later chapters, being deemed autonomous with regard to one's reproduction often depends on whether one acts in ways that reflect dominant norms.

Furthermore, the idea of autonomy as proper self-governance would seem to require the existence of some person or group who would judge who has the requisite capacities or competency for autonomy. In historic and contemporary regulations of reproduction, experts tend to assume that they have the ability to know others' interests better than individuals know their own interests. They often seek, in a Rousseauian fashion, to manipulate the decisions of those who come under their management so that they accord with the experts' own ideas of proper self-governance. The autonomy as proper self-governance tradition lays the groundwork for judgments about who is capable or incapable of making the right kinds of decisions or reflecting properly.

As I show in coming chapters, this tradition resonates with the way autonomy is conceived in much reproductive legal discourse. Subsequent chapters examine how autonomy operates politically and legally; in doing so, they illustrate the problem with thinking that the ascription of autonomy can be determined philosophically or without attention to how relations of power affect accounts of knowledge and assessments of who is autonomous. The rest of this book illustrates the problem that arises when concerns about the concept of autonomy are severed from the political and legal consequences of being deemed nonautonomous. I thus question the division scholars sometimes make between personal and political autonomy. Additionally, the conceptualizations of autonomy examined thus far are so focused on individuals and determining who is autonomous that they deflect attention away from possibilities for challenging existing social structures. They tend to take the existing social context for granted and therefore do not attend to the potential role of individual conduct in challenging norms. I now turn to poststructuralist understandings of the subject, which direct more attention to social forces, their role in constituting the subject, and the political potential of individual conduct.

Productive Power, Performativity, and the Subject

The individual is not to be conceived as a sort of elementary nucleus, a primitive atom, a multiple and inert material on which power comes to fasten or against which it happens to strike, and in so doing subdues or crushes individuals. In fact, it is already one of the prime effects of power that certain bodies, certain gestures, certain discourses, certain desires, come to be identified and constituted as individuals. The individual, that is, is not the *vis-à-vis* of power; it is, I believe, one of its prime effects. The individual is an effect of power, and at the same time, or precisely to the extent to which it is that effect, it is the element of its articulation. The individual which power has constituted is at the same time its vehicle.
—Michel Foucault, "Two Lectures"

Poststructuralism emphasizes the deep political and social construction of the subject. As such, poststructuralists like Foucault eschew the philosophical view that presupposes the subject and conceives of it as a pre-social phenomenon. The subject does not exist outside power relations. Instead, power relations constitute the subject. As such, a subject does not merely exercise power, but also simultaneously undergoes that power. In other words, the subject both articulates and is produced by power (Foucault 1980). Foucault himself was interested in discovering how "subjects are gradually, progressively, really and materially constituted through a multiplicity of organisms, forces, energies, material, desires, thoughts etc." (1980, 97). In this section, I examine Foucault's, as well as Butler's, descriptions of the subject and power.

A corollary to Foucault's conception of the subject is the idea of productive power, which constitutes the subject and "produces effects" at the levels of desire and knowledge (1980, 59). Foucault contrasts productive power with what he claims is the more traditional view of power as repressive. Repressive power is that which prohibits and is largely associated with sovereign power and the rule of law. Although Foucault focuses on nonlegal articulations of productive power and at times seems to align repressive power with the law, the law is an instance of both repressive and productive power. Insofar as power and knowledge operate through the circulation of legal discourses and rationales, the law is a productive force that should be interrogated on that basis.

For Foucault, both knowledge and knowledge-production are bound up with the constitution of the subject. In *The History of Sexuality*, for example, he argues that others' knowledge and expertise, as well as individuals' knowledge of themselves, steer and guide individuals. To the extent we are produced by power, we internalize norms and monitor ourselves. For example, individuals can be disciplined as objects of scientific study and techniques; in the process, we internalize regulatory norms and become self-regulating subjects. Accordingly, to understand self-knowledge as the key to freedom or autonomy is to misunderstand self-knowledge. Rather than being authentic or liberatory, self-knowledge is itself an effect of power. To take the voicing of some presumed truth of oneself and one's experience as freedom is to ignore the power endemic to that truth.

On this view, autonomy theory cannot simply rely on individual consideration of norms and wants because of the complicated relation between external forces and individual preference. Since autonomy is about—indeed is defined as—*self*-government, attention to the production of the self would be crucial. An account of autonomy narrowly focused on individual self-reflection would exclude a consideration of the processes that constitute us and would thereby preclude an analysis and critique of those processes. Such a focus forecloses the possibility of a more robust autonomy—the kind that might be found to be possible if we engaged critically with the social constitution of the subject.[5]

Drawing on Foucault, Butler develops an account of the subject and subjectivity that is especially concerned with issues of sex and gender. Like Foucault, she rejects the strand of social constructionism that seeks to place "Culture or Discourse or Power" in the agentive place of the subject. There is no single entity that acts and creates the subject; rather, there is only a process, an acting through which "both 'subjects' and 'acts' come to appear at all. There is no power that acts, but only a re-iterated acting that is power in its persistence and instability" (1993, 9). More specifically, Butler locates this production of the subject in per-formativity: it is through our very performance of gendered norms that we, as gendered subjects, come into being. In her words, "identity is performatively constituted by the very 'expressions' that are said to be its results" (1990, 24–25). Gender is brought into being by the very per-formances, which consist in the reiteration of norms, that are taken to be its result.

Consequently—and contrary to prevalent understandings of the terms—Butler does not view sex as pre-cultural and gender as a so-cial construction that maps onto sexed selves. Rather, she argues that sex itself is brought into being through social productions. Following Foucault, she writes that gender is the "very apparatus of production whereby the sexes themselves are established. . . . [G]ender is the dis-cursive/cultural means by which 'sexed nature' or 'natural sex' is pro-duced and established as 'prediscursive,' prior to culture, a politically neutral surface *on which* culture acts" (1990, 7). Matter itself should not be seen as given, but as something that is established through a process that gives the appearance that matter is fixed. This view leads her to raise questions about the norms by which sex is materialized and to question the oft-unquestioned presupposition of the givenness of sexed bodies (1993). She views the body itself not as a passive, pre-societal entity, but as a construction. She writes that "[b]odies cannot be said to have a sig-nifiable existence prior to the mark of their gender" (1990, 8).

Norms cannot sustain themselves, but require our performances for their sustainability. In Butler's terms, norms are reiterated in nonuni-form and unstable ways. Reiteration does not amount to perfect replication. Therefore, in reiteration lies the possibility of subversion of the very norms that construct us. Put in other words, in our performances lies the possibility of impeding and subverting prevailing norms.

On the topic of subversion, Butler writes,

> "Intelligible" genders are those which in some sense institute and maintain relations of coherence and continuity among sex, gender, sexual practice, and desire. . . . [B]ecause certain "gender identities" fail to conform to those norms of cultural intelligibility, they appear only as developmental failures or logical impossibilities from within that domain. Their persistence and proliferation, however, provide critical opportunities to expose the limits and regulatory aims of that domain of intelligibility and, hence, to open up within the very terms of that matrix of intelligibility rival and subversive matrices of gender disorder. (1990, 17)

Gender performance is subversive "to the extent that it reflects on the imitative structure by which hegemonic gender is itself produced and disputes heterosexuality's claim on naturalness" (1993, 125).

While Butler is focused on how heterosexuality comes to appear as natural, she is also critical of approaches that take maternal desire as given. She argues that we should consider "mechanism[s] for the compulsory cultural construction of the female body *as* a maternal body" (1990, 90). While the production of maternal desire as natural to womanhood and as located in the female body masks its very production,[6] Butler argues that if we heed Foucault's insights, the maternal body

> would be understood . . . as an effect or consequence of a system of sexuality in which the female body is required to assume maternity as the essence of its self and the law of its desire. . . . [W]e are compelled to redescribe the maternal libidinal economy as a product of an historically specific organization of sexuality. (1990, 92)

On this view, compulsory heterosexuality and compulsory motherhood are intertwined with one another.

Butler also builds on Foucault's insight that power produces the very subjects that it then claims to represent to argue that the "feminist subject is discursively constituted by the very political system that is supposed to facilitate its emancipation" (1990, 2). Butler does not presuppose the subject, and the agency possible in her account does not consist in the voluntary action of a self-determining individual. Rather, "the subject who would resist [regulatory] norms is itself enabled, if not produced, by such norms" (1993, 15). This does not mean agency is impossible, but that agency is "a reiterative or rearticulatory practice, immanent to power, and not a relation of external opposition to power" (1993, 15).

In her more recent work, Butler has elaborated her Foucaultian understanding of agency in relation to the notion of subjection, which involves both subjectivity—"the process of becoming a subject"—and subjugation—"the process of becoming subordinated by power" (1998, 2). She argues that subjectivity and subjugation are inevitably intertwined: it is through a subordination to power that the subject comes into being. On this account, "[s]ubjection consists precisely in this fundamental dependency on a discourse we never chose but that, paradoxically, initiates and sustains our agency" (1998, 2). According to Butler,

> Where conditions of subordination make possible the assumption of power, the power assumed remains tied to these conditions, but in an ambivalent way; in fact, the power assumed may at once retain and resist that subordination. This conclusion is not to be thought of as (a) a resistance that is *really* a recuperation of power or (b) a recuperation that is *really* a resistance. It is both at once, and this ambivalence forms the bind of agency. (1998, 13)

Thus, replication and subversion, the doing and undoing of norms, are inescapably bound up with one another. Because power is the precondition of agency, the agent, even in resisting, cannot escape power.

A crucial aspect of Butler's theorization of agency is the idea that constitution through norms enables agency. Butler's theorization of agency does not lead her into the determinism/agency paradox that is often thought to ensue from the constructionist project. Since she understands the constitution of the subject as the site and precondition of agency, the constitution of the self no longer presents a bar to agency; rather, agency cannot occur without this discursive production. The political project for Butler, then, is not to free subjects from power, because power is also the condition of possibility of agency. Agency is not strictly opposed or external to power. Owing to reiteration, "what is enacted by the subject is enabled but not finally constrained by the prior working of power" (1998, 15). Power thus enables but does not determine the subject's actions.

Autonomy as Critique and Transformation

As noted above, Foucault was interested in discovering how "subjects are gradually, progressively, really and materially constituted through a multiplicity of organisms, forces, energies, material, desires, thoughts etc." (1980, 97). Although this understanding of the subject rejects views of autonomy that presuppose the subject, it does not eliminate the possibility of autonomy. In fact, Foucault articulated a version of autonomy compatible with his work on power and knowledge. Relying on a close reading of much of Foucault's work, particularly his writings on Kant, Amy Allen argues that Foucault was interested in autonomy as both "the capacity for critical reflection" and "the capacity for deliberate self-transformation" (2008, 47). Because the subject is never outside power and is constituted by power, Allen argues that Foucault views this capacity for self-transformation to "necessarily involve[] taking up in a transformative way the relations of subjection that have made us who we are" (2008, 67–68).

In his essay "What Is Enlightenment?," Foucault links critique to "a permanent creation of ourselves in our autonomy" (1984, 44), and in doing so connects the capacities of critical reflection and self-transformation that Allen identifies. Foucault notes further that "this critique . . . will separate out, from the contingency that has made us what we are, the possibility of no longer being, doing, or thinking what we are, do, or think. . . . [I]t is seeking to give new impetus, as far and wide as possible, to the undefined work of freedom" (1984, 46). Because this capacity for autonomy is always tied to power, it is not a capacity for self-determination unmarked by or outside power. Instead, deliberate self-transformation involves resistance to and transformation of social forces that themselves constitute the subject and delineate modes of conduct (Allen 2008, 65). While critique "is the movement through which the subject gives itself the right to question truth concerning its power effects and to question power about its discourses of truth" (Foucault 1996, 386), deliberate self-transformation involves the potential transgression of the limitations of truth and power (see Allen 2008, 65).

This Foucaultian notion of self-governance does not eschew the view of autonomy as the imposition of self-given law. Rasmussen argues that Foucault's notion of autonomy "is a double-edged sword that on the one hand compels the self to exercise power over itself (and others) while at the same time provoking resistance to that power in selves that, using the compulsion to self-legislate, may always legislate in different ways" (2011, 18). Nevertheless, this Foucaultian focus on transformation and critique[7] challenges the notion that autonomy inheres in *proper* self-governance.

In fact, Foucault has demonstrated how the liberal art of governance is geared toward prompting subjects to govern themselves in appropriate and optimal ways (1988, 2003). In his work on governmentality, Foucault argues that, in Rasmussen's words, "the norm of self-governance is itself an instrument of power through which the liberal subject is constructed" (2011, 13). We are encouraged to govern ourselves in the best and most optimal ways, which presupposes that we have choice. Governance is exercised, not through the denial of options or a rejection of self-governance, but instead through the existence of options and freedom. It is the subject's ability to make choices that creates the conditions for the exercise of power.

Thinking of autonomy as critique and transformation exposes and promotes the possibility of reflecting upon and resisting accepted notions of what constitutes appropriate and optimal governance. Transformation, then, "is absolutely indispensable" from a critique of social forces and accepted practices (Foucault 1990, 155). Self-transformation in this sense is a form of autonomy because the critique to which it is tied is a form of liberating one's thought from "familiar, unchallenged, unconsidered modes of thought" and the practices upon which they rest (Foucault 1990, 154).[8] Since the kind of self-transformation that is a form of autonomy is connected to critique, not every instance of what may be commonly called self-transformation will be autonomous in Foucault's sense.

Because this interpretation of a Foucaultian approach to autonomy as self-transformation involves taking up and transforming force relations, it can be connected to Foucault's notion of counter-conduct. Conduct involves leading others and is also "a way of behaving within a more or less open field of possibilities" (Foucault 1982, 789). As he writes, "The exercise of power consists in guiding the possibility of conduct and putting in order the possible outcome" (1982, 789). Counter-conduct is a form of resistance to this exercise of power and as such it shifts the possibilities of conduct. In resisting the exercise of power, counter-conduct modifies the relations of power and affects the range of possible action. As Arnold Davidson explains, "force relations structure the possible field of actions of individuals. Resistance and counter-conduct modify these force relations, counter the locally stabilized organizations of power, and thereby affect, in a new way, the possibilities of action of others" (2007, xxii).

Modes of life and cultural forms are two things that arrange the "field of possibilities" and thus affect the possible actions of others. Since cultural forms play a role in guiding conduct, counter-conduct aimed at the re-creation of cultural forms affects the possible actions of others. By taking up and challenging the very force relations and cultural forms that structure options and constitute the self, we can partake in self-transformation and achieve a kind of autonomy. In this way, the creation of cultural forms is tied to self-transformation. While discourse frames and gives meaning to experience, critique and counter-conduct can challenge certain discursive understandings and be an expression of autonomy. For example, counter-conduct that did not rest on a fundamental identity between women and reproductive capacity would shift force relations and open up alternative modes of life for women.

Understanding the link between autonomy as the capacity for intentional self-transformation and counter-conduct reveals how intertwined the individual and the political are to this view of autonomy. Deliberate self-transformation may at once shift force relations and be an expression of autonomy. Put in other words, to take part in the creation of new ways of life is at once an expression of autonomy as self-transformation and a political act that affects the possibilities for others' conduct and thus their capacity for self-transformation. As Davidson writes, "even apparently personal or individual forms of counter-conduct . . . have a political dimension, that is, modify force relations between individuals, acting on the possibilities of action" (2007, xxiii). Autonomy and opening up new cultural understandings are valuable, on this account, as a way of countering and resisting, in Allen's words, "those limits that turn out to be both contingent and linked to objectionable forms of constraint" (2008, 65).

In interpreting Foucault in this way, I am following a number of theorists in highlighting the social and political aspects of Foucault's later thought. Although, as Jean Grimshaw (1993) and Ella Myers (2008, 2013) note, Foucault's ethical thought is focused on individual cultivation of a reflexive relationship to norms and sometimes seems not to take into account "the importance of collective goals or aspirations" (Grimshaw 1993, 68), the individual care of the self has wider political and social import. Moreover, though Foucault does not always emphasize collective action, his ethical thought does not preclude collaboration or association. Bevir argues that Foucault's position on collective struggles is that "we should be free to join, or stand apart from, struggles made on behalf of any collective to which we are supposed to belong." It is important, though, "that we should decide, critically and for ourselves, whether or not we wish to be part of any particular cooperative endeavor" (1999, 77–78).[9]

The Foucaultian reading of autonomy provided here is in line with Butler's work on subversion and agency. Although Butler generally favors the notion of agency over autonomy, she has employed the notion of autonomy favorably in some of her more recent work. In fact, there are traces in Butler's work of two different understandings of autonomy. One is a radically individualistic autonomy that she dismisses and differentiates from agency, while the other is a socially embedded autonomy that she at times aligns with agency. As an example of her radically individualistic understanding of autonomy, consider her statement in her essay "Contingent Foundations" that "autonomy is the logical consequence of a disavowed dependency, which is to say that the autonomous subject can maintain the illusion of its autonomy insofar as it covers over the break out of which it is constituted" (1995, 46). Furthermore, she makes clear in *Excitable Speech* that "agency is not the restoration of a sovereign autonomy" (1997, 15).

In *Undoing Gender*, however, Butler differentiates this sovereign autonomy from a socially constituted one on which she looks more approvingly. She writes of "the concrete limits to any notion of autonomy that establishes the individual as alone, free of social conditions, without dependency on social instruments of various kinds. Autonomy is a socially conditioned way of living in the world" (2004, 77). In the same book she discusses bodily autonomy in the context of reproductive rights, noting that "we are referring to forms of autonomy that require social (and legal) support and protection, and that exercise a transformation on the norms that govern how agency itself is differentially allocated among genders" (2004, 12). Butler, then, has more recently written positively of an always socially constituted autonomy that nonetheless holds out the possibility for social transformation. Indeed, the possibility for this transformation relies on her understanding of social constitution not as antithetical to agency but as a precondition of agency. That is, her view of the subject's constitution is compatible with a view of autonomy as involving critique and transformation of cultural forms.

On the view advanced here, autonomy does not inhere in an individual's isolated ability to do as she pleases, nor does it involve self-legislating in an appropriate fashion. Rather, and in contrast to the philosophical accounts of autonomy explored above, autonomy inheres in calling into question problematic cultural forms and norms. Although contemporary philosophical accounts of autonomy focused on relationality would seem to require a change in social relations to achieve wider autonomy, those approaches do not conceive of conduct itself as a means of social transformation, nor are they necessarily focused on bringing about such change. The poststructural accounts of autonomy, however, emphasize the social production of the self and the fact that individual actions have ramifications beyond the self. Autonomy is to be valued, not just because in acting autonomously an individual is pushing back against norms for herself, but because doing so has the potential to call into question broader social norms and relations of power. This may counter broader social threats to autonomy. Autonomy, on this view, is fundamentally political and social. As Butler describes, the social constitution of the subject enables the subject's agency. The subject can turn back upon itself to question and push back against the very forces that have constituted the subject. In doing so, existing hierarchies and relations of power may be challenged rather than reinforced.

Liberty and Eccentricity

In his writings on liberty and society, Mill articulates an understanding of autonomy that is similar to Foucault's account of counter-conduct, although he also uses the notion of autonomy in an exclusionary way. Mill is concerned with establishing a realm of self-governance for the individual and thus takes a strong stance against paternalism, but only for certain people. Mill writes early in *On Liberty* that "[t]hose who are still in a state to require being taken care of by others, must be protected against their own actions" (1998, 14). Young people below the age of maturity, as well as "those backward states of society in which the race itself may be considered as in its nonage," fall into this category (14). He concludes that "[d]espotism is a legitimate mode of government in dealing with barbarians" (14–15). Mill, who so forcefully attacks paternalism, also justifies it for those who he deems not to have "attained the capacity of being guided to their own improvement by conviction or persuasion" (15). Mill's defense of liberty in *On Liberty* is thus not universal and would be applied to perpetuate subordination under the guise of paternalism. Mill can be seen as a kind of transitional figure: he is concerned with determining who is a proper political subject and also provides an account of the transformative possibility of autonomy.

In *On Liberty*, Mill argues that the state must be a guardian of liberty by staying out of private affairs so long as the private action at issue does not harm others. He strongly believes that certain individuals know what is best for themselves and that the state, insofar as it has the power to encroach on the individual's sphere of autonomy, is a threat to self-sovereignty. Mill asserts that "[o]ver himself, his own body and mind, the individual is sovereign" (1998, 14).

Mill encourages diversity in modes of living because uniform adherence to the customary mode of life impedes progress and human happiness (1998, 63). Mill is thus concerned that the majority views "individual spontaneity" as undeserving of regard: "The majority, being satisfied with the ways of mankind as they now are (for it is they who make them what they are) cannot comprehend why those ways should not be good enough for everybody" (1998, 63). This statement suggests the formative role of the majority and sets the stage for his argument that eccentricity is necessary for the sake of liberty. He says the following of most people:

> I do not mean that they choose what is customary, in preference to what suits their own inclination. It does not occur to them to have any inclination, except for what is customary. Thus the mind itself is bowed to the yoke: even in what people do for pleasure, conformity is the first thing thought of; they like in crowds; they exercise choice only among things commonly done: peculiarity of taste, eccentricity of conduct, are shunned equally with crimes. (1998, 68)

The problem for Mill is not necessarily that the majority way is wrong or less advantageous than other ways. The problem instead is that the majority do not even consider the possibility of alternatives since dominant modes of thinking blind people so much that they do not think to conceive of alternatives.

There is an important resonance between Millian eccentricity and Foucaultian counter-conduct. Davidson (2011) argues that "'[e]ccentricity of conduct' is Mill's name for counter-conduct" and that Mill and Foucault are both notable for their attention to "the autonomous sphere of conduct" (31). For both, this conduct is political in that "it is the active intervention of individuals and constellations of individuals in the domain of the ethical and political practices and forces that shape us" (2011, 32).[10]

Like Foucault, Mill is concerned with stressing liberty because of the potentially pernicious effects of society and the customary. Counter-majoritarian conduct is thus especially valuable. According to Mill, "In this age, the mere example of non-conformity, the mere refusal to bend the knee to custom, is itself a service. Precisely because the tyranny of opinion is such as to make eccentricity a reproach, it is desirable, in order to break through that tyranny, that people should be eccentric" (1998, 74). Eccentricity and diversity derive value, according to Mill, from the role they play in reducing and challenging conformity. Mill argues that "[i]f resistance waits till life is reduced *nearly* to one uniform type, all deviations from that type will come to be considered impious, immoral, even monstrous and contrary to nature" (1998, 82). In this way, what is customary can come to be taken as natural and thus incontrovertible, even unquestionable. Eccentricity is crucial in order to avoid the equation of the customary with the natural. Bound up with this need for eccentricity as a way to counter the tyranny of the majority is the value of diversity: diversity of modes of life entails a wider variety of options. It is diversity that induces reflection, which is one of the key components of Mill's understanding of self-direction. While acting eccentrically may be an instance of liberty, it is also necessary to maintain liberty for the general populace because of its role in calling into question accepted customs.

Mill further elaborates on injurious practices of socialization in *The Subjection of Women*, in which he argues that women are taught to be obedient and repress any desire for liberty they may have such that "[w]hat is now called the nature of women is an eminently artificial thing" (1998, 493). Due to a sort of mental control that men exercise over women, women internalize the idea that they are to be the opposite of men; they are taught to be submissive and self-sacrificing instead of self-governing. Mill thinks that lifting legal barriers to women's liberty, along with educational reforms, would lead to what he labels a "morality of justice" and would make women less self-sacrificing and men less selfish. A society of equals would also make women less dependent. Even so, Mill seems to naturalize women's place in the home, maintaining that if women were permitted greater opportunities outside the home, the majority would devote themselves primarily to household pursuits.

In both *On Liberty* and *The Subjection of Women* Mill grapples with the threat that socialization poses to liberty. Moreover—and this is a crucial point—Mill emphasizes the value of individuality, not because he sees us as fully forming ourselves, but because individuality needs to be stressed in light of the pervasive and pernicious forces of public opinion and social institutions. As Bruce Baum argues, Mill's "analysis of the necessary conditions for freedom in modern societies is informed by a profound understanding of how people's powers of self-determination and self-development are shaped by the power dynamics they encounter in their political, economic, educational, gender, and family relationships" (2000, 4). It is through eccentric, counter-majoritarian conduct that space for alternative modes of being is opened.[11] With this arises the possibility of liberty—of people realizing they have choices, reflecting upon them, and ultimately choosing a course of conduct rather than it being prescribed to them by their social position. It is not only such deliberative reflective action that is valuable from the standpoint of liberty. Mill repeatedly mentions spontaneity and impulse in his discussion of eccentric conduct. In doing so he suggests that moments of impulsive rebellion can disrupt majoritarian thinking. Even these moments demonstrate that there is an alternative to the dominant mode of life. They thereby increase space for autonomy for the self and others, even if the spontaneous action is not itself autonomous because not preceded by reflection.

Despite the negative effects of custom, Mill argues, in what is commonly referred to as his epistemological argument, that individuals know their own interests better than others. Individuals should therefore be allowed to act on their own interests without interference from others and should be afforded as much liberty in the direction of their lives as is compatible with a similar liberty for others. He writes, "The strongest of all arguments against the interference of the public with purely personal conduct is that when it does interfere, the odds are that it interferes wrongly, and in the wrong place" (1998, 92). There is tension between this claim that the individual knows his own interests best and his argument about the blinding capacity of custom. If we are so influenced by custom, then why trust our own judgments?

One response to this line of critique is the following: When others have the power to coerce the individual, they are likely to do so in a way that shores up and reflects custom and dominant norms. Although individual actors often act in ways that reflect custom, permitting interference in individual conduct would generally strengthen the compulsion to act in accordance with custom. It is likely that others will actively intervene primarily in individual conduct that challenges custom. The superior self-knowledge of individuals should be presumed because doing so results in a greater ability to challenge custom. In fact, in subsequent chapters, I offer a defense of this perspective. I show that, in contemporary reproductive regulation, coercive paternalism is indeed exercised in a way that strengthens existing hierarchies and oppressive norms. This key point supports the presumption in favor of women's superior self-knowledge and personal decision-making ability that I defend.

Resistance, Subversion, and Eccentricity

With regard to their respective and similar notions of counter-conduct, subversion, and eccentric conduct, Foucault, Butler, and Mill reveal the possibility and potential importance of autonomy as critique and transformation. The mutual shaping of self and society, far from making a discussion of autonomy and individual decisions irrelevant, actually demonstrates the importance of autonomy. Autonomy as critique and transformation carried out through counter-conduct is important and possible because of this mutual shaping. Were individual conduct cut off from society and not a reflection or reiteration of norms, then there would be less transformative potential within individual conduct. It is individuals' very involvement in the ongoing reiteration or reconstitution of norms that creates the possibility of autonomy.

The concepts of eccentricity, counter-conduct, and subversion are closely aligned with one another due to the shared concern of their respective theorists with something like counter-majoritarian conduct. Mill characterizes eccentricity as "the mere example of non-conformity, the mere refusal to bend the knee to custom" (1998, 74). Foucault talks of the importance of "look[ing] like a girl when one is a boy (and vice versa)" (1971, 201). Butler writes of subversion through parodic practices such as drag. These practices are all emphasized because of their potential challenge to power. The value of eccentricity or resistance or subversion is the potential of such practices to unmask the effects of power, which may otherwise appear natural, by revealing their contingency.

Autonomy requires grappling with the collectivities of which we are a part, not just because they form us, but because we have a role—even if always partial and contingent—in shaping them. It is crucial to keep in mind that on the poststructuralist account individuals can never be fully aware of the extent of this mutual shaping, in part because mechanisms of power work by obscuring their processes. We will never be fully conscious of productive power or how it works through us, and we will be constrained in that we will be reacting to dominant forces. As Foucault argues, we are never outside power, although that does not mean that outside forces wholly govern our actions. The resistive or subversive potential fundamental to the Foucaultian and Butlerian accounts of power is important: in challenging norms and their accompanying external and psychological constraints, subversion has the potential to increase autonomy. Subversion can call into question dominant modes of thinking and reveal alternatives to that thinking. Consequently, some room for maneuver and reflection on that shaping remains possible.[12]

On this reading, what is at stake in reproductive autonomy is not only individual control over one's own life, but also the ability to engage in the construction of cultural forms that have ramifications for shared public life. For example, to the extent understandings of women are bound to reproductive capacity and motherhood, some reproductive practices may disrupt that link and contribute to the creation of different cultural understandings of women and maternity. They would thereby shift or, in Butler's terms, subvert force relations such that others' possibilities of action are affected. Thus, such subversive or eccentric acts are political. As Butler writes, "drag, butch, femme, transgender, transsexual persons . . . make us not only question what is real, and what 'must' be, but they also show us how the norms that govern contemporary notions of reality can be questioned and how new modes of reality can become instituted" (Butler 2004, 29). In this way, such practices "enter into the political field" (29).

This link between autonomy and subversion can provide an answer to a question that is frequently asked of Butler: why is the resignification of norms good?[13] In *Excitable Speech* Butler provides a possible answer:

> the interval between instances of utterance not only makes the repetition and resignification possible, but shows how words might, through time, become disjoined from their power to injure and recontextualized in more affirmative modes. I hope to make clear that by affirmative, I mean "opening up the possibility of agency," where agency is not the restoration of a sovereign autonomy in speech, a replication of conventional notions of mastery. (1997, 15)

Transgression and resignification are valuable because they can create more room for agency for others while also being an expression of agency. Dominant norms pose a variety of threats to agency, and resignification potentially counters those threats. Bevir makes a similar defense of Foucault when he argues,

To explain the value of transgression, we need to portray it as an expression of agency in a world where the impact of a normalizing power makes agency highly vulnerable to various forms of distortion. And to distinguish good transgressions from bad, we need to appeal to the impact different actions have on the space for agency left to others. (1999, 80)

Mill's account of the importance of eccentricity complements this interpretation of Foucault and my interpretation of Butler. Mill is concerned that when people act, they tend to be unreflective and shore up existing norms. Eccentric conduct can be a manifestation of reflection and thus an instance of autonomy. At the same time, eccentricity can prompt reflection and critique in others, thus providing a potential counter to dominant norms and increasing autonomy for others.

This interpretation of autonomy is quite at odds with the Rousseauian version of autonomy as proper self-governance. Autonomy in its critical register would promote "improper" actions in order to induce critical reflection on norms and open up more room for autonomy. Unlike the proper self-legislation tradition of autonomy, autonomy as transformation is not concerned with ascribing autonomy to individuals. Autonomy as transformation is understood as a political practice, not an attribute. Although transformation is favored, not engaging in transformative practices is not grounds for being denied political subjectivity. One of the concerns of common philosophical accounts of autonomy is whether those who have desires that reflect oppressive forces can be considered autonomous. Rather than being concerned with whether such individuals can be deemed autonomous, critical autonomy emphasizes the importance of "the autonomous sphere of conduct" (Davidson 2011, 31) for transforming the oppressive force relations that may be internalized. Mill warns against letting the state decide whose desires are problematic, since doing so would tend to reflect existing and often oppressive norms rather than counter them.

Furthermore, autonomy as critique and transformation necessitates thinking of knowledge as situated. As Haraway writes,

situated knowledges require that the object of knowledge be pictured as an actor and agent, not a screen or a ground or a resource, never finally as slave to the master that closes off the dialectic in his unique agency and authorship of "objective" knowledge. . . . Accounts of a "real" world do not, then, depend on a logic of "discovery," but on a power-charged social relation of "conversation." (1991, 198)

Such situated knowledges will always be partial and, for Haraway, offer a type of objectivity that is both feminist and "not about transcendence and splitting of subject and object" (1991, 190). Self-knowledge in the critical autonomy tradition would be partial, unstable, and fluid. This type of knowledge originates in a "power-charged" conversation between oneself and others. With regard to conversation with oneself, there is no passive or real self to be discovered, but only an active self engaged in a conversation. Autonomy requires acknowledging one's location; there is not a splitting of self as object from self as subject, but a less easily described and messy conversation in which no part of the self is understood as passive, simply there to be discovered. Situated conversation also involves conversation—where conversation is understood broadly—with others. Because the self is always partial and constructed, it is "therefore able to join with another, to see together without claiming to be another" (1991, 193).

This aspect of situated conversation reveals the importance of engendering a context conducive to reflection. Situated knowledge is thus consistent with and complements Mill's thoughts on epistemology and the value of eccentricity. Although, as a political matter, Mill emphasizes the importance of protection from interference in one's "self-regarding" sphere, he also recognizes the importance of encountering other ways of doing and being. Situated conversation, like Mill's ideas about self-knowledge, involves both trusting individuals' own understandings and recognizing the potential for and importance of reflection. The danger with "tyranny of opinion" or hegemonic norms is that they function to "naturalize" the customary. The customary or the compulsory may become so accepted that other possibilities cannot be conceived. In this way and to the extent norms produce the self, the situatedness of knowledge is obscured. The knowledge that accompanies the naturalized customary is viewed not as partial but as universal. Subversive or eccentric conduct may prompt reflection on that which is otherwise taken as natural.

The kind of reflection involved in autonomy as critique and transformation, then, may be understood as situated: reflection is undertaken from a perspective and will result in partial knowledge of a self that is itself agentic and that may change in and through the very process of reflecting. While another's perspective can provoke critical reflection precisely because it is removed from one's own experience, the other should not be understood as unsituated. The other will have a distinctive view, not because the other is without perspective but because the other has a different situated perspective. Confrontation with the eccentric or subversive may lead to an encounter with another partial perspective. This may provoke awareness of one's own situatedness and reflection on what has been taken for granted.

Conclusion: The Importance of Reproductive Autonomy

A question that arises in viewing autonomy in terms of critique and transformation is, How do we determine which constraints are objectionable and should thus be subject to transformation? On Foucault's account, criticism involves "a historical investigation into the events that have led us to constitute ourselves and to recognize ourselves as subjects of what we are doing, thinking, saying. In this sense the criticism is not transcendental" (1984, 46). This suggests that the question of which constraints turn out to be objectionable depends on context. In considering reproductive restraints and autonomy, we should investigate the context and history of reproductive regulations and norms. The rest of this book takes up that task in various arenas. Here I discuss why, more generally, it is important to value reproductive autonomy, where autonomy is understood as critique and transformation facilitated by counter-conduct or eccentricity.

All norms place limitations on individuals, but that alone may not provide grounds for opposing them. However, the limitation of procreative possibilities through norms and their attendant regulatory practices—like abortion restrictions, forced sterilization, or certain restrictions on voluntary sterilization—do, I argue, provide grounds for their opposition. This is in part because the experiences of pregnancy and motherhood, and thus also their absence, bear significantly on how one's life is lived and how one's body is embodied. Attention to the bodily, material process of reproduction is critical in part because it is the very transformation of the body in pregnancy that makes the privileging of reproductive autonomy over many other values so important. As Drucilla Cornell has argued with regard to abortion, a woman's ability to decide the outcome of her pregnancy is crucial to her sense of self. Although individuals cannot have a radically voluntarist ability to determine the meanings of their actions because they will always be informed by cultural context, many reproductive restrictions identify women with reproductive capacity and thereby deny them full personhood. Cornell explains that "a woman must not be reduced to this physical capacity because such a definition identifies her with a function rather than as a self who projects and continuously re-imagines herself and the meaning of her embodiment" (1995, 65). Abortion prohibitions restrict individuals' ability to decide the meaning of pregnancy and violate their bodily integrity. Individuals should have the space to decide the symbolic meaning of their pregnancies, and restrictions on abortion deny that possibility (1995, 31–91). Sterilization restrictions present a similar issue. Both forced sterilization and the denial of voluntary sterilization treat individuals, primarily cisgender women, as violable in a way that denies them the ability to decide their bodily configurations and meanings.

Whereas autonomy as proper self-governance or self-limitation generally results in imposing normative expectations on individuals, the transformative and critical account of autonomy requires examining context and being critical of the way norms and judgments operate to preclude certain people from directing their own lives. In fact, rather than shoring up power relations, autonomy as critique reveals the importance of disrupting and questioning certain norms. In presenting an alternative to autonomy as proper self-limitation, this version of autonomy also requires recognizing all "as capable of generating our own evaluations of our life plans" (Cornell 1998, 18). Without this recognition, the force of autonomy as critique would fall away. Once others are regarded as always already potentially incapable of generating their own life plans, then it is a short move to the frequent paternalism of autonomy as proper self-governance. In practice this paternalism tends to reflect and reinforce dominant norms.

Cornell supports the idea that, as a political matter, all should be recognized as capable of directing their own lives by reference to Kant's notion that individuals possess equal intrinsic value. In contrast to Kant, she has justified this idea "not [as] a metaphysical proposition, but [as] an aspect of the politically conceived free person" (1998, 19). This leaves intact Kant's general argument that

> [m]an's *freedom* as a human being, as a principle for the constitution of a commonwealth, can be expressed in the following formula. No-one can compel me to be happy in accordance with his conception of the welfare of others, for each may seek his happiness in whatever way he sees fit, so long as he does not infringe upon the freedom of others to pursue a similar end which can be reconciled with the freedom of everyone else within a workable general law—i.e. he must accord to others the same right as he enjoys himself. (1991b, 74)

This idea of individuals possessing equal intrinsic value and being conceived of as capable of directing their lives can serve an important role within the critical tradition of autonomy. The recognition of the equal intrinsic value of individuals reveals the importance of counter-conduct and subversive acts: in some instances they push back against those norms that treat certain people as though they are of lesser value or have lesser ability to evaluate and direct their own lives. As I argue in coming chapters, contemporary reproductive regulations tend to treat women as though they have a lesser ability to direct their own lives. Such regulations impose restrictive understandings of gender and reproduction on women. Accordingly, eccentric acts have a privileged status because of their potential to challenge norms that treat people as though they are of unequal value. Counter-conduct can lead to cultural transformations that may overturn norms and regulations that treat certain individuals as having a lesser ability for self-governance.

The denial of reproductive autonomy to women is premised on the notion that women's reproductive capacity justifies government management of women's bodies in order to govern the population. The way that management is carried out varies based on race, class, ability, and sexuality such that regulations perpetuate racial and other hierarchies. As Roberts explains, reproductive justice can be brought about only if the link between equality and liberty is recognized. She explains that prioritizing a narrow understanding of liberty over equality has justified many of the abuses of reproductive law and policy. She urges "theorists committed to protecting individual autonomy . . . to explore how social justice could be made central to their conception of rights, of harms, and of the value of procreation" (1998, 312). This book explores how an alternative tradition of autonomy could serve as a counter to traditional understandings of autonomy that justify social injustice and in doing so answers Roberts's call. Moreover, noting that autonomy as critique requires a commitment to equality highlights the fact that justice is an important part of what is at stake in how we think about autonomy. The social injustice of group subordination often happens in conjunction with and through a refusal to recognize individuals in that group as capable of proper self-government. Autonomy as critique and transformation values both individual decision making and social transformation, especially transformation that would upend group subordination.

Because judgments of who is properly autonomous tend to reflect and reinforce existing power relations, the already marginalized are more likely to be deemed less than full political subjects. The autonomy as proper self-governance or self-limitation tradition excludes many from full political subjectivity. While historically women were presumed to lack the requisite rationality for autonomy, it is now unacceptable to claim explicitly that women are incapable of reason and therefore autonomy. Yet women and other marginalized groups are likely to be deemed less than fully autonomous when their conduct does not adhere to norms. Adherence to norms then operates as the measure of whether one is rational and autonomous. As Rasmussen demonstrates, autonomy has often functioned as an exclusionary idea, in which "[f]ulfilling the expectations of autonomy is to submit oneself to norms, while violating those norms is grounds for marginalization and exclusion" (2011, 95). The next chapter examines how some women's failure to submit themselves to reproductive norms has provided grounds for the judicial restriction of reproductive rights.

2

Abortion and the Juridical

Reproductive Autonomy and Protection from Injury

Proponents of legalized abortion often assume that the existence of the right to abortion increases women's autonomy in the sense that the right allows women greater control of their own bodies and lives. However, the existence of the right to abortion has coincided with and enabled the state's management and governance of those deemed unable to govern their reproduction properly. Moreover, it may be that the deeper significance and meaning of the right to abortion has not yet been realized. For Ann Snitow, this larger meaning involves the creation of alternative female identities and the ability "to imagine full and deeply meaningful li[ves] without motherhood, without children" (1992, 33). On this account, which has historically been shared by many feminist advocates for reproductive rights, the significance of the right to abortion is not limited to individual control over one's own reproductive processes, but also includes the right's potential to play a role in opening up new cultural understandings of womanhood and reproduction. On understandings of autonomy that emphasize critique and transformation, the creation of cultural conceptions and forms is crucial. Although autonomy is often understood in a narrow sense to involve merely individual self-governance divorced from larger concerns, from another perspective autonomous acts are understood as themselves playing a role in the creation of cultural forms that shift force relations.

This autonomy as transformation perspective suggests a more complex relation between reproductive autonomy and legal formulations of abortion than that which is commonly assumed. In particular, it suggests that legal formulations of abortion affect the extent to which reproductive autonomy is enhanced, even when the right to abortion is strongly defended. From this perspective, the evaluation of legal formulations requires asking questions like: Does the framing reinforce or push back against expert judgments of proper reproductive self-governance and appropriate reproduction? Does the legal framing of abortion tend to reinscribe dominant cultural conceptions? Is the potential for the right to abortion to play a role in disrupting the cultural link between female identity and maternity undermined? I argue that taking into account the connection between the construction of cultural forms and autonomy, as well as the productive power of law, results in a fuller understanding of how the right to abortion relates to reproductive autonomy. Through the examination of two prominent legal approaches to the right to abortion in the United States, I demonstrate how each relies on limiting views of abortion and reproduction. Each would encode in the law a circumscribed vision of the political import of the right to abortion, thereby diminishing its potential to enhance autonomy understood in terms of critique and transformation.

The following analysis of legal approaches to abortion complicates common understandings of what it means to be autonomous and of what it means to seek autonomy through law. While the right to abortion is often understood as enhancing individual self-governance, scholars have not examined the relation between the legal discourse of abortion and autonomy as the creation of cultural forms through self-transformation. Through the examination of legal understandings of the right to abortion, I argue that there is a complex relationship between rights and challenging existing cultural norms through counter-conduct. Rights may be a first step toward larger social transformation, but their potential to lead to more transformative outcomes will depend in part on the legal understanding of the right and how the action in question is framed. Rights may, as Patricia Williams states, be "the magic wand of visibility and invisibility, of inclusion and exclusion, of power and no power" (1991, 164). Yet they can be interpreted so that their powers of visibility and inclusion are weakened.

Legal formulations are crucial because of the productive power of law. On such a Foucaultian understanding of power, the law can be understood not merely as a repressive force—a force that operates through restriction—but also as a productive force. That is, both the right to abortion and the rationale for the right do not act on subjects constituted outside or before the law, but are constitutive of subjects. Legal discourse plays a role in constructing that which it names and regulates.

Since legal formulations are part of a complex of forces and discourses that produce subjects, they play a role in the production of women as subjects. The legal discourse of abortion also frames how the act of abortion is understood, and how the act is understood is itself bound up with how women are viewed.

Although Foucault understood legal discourse as productive, he nevertheless downplayed at times the importance of legal formulations of rights for the creation of cultural forms. As he noted in speaking of gay rights, the struggle for rights is only a first stage because "a right, in its real effects, is much more linked to attitudes and patterns of behavior" (1998, 157). The battle for rights is a stage in a more robust enterprise of establishing new lifestyles and "constructing cultural forms" (1998, 157). In fact, on at least one occasion Foucault diminished the importance of rights and their legal formulations for this construction of cultural forms, saying, "That in the name of respect for individual rights someone is allowed to do as he wants, great! But if what we want to do is to create a new way of life, then the question of individual rights is not pertinent" (1998, 157). Although noting the importance of rights, especially as a stage in a larger cultural struggle, Foucault at times separated rights from the construction of new cultural forms and lifestyles and thus from counter-conduct. Davidson notes that Foucault takes "the threat of counter-conduct, and not the legal status," as more "disruptive and unsettling" to existing social frameworks (2007, xxix).

Legal discourse can have important social ramifications because law and society are co-constitutive. As Jane Scoular argues, the law "may take a more potent form as it increasingly operates alongside other normative ordering practices to shape subjects, identities, practices, and spaces" (2010, 38). In fact, Foucault sometimes acknowledges the continued importance of the law to society and contemporary forms of power. He argues that "the law operates more and more as a norm, and the judicial institution is increasingly incorporated into a continuum of apparatuses (medical, administrative, and so on) whose functions are for the most part regulatory" (1980, 144). Modern forms of power, including normalization, operate in part through law.[1] Therefore, transformations in law can have a wide-ranging effect on how that power operates.

Thinking of abortion in terms of counter-conduct shows that what is at stake in cultural understandings and legal formulations of abortion is not only the ability of individual women to control their own bodies and lives but also, as feminists have often argued, the construction of cultural forms that have ramifications for shared public life.[2] The act of abortion can thus be understood as an expression of autonomy and as a form of counter-conduct that alters force relations and affects others' possibilities of action. Conduct that counters the constraining and seemingly natural connection between womanhood and motherhood affects force relations. Such conduct can also be an expression of autonomy as self-transformation. However, the transgressive possibilities of an act such as abortion, which potentially challenges the identification of woman and mother, is dependent in part on the discourse of abortion, including legal understandings of abortion. Legal understandings of abortion may play a role in either reinforcing or disrupting the link between women and motherhood. To the extent legal discourse disrupts that link and frames abortion as an act with larger cultural meaning, it may contribute to the creation of different cultural understandings that shift force relations and affect others' possibilities of action. In contrast, when legal frameworks present abortion as against women's nature or merely as an escape from oppression, they reinforce a limiting view of women and ignore abortion's transformative potential. Furthermore, the framing of abortion as a "choice" has coincided with the postfeminist interpretation of reproductive rights (which is examined more in the following chapter) that invokes feminist language but strips it of its critical and transformative edge. Such interpretations of reproductive rights eschew social context and the import of social change.

Underlying my argument is the idea that one thing that is at stake in the legal regulation and act of abortion is cultural views of cisgender women. This is an idea rooted in radical feminist arguments. When abortion is restricted, the state compels women to bear children and the woman-mother link is reinforced. One way abortion might be understood is as a refusal to be compelled to bear children. It may be an act of autonomy that resists cultural understandings that identify women with reproductive capacity. In the coming sections I argue that two prominent legal understandings of abortion limit the potential for the act of abortion to be understood as a challenge to common cultural understandings of gender and reproduction. Rather than understanding that at least one thing that is at stake in the legal regulation of abortion is cultural views of women, each argument I analyze below reinforces a contingent and limiting view of women and reproduction. Each argument frames the act of abortion narrowly.

Although I maintain that one thing that is at stake in the practice of abortion—and therefore also in the legal discourse of abortion—is the re-creation of cultural norms, I do not claim that women do or should abort simply to resist the cultural identification of women and mothers. Moreover, recognizing that part of what is at stake in the act as well as the framing of abortion is the re-creation of cultural forms does not necessarily entail ignoring the range of ethical issues involved in terminating pregnancies. I acknowledge that the termination of pregnancies raises ethical concerns beyond those considered here. Nonetheless, a narrow focus on the ethics of killing fetuses, separated from the ethical concerns that arise when women are denied reproductive autonomy, relies on a symbolic separation of fetuses from pregnant women. Such a narrow focus and symbolic separation cast aside the set of ethical issues surrounding the status and cultural understandings of women that must also be considered in discussions of the ethics of abortion.[3] In this chapter I explore the ethical and political issues that arise from two different legal understandings of abortion with the recognition that the full ethical complexity of abortion cannot be adequately addressed here but that the issues I explore regarding autonomy nonetheless merit attention.

This chapter examines legal arguments on the right and left that neglect the larger potential cultural significance of the right to abortion—which would involve the reconstruction of cultural forms—because of different but sometimes parallel understandings of abortion's relation to women and motherhood. I investigate, first, the 2007 U.S. Supreme Court case of *Gonzales v. Carhart*—which upheld the congressional Partial Birth Abortion Ban Act—and the woman-protective argument it advances. That approach to abortion relies on an understanding of women as victims and as essentially maternal. It reinforces the discursive mother-woman link and undermines efforts to reconstruct cultural conceptions of women and reproduction. I then examine how the defense of the right to abortion based on an antisubordination interpretation of the Fourteenth Amendment of the U.S. Constitution similarly reinforces this link and how an antidiscrimination defense is more promising. The antisubordination approach circumscribes the significance of the right to abortion by premising it on a subordinating social structure and presenting the right as a necessary escape hatch, whereas an antidiscrimination interpretation would invalidate laws that are premised on or reinforce sex stereotypes. Crucially, both the antiabortion woman-protective argument and the antisubordination defense of the abortion right depoliticize abortion by casting it as an act marked indelibly by injury.

In addition, the chapter explores how the right to abortion operates differently for different individuals. Using Foucault's notion of governmentality, I argue that the option to abort creates possibilities for governance and changes the way a woman's actions with regard to pregnancy are evaluated. Given that some women's reproduction is devalued and encoded as "irresponsible," this change in moral evaluation could lead to pressure to choose in a "responsible" manner. The chapter concludes with a discussion of an approach to the right to abortion that emphasizes autonomy as critique and transformation. On this account, the right is defended not just because it protects an individual from interference or domination, but also because that protection is crucial in part for the larger political significance that is captured in the notions of counter-conduct and eccentricity. In this, I follow Williams in seeking to transform rights to be more inclusive and insisting on their ongoing utility (1991), even as I uncover their current exclusionary tendencies and recognize their limits for radical social change.

Woman's Nature and the Woman-Protective Antiabortion Argument

In the immediate post–*Roe v. Wade* period, the most prominent arguments against abortion in the United States centered on the humanity, life, and consequent rights of the fetus. A segment of the antiabortion movement has more recently turned to what Reva Siegel has termed the "woman-protective antiabortion argument" (WPAA), according to which abortion should be prohibited because it harms women (2008). Proponents of this argument claim that women undergo psychological trauma and severe regret after abortion (known as "post-abortion syndrome") and are at higher risk of suicide and substance abuse. Proponents of the WPAA also assert that women are at high risk of severe or even life-threatening complications arising from abortion. These claims are joined with the assertion that women are frequently coerced or pressured into aborting: it is not the pregnancy that is unwanted, but the abortion.

Siegel traces the rise in the woman-protective argument to a deliberate change in strategy among substantial segments of the pro-life movement.[4] As leaders became aware that the movement's previous concentration on fetal-protective arguments—which largely ignored the role and situation of pregnant women—alienated many moderates on the issue, the movement's leaders began advancing the woman-protective argument for its supposed strategic value. The rationale of the WPAA is summed up well in the slogan of the pro-life organization the Elliot Institute: "Abortion is the unchoice. Unwanted. Unsafe. Unfair." The same organization has produced a number of advertisements to propound this antiabortion argument, many of which claim that over 60 percent of abortions are coerced. The ads blame boyfriends, parents, and husbands for using physical or psychological abuse to force women to have abortions. They also claim that doctors misrepresent the risks and the details of the procedure. One poster reads, "She believed . . . the guy in the white coat who said it was just a blob of tissue." Some ads even hint at pressures to abort that stem from wider social issues like poverty and women's increased risk of losing employment due to pregnancy (Elliot Institute 2010).

The woman-protective argument's success in shaping public discourse about abortion is clear from its appearance in the reasoning of the U.S. Supreme Court in *Gonzales v. Carhart* (2007).[5] In upholding the federal ban on intact dilations and extractions (D&Es)—as "partial birth abortions" are known in the medical community—the court goes so far as to reject the medical opinion that banning the procedure would constitute a threat to many women's health. The court's decision also allegedly relies on the framework set forth in *Planned Parenthood v. Casey* (1992).[6] The *Casey* framework seeks to balance the individual interest in abortion access against the state's interest in protecting fetal life. However, Justice Kennedy, writing for the majority in *Carhart*, actually recasts the state interest such that it involves not merely protecting fetal life but also demonstrating "profound respect for the life within the woman" (157). Because the act does not purport to save any fetal life, using this broader standard places the act more clearly in the category of legitimate state action.[7]

The state's interest in showing respect for fetal life is balanced against the individual interest, which is presented as a privacy interest in determining what happens to one's body. As cast in *Casey* and *Carhart*, the individual interest is decidedly not connected to opening up new ways of life. The court does not understand that the individual interest in abortion is bound up with understandings of womanhood and motherhood and thus with the potential for the re-creation of those understandings. Instead, *Carhart* and the jurisprudence of abortion more generally rely on and reinscribe an aporia between individual and political. The individual interest is presented as something to be balanced against the public interest, but not as something that has implications for public life.

If instead abortion is conceptualized as having broader cultural import for conceptions of womanhood and motherhood, abortion's significance shifts. As Snitow has written of abortion, "just like with the vote, there will be much resistance to letting the right to abortion expand to its larger potential meaning. We seem—this time around—to really want abortion. And this right carries within it the seed of new identities for women" (1992, 43). Put in other words, abortion's political significance is not simply about control of one's body and self-determination. In addition, abortion's political significance includes counter-conduct or eccentricity. Counter-conduct is a form of resistance that aims at shifting force relations through the construction of new cultural forms and ways of conducting oneself. Counter-conduct involves the construction of new ways of life rather than just fitting new rights into existing cultural conceptions and dominant ways of conducting one's life.

According to even the circumscribed notion of individual interest articulated in *Casey*, the *Carhart* decision hinders autonomy in part because, in its exercise of repressive power, the court does not permit women, in the words Justice Ginsburg uses in her dissent, "to make an autonomous choice."[8] Although consistent with the idea that autonomy inheres in *proper* self-governance, *Carhart* restricts individuals' ability to control the outcomes of their pregnancies. The reasoning of the decision in *Carhart* also shores up common views of women as both mothers and victims such that the potential for disrupting the link between womanhood and motherhood is undermined. The court's reasoning reflects the woman-protective antiabortion argument and is apparent in Justice Kennedy's statement in *Carhart* that

> [r]espect for human life finds an ultimate expression in the bond of love the mother has for her child. . . . Whether to have an abortion requires a difficult and painful moral decision. While we find no reliable data to measure the phenomenon, it seems unexceptionable to conclude some women come to regret their choice to abort the infant life they once created and sustained. Severe depression and loss of esteem can follow. (159)

By prefacing this unsupported claim regarding the existence of something akin to "post-abortion syndrome" with the claim about maternal love, Kennedy draws on, and in the process reinforces, the notion that women are maternal and cannot help but regret ending a pregnancy. Reflecting the language of the statute,[9] Kennedy consistently refers to the woman who has undergone an intact D&E as a "mother."[10] Especially when read in light of other instantiations of the woman-protective antiabortion argument,[11] this language suggests an identification of women with motherhood such that to be a woman is to be a (potential) mother. Even the pregnant woman who has elected to abort her "unborn child" is a mother.[12]

Rendering maternity part of women's essence serves only to contribute to and obscure the processes by which the production of that identity occurs. While the logic of Kennedy's opinion might be compatible with an understanding of liberty posited upon women's maternal essence, from the perspective on autonomy advanced here, such essentialized notions of the self are objectionable. An appeal to maternal essence reinscribes rather than resists the dominant discourse of womanhood. The reliance on an essentialized notion of women undermines the possibility for abortion to be understood as a practice that is significant in part because it may play a role in the re-creation of identities for women. This in turn limits autonomy when autonomy is understood as self-transformation that involves shifting the force relations that play a role in the constitution of the subject.

Consistent with the view that autonomy inheres in *proper* self-management, Kennedy implies that women's freedom is legitimately curbed in order to protect women from the regret that inevitably follows from violating the essence of the mother-child relationship. Kennedy's assumption of the existence of "post-abortion syndrome"—based largely on the natural maternal bond—perpetuates and plays a role in producing post-abortion guilt. His discussion of regret locates grief in the essence of the mother-child relationship, which is closely connected in the woman-protective frame with women's biology.[13] Kennedy's assumption of the existence of "post-abortion syndrome" functions to keep women's actions in line with normative expectations. In contrast to that view, this guilt can be understood as produced: antiabortion discourse and pro-choice reluctance to counter the post-abortion guilt narrative contribute to the production of the guilt women may feel after an abortion.[14] Although potential guilt and regret present important issues, portraying regret as emanating from maternal love naturalizes it as the product of women's essence, thereby covering over its production. This naturalization of regret serves to keep women's actions in line with their supposed maternal nature and discursively links women and maternity. Just as Mill warned, this state interference in individual decisions reinforces common norms.

Furthermore, Kennedy's reliance on the risk of regret is problematic because he is not willing to allow women to make a decision that they may come to regret. His impulse is to protect women from potential regret rather than let them make a decision for themselves. Privileging women's autonomy understood as critique and transformation and rejecting the notion of autonomy as proper self-governance in a discussion of abortion means protecting against such interference. In this case, the possibility of regret should not be taken as a reason for overriding women's expressed desires. Autonomy on this view entails living with the consequences of decisions instead of being relentlessly protected from potential adverse outcomes. If Kennedy's concern were with this kind of autonomy, he would recognize regret as a potential consequence of being autonomous and of making choices of one's own.

This decision is part of a larger cultural trend to experience life as fraught with risk and danger. As Foucault writes of individuals in liberal societies, "they are conditioned to experience their situation, their life, their present, and their future as containing danger" (2010, 66). Kennedy's opinion takes part in conditioning women to experience abortion as fraught with the risk of overwhelming guilt, regret, and depression.

However, Kennedy asserts the existence of post-abortion regret and depression without relying on expert or statistical analyses of risk. Rather, the management of risk is tied simply to the asserted risk factors of womanhood and a history of an intact dilation and extraction. The majority manages risk by eliminating the possibility of obtaining an intact dilation and extraction.

The discourse of maternal nature that is present in *Carhart* is entwined not only with "post-abortion syndrome," but also with the claim that women are victimized. Kennedy writes, "In a decision so fraught with emotional consequence some doctors may prefer not to disclose precise details of the means that will be used" (159). Although not explicit in the decision itself, the WPAA as described by certain pro-life organizations makes it clear that this victimization is two-tiered. At the first level are those women who do not want to abort, but who are pressured into aborting by others. At the second, deeper level are the women who think they do want to abort: these women have been manipulated at the level of desire or will. As the activist David Reardon argues, some women will need "a tremendous amount of love and help to see" that their interests are best served by bringing their pregnancies to term (1996, 5).[15]

Pro-life activists claim that mainstream society oppresses women and creates in women desires that run counter to their interests. In claiming that women's desires have been distorted and manipulated in this way, pro-life activists implicitly invoke the notion of false consciousness on which some feminists also rely. Catharine MacKinnon, for example, relies on something like false consciousness—even as she critiques the very concept—in her account of social construction (1989). She sees women as so thoroughly produced by male dominance that some have desires (for pornography or sadomasochism, for example) that run counter to women's interests. Here we see a convergence of right and left regarding oppression and its effects on the will. Each of these approaches wants to protect people from making certain decisions about their own plan of life because each camp understands certain preferences as necessarily produced by oppressive circumstances. This turn in pro-life strategy, then, resonates with the underpinnings of certain feminist orientations concerning consciousness and desire. This view also comports with the understanding of autonomy as a self-imposed law. On this account, autonomy should not be offered to those who are judged unable to govern themselves adequately, whatever the cause of their inability.

The woman-protective framework renders women who undergo abortions victims. The phenomenon of women having abortions would otherwise appear as a logical impossibility within the woman-protective frame that casts women as maternal. Suggesting that women themselves do not make the decision to abort allows Kennedy to escape the contradiction of mothers acting against their nature and killing their babies. Victimization renders intelligible the unnatural acts of women, even as maternal nature serves as evidence for the manipulation of women. There is scant evidence that this victimization actually occurs, and it is hypostatized to provide a basis for precluding women from deciding for themselves. If doctors were manipulating women, mandating detailed consent forms or other such safeguards might be necessary to ensure that women make informed decisions. In the absence of such evidence, these safeguards undermine women's agency. Thus it is not the case that all abortion restrictions are prima facie wrong. For example, there are difficult ethical concerns that arise with regard to later-term abortions. However, recognizing those concerns need not result in ignoring the ethical concerns regarding autonomy and cultural change.

Taking a robust, political view of autonomy reveals the ways the prohibition in question in *Carhart* not only is an affront to women's individual decision-making capacity but also constrains individuals' ability to participate in the creation of cultural understandings of gender and reproduction. As Valerie Hartouni has argued with regard to other court rulings involving reproduction, court decisions are "site[s] for the production of cultural meaning" and can at times be understood to "(re)consolidate cultural meaning even as they . . . simultaneously produce it" (1997, 70). While the practice of abortion could be framed in a way that renders it potentially destabilizing to the mutual constitution of womanhood and motherhood, the court's rationalizations neutralize this possibility, turning the act into a symptom of women's coerced denial of their maternal nature and reconsolidating cultural views of women and reproduction.

Depoliticization and Antisubordination

Many critical race and feminist legal theorists in the United States have taken up an antisubordination interpretation of the Fourteenth Amendment's Equal Protection Clause in order to advocate for a more progressive constitutional analysis of issues of racial and gender equality. As applied to abortion, the antisubordination analysis contextualizes the right to abortion to a greater degree than do privacy rationales like that in *Roe v. Wade* (1973).[16] Although the antisubordination approach to abortion is promising in many ways, I turn my attention to it in order to show its limitations and its surprising resonances with the woman-protective antiabortion argument. Although unlike the woman-protective antiabortion argument, antisubordination arguments defend the right to abortion and uphold women's right to control their bodies, the antisubordination approach shares some similarities with the antiabortion argument. Importantly, even though its goal is to secure the right to abortion, the antisubordination framework delimits the larger cultural and symbolic significance of abortion.

Siegel, who has adeptly critiqued the turn toward the woman-protective antiabortion argument, is herself a proponent of the antisubordination argument and has developed it in the context of abortion more extensively than other scholars. In her article "Reasoning from the Body," Siegel argues that abortion restrictions violate the Equal Protection Clause. In her view, the Constitution's guarantee of equal protection is animated by the dual ideals of antidiscrimination and antisubordination. Antidiscrimination is "concerned with the reasoning of state actors, prohibiting them from acting on the basis of prejudicial or traditional habits of thought that deny the full humanity, individual worth, or dignity of members of particular social groups"; antisubordination is "concerned with the material and dignitary injuries inflicted on members of particular social groups by public actions premised on such prejudicial habits of thought" (1992, 353). Restrictions on the right to abortion violate the antidiscrimination principle since their legislative purpose "is to pressure or compel women to carry a pregnancy to term" (357–58). This purpose itself embodies "'archaic and stereotypic notions' about the sexes" (355)[17] that are prohibited under the antidiscrimination principle. Siegel argues, though, that the "most important" way abortion restrictions violate the Equal Protection Clause is not the stereotypes they reflect but the harm they impose on women—namely, compelling women to bear and rear children (368). Antisubordination is thus the lynchpin of her approach.

Siegel has a three-part argument regarding how abortion restrictions harm women. To quote her at length:

> First, restrictions on abortion do not merely force women to bear children; powerful gender norms in this society ensure that almost all women who are forced to bear children will raise them as well, a result that legislatures adopting restrictions on abortion both desire and expect. Second, the work legislatures would force women to perform defines women's social status along predictable, gender-delineated lines. Women who perform the socially essential labor of bearing and rearing children face diverse forms of stigmatization and injury, none of which is ordained by the physiology of gestation, and all of which is the doing of the society that would force women to bear children. Third, when states adopt restrictions on abortion, they compel women to become mothers, while in no respect altering the conditions that make the institution of motherhood a principal cause of women's subordinate social status. When the gender-based impositions of abortion-restrictive regulation are considered in light of the forms of gender bias that may animate it, it is clear abortion-restrictive regulation is and remains caste legislation which subordinates women in ways that offend constitutional guarantees of equal protection. (1992, 370)

In short, the subordination that accompanies motherhood, such as the ways "a woman's identity, relations, and prospects are defined by becoming a parent in a way that a man's are not" (376), necessitates the right to abortion.

From within the framework of Fourteenth Amendment jurisprudence, Siegel's argument is compelling. In fact, current Equal Protection Clause jurisprudence provides increased scrutiny for actions that target "suspect classifications" and thus invites analysis of this kind. The determination of whether a classification is suspect depends on a history of subjugation. The antisubordination approach is powerful from within that framework because it presents a strong argument that the social consequences of motherhood and pregnancy subordinate women. While it is important to place the argument in jurisprudential context, neither Fourteenth Amendment jurisprudence nor the antisubordination analysis should thus be insulated from critique. Perhaps many of the faults of the antisubordination approach can be traced to faults with Fourteenth Amendment jurisprudence. Nevertheless, the antisubordination argument remains an appropriate and important object of critical inquiry.

While Siegel's project is promising and persuasive, especially when placed in the context of current constitutional jurisprudence, her understanding of the antisubordination approach to abortion reduces the significance of abortion to escape. Siegel acknowledges that the right to abortion serves liberty, but it is a very limited liberty, affording women only "some rudimentary control over the sex-role constraints this society imposes on those who bear and rear children" (1992, 378).[18] Considered in this way, the right to abortion hinges on a social structure that subordinates mothers and is necessary because it allows women to avoid the socially imposed harms that attend pregnancy and motherhood. Abortion is not framed as a potential form of resistance, as itself a tool for re-conceiving motherhood or womanhood, but as an escape hatch. The framework that presents abortion as an escape from overwhelming social forces denies the possibility of understanding abortion as an act with more political significance. While the right to choose abortion is crucial in part because of the reasons Siegel examines, to focus primarily on the importance of being able to escape subordination through abortion is overly limiting. Rights are significant not just because they protect individual choice, but also because they can be part of the process of "the creation of new forms of life, relationships, friendships in society, art, culture, and so on" (Foucault 1998, 164).

Siegel's dedication to both antidiscrimination and antisubordination analyses creates tension within her approach. Antidiscrimination is concerned with combating stereotypes that would reinforce limiting and traditional gender roles. The central point of an antidiscrimination analysis, which I favor, is not that motherhood is necessarily subordinating but that states act on the basis of stereotypes about women's identity and roles when they ban abortion and compel motherhood. On the antidiscrimination account, then, the right to abortion could still be grounded in an equality analysis even if we lived in a society with true gender equality. I am arguing that, even if all of the socially imposed harms of pregnancy and motherhood were addressed, prohibiting abortion would still be a violation of equality.

Antisubordination analysis, however, is premised on the continued existence of limiting gender roles. That is, the logic of escape from subordination is premised on the seemingly unassailable oppression of motherhood. Crucially, the antisubordination approach has a vested interest in casting the social context that subordinates mothers as intractable. Because abortion rights rest on claims about the oppressive social circumstances of pregnancy and motherhood, presenting the social context as static and lasting, as Siegel tends to do, strengthens the basis of the right. The possibility and importance of resisting the oppressive social aspects of motherhood are obscured and the subordinating social consequences of pregnancy and motherhood are rendered relatively stable and enduring. The logic of escape reaffirms the profound link between motherhood and subordination, thereby again restricting abortion's meaning. The gendered character of child rearing and the constrained life choices of mothers are presented as unassailable and, in the process, depoliticized.

The antisubordination prong of Siegel's argument thus pits the transformation of oppressive social forces against the right to abortion. To the extent that the powers and context that make motherhood subordinating are successfully challenged, the basis of women's claim of right would simultaneously be eviscerated. In fact, a key part of Siegel's argument is that legislatures have not accompanied restrictions on abortion with "any provision that would mitigate or offset the social consequences of enforced motherhood for women" (1992, 377). Her argument does not stand or fall on this claim, but it nonetheless raises the question of what would result for the right to abortion if legislatures did thoroughly address motherhood's social consequences. Premising the right to abortion upon the maternal subject's subordination places feminists in a double bind between agitating for changes in the broader social context and upholding the basis for the right to abortion. Comparable to the way the woman-protective antiabortion argument does not aim to provide women with resources that would mitigate the coercion they supposedly face in deciding to abort, the antisubordination approach to combating harm is quite narrow. Siegel's general point that women have been subordinated in part through practices of childbearing and child rearing is correct. Her preferred legal approach, however, works at cross-purposes to more emancipatory goals that she surely supports.

Additionally, in the process of defending a particular understanding of women's relation to motherhood, certain experiences of pregnancy and motherhood become more salient. In the woman-protective antiabortion approach, women's purported experiences of harm from abortion are salient, whereas the antisubordination argument privileges the experiences of subordinated motherhood. These legal arguments emphasize the establishment of a specific type of harm because the desired legal outcome depends on it. In doing so, they tend to present a universalizing account of women's experiences in a way that obscures the process by which they become salient as well as the theorist's or advocate's role in that process.[19] Might an emphasis on establishing injury neglect the diversity among women's experiences with reproduction and implicitly rely on a privileged perspective?

In fact, the antisubordination part of Siegel's defense of abortion has faults similar to the woman-protective antiabortion argument in that it relies on a simplistic and unfounded picture of women's experience of abortion. The antisubordination analysis, which is premised on establishing pregnancy and motherhood as injuries, obscures the fact that some women—in particular, lesbians, women of color, and poor women—are often harmed via denial or discouragement of motherhood.[20] By making the analysis turn on an establishment of subordination and by rendering abortion, not so much a matter of liberty, but an escape, the antisubordination framework cannot grapple with harm stemming from the denial of motherhood. Because of the deep investment in establishing pregnancy and motherhood as harms, the antisubordination framework cannot account for harms from nonmaternity or even for those that result from the existence of the right to abortion.

The antisubordination approach may thus reflect gender essentialism, which Angela Harris has defined as "the notion that a unitary, 'essential' women's experience can be isolated and described independent of race, class, sexual orientation, and other realities of experience" (1990, 585). The tendency to take the experiences of relatively privileged women to stand in for the experiences of all women is a characteristic of gender essentialism. That women have different experiences of abortion and motherhood is at odds with a defense of abortion premised upon the unequivocal subordination of motherhood. This is not to say that Siegel discusses only privileged women. For example, in discussing drug-dependent pregnant women, Siegel notes that pregnant women of color are disproportionately targeted for prosecutions related to drug dependency during pregnancy. In a footnote she observes that

> [s]ome advocates of fetal-protective regulation do in fact argue that the pregnant woman has assumed the duties, burdens, and penalties they would inflict on her because she has failed to obtain an abortion. Considered from this perspective, fetal-protective regulation can be understood as providing incentives for abortion which at least some of its proponents may intend as a matter of conscious design. (1992, 344n341)

In this instance, the option to abort creates the circumstances under which a woman can be prosecuted for bringing a pregnancy to term. Without the option to abort, bringing a pregnancy to term would more likely be understood as a consequence of fate.[21] Once the option to abort exists, however, giving birth becomes a decision and thereby opens up a woman to social evaluations—and, in the extreme, prosecution—stemming from her decision not to terminate her pregnancy. With the above statement, Siegel acknowledges that the option to abort can itself lead to coercion and harm for some women such that access to abortion is not an unequivocal good. That she fails to address this issue fully and only mentions it in a footnote suggests that it cannot be analyzed sufficiently from within the antisubordination framework. Antisubordination is heavily invested in establishing compelled motherhood as a harm and thus cannot grapple well with the possibility of oppression arising from denied motherhood or the option to abort.

While legal arguments and analyses depend upon singling out certain aspects of complex situations, the assumptions of the antisubordination analysis of abortion-restrictive legislation may ultimately compromise the larger goal of reproductive autonomy. Although one may argue that my critique is misplaced because the law simply cannot grapple with such complexity or nuance, such an objection relies on a simplistic and overly conservative view of the law. In fact, critical legal theory has shown how an uncritical reliance on legal categories often perpetuates subordination and renders the law a less effective tool for social transformation than it might otherwise be.[22] The law must make recourse to categories, but those categories can and should be critically analyzed. When legal categories go unchallenged, the law often ends up perpetuating oppression. Only through grappling with the complexity of social subordination can legal theory ever hope to move law in a more emancipatory direction.

Therefore, a serious consideration of Siegel's legal defense of abortion is crucial. As I have argued, her antisubordination defense is depoliticizing in two distinct senses. First, it makes the social context that oppresses mothers appear immutable and universal. As argued here, the antisubordination approach frames abortion as affording women an escape from motherhood and thus subordination, but it does not cohere well with a framework that would combat the oppression that attends pregnancy and motherhood. It tends to depoliticize the context in which individuals decide to abort by presenting that context as universal and also taking it for granted. Second, in rendering abortion an escape from one kind of subordination, that which accompanies childbearing and child rearing, the antisubordination approach not only depoliticizes the context that makes motherhood oppressive, it also depoliticizes abortion itself. According to the antisubordination analysis, the right to abortion merely presents women with a choice between subordinated motherhood or no motherhood. While that is better than the simple imposition of subordinated motherhood, it nonetheless restricts abortion's importance.

Put in other words, this defense of abortion would result in protecting only a limited sense of autonomy as individual control over the body. Through its depoliticization of abortion, the antisubordination analysis circumscribes the meaning of abortion. The importance of access to abortion centers on avoidance, not on the potential to construct new cultural forms, create new ways of life, or otherwise transform the social context. This analysis thereby less readily conduces to a more political and emancipatory vision of autonomy that would understand the cultural significance of the practice of abortion as bound to the cultural production of reproduction. If one aim of the right to abortion is to enhance autonomy, where autonomy is understood as self-transformation that involves counter-conduct, the right to abortion must be understood as having significance beyond affording women a narrow escape from oppression.

The antisubordination argument shares with the woman-protective antiabortion argument an emphasis on the establishment of harm to women. In the case of the woman-protective antiabortion approach, abortion unavoidably harms women. In the case of the antisubordination analysis, pregnancy and motherhood almost certainly harm women. In framing abortion regulation in terms of protection from harm, both the woman-protective argument and the antisubordination approach become invested in demonstrating injury. This emphasis on harm obscures the fact that part of the reason the right to abortion is important is that it has the potential to play a role in disrupting the link between woman and mother. This focus on injury is an instance of what Jodi Dean describes as "[s]hrinking the scope of political claims to those of victims needing recognition and redress." The effect of this is to "trap[] claimants in a double bind: to speak at all they have to demonstrate how they are weak, inadequate, or suffering. They must speak as those who have lost, those who are losers" (2009, 5). As Dean argues, this emphasis on victimization and the reduction of "political speech to testimony to the suffering of victims" delimits the political power of activist movements (5). In this case, claiming that abortion is needed primarily to escape injury is in tension with a claim that abortion can be a means of social transformation and that a movement can arise to change the social status of pregnancy and motherhood. The framework of injury thereby neglects the idea that the importance of abortion is tied to the ability to transform oneself and in doing so modify force relations.

Moreover, the left emphasis on the harmful physiological and social effects of pregnancy and motherhood that is apparent in the antisubordination analysis places in perspective the pro-life turn to a counter-discourse that casts abortion as the real site of women's injury. Once abortion is viewed through a framework of injury, the debate turns on whether it is abortion access or abortion restrictions that really harm women. The insistence on viewing abortion as necessary to escape injury makes the left framework vulnerable to attack from those who have been harmed by abortion. This may be an example of a kind of ideological victory that in Dean's words, "can look just like ideological defeat.

When one's enemy accepts one's terms, one's point of critique and resistance is lost, subsumed" (2009, 9). Here, the claim to an injured status loses any critical power. Both sides accept that women are injured and subordinated; the question becomes by whom and what. In either case, the goal is simply to redress women's injury, which minimizes women's power as political actors. Furthermore—and paradoxically—the focus on injury obscures the complexity of the connection between injury and abortion. Each approach neglects the possibility that some women experience injury through abortion and some through pregnancy, as well as the possibility that someone may experience both injury and emancipation in a single instance of either abortion or childbearing. The disputants in this controversy cannot allow for such nuance or ambiguity since the matter of abortion's legality turns on a somewhat absolute assessment: either abortion harms or helps women.

Governance, Options, and Autonomy

An overwhelming emphasis on the harm resulting from the lack of abortion can preclude an analysis of the complicated implications of the option to abort. Importantly, as Foucault explained with his notion of governmentality, choice creates the conditions for governance. That is, we can be governed through choice. Power can act only when directed at subjects who have some choice as to how they act, and power presupposes the subject who is free. As he notes of liberalism, it must produce freedom, but this very act entails "the establishment of limitations, controls, forms of coercion, and obligations relying on threats" (2010, 64). The art of government involves the production and management of freedom. As Catriona Macleod and Kevin Durrheim explain of governmentality, "Although the individual ostensibly has more formal rights than previously, there is less room for deviance and disorder" (2002, 48). In this section, I look at the social context in which decisions about pregnancy are made. In doing so, I explore the ways the right to abortion enables governance and constrains the ability to deviate from norms despite its creation of more options. The view of autonomy taken up in this book precipitates this examination. Focusing on autonomy as critique and transformation requires that we pay attention to the context in which options or rights are afforded. Rights do not necessarily promote autonomy. As Wendy Brown advises, "[I]t makes little sense to argue for or against [rights] separately from an analysis of the historical conditions, social powers, and political discourses with which they converge or which they interdict" (1995, 98).

Increasing options does not necessarily reduce constraints on action because the existence of a choice entails heightened responsibility for the consequences of a choice (see Dworkin 1982). Without a viable option to abort, bringing a pregnancy to term is generally regarded as a consequence of fate. However, legalized abortion in conjunction with the abortion discourse of choice renders a woman's decision to carry her pregnancy to term a choice. This opens up a woman's decision regarding the outcome of her pregnancy to moral evaluation—to assessments of whether or not she is choosing responsibly. To the extent that assessments of whose reproduction is "responsible" continue to be connected to eugenic notions of fitness for reproduction, legal and state actors as well as many people in the general populace regard many women—such as poor women, women of color, and women with disabilities—as acting irresponsibly when they choose birth.[23]

This view of women's irresponsibility is connected to ideas about their autonomy. The historian Rickie Solinger has argued that because women formally have the options to abort and use birth control, many people view indigent women as making poor choices when they have children: they are assumed to be irrational, bad at governing themselves, and even unfree (2001). Moreover, because of some women's (presumed) dependency on the state—due to poverty, disability, single status, or race—and prevailing beliefs about the value of their and their potential children's lives, any effort to justify their choice not to abort may be futile. This combines with pervasive societal doubt in such women's rational capabilities (Who would have a child on welfare? Why would a disabled woman ever procreate?) to further undermine their self-governance. The presumptive existence of the option to abort changes the evaluation of the actions of both those who exercise the option and those who do not. The option creates the possibility of being judged as bad at governing oneself.

It is worth surveying here some of the ways that certain women's reproduction is devalued and discouraged. One way state legislatures have devalued the reproduction of women in poverty is through "family cap" legislation that denies women or families increased benefits when they bear additional children. Fifteen states currently have family caps in place (Bapat 2013). Advocates for family caps put forth disturbing rationales for the caps. A citizen at a Louisiana committee hearing on a family cap proposal stated, "How long can we spend taxpayers' money on irresponsible people? We're sick and tired of working for other people. If you're not going to work, you can at least refrain from bringing other people into the world" (Saletan 2004, 207). As Linda McClain explains, "public alarm and indignation about 'irresponsible' reproduction reaches a fevered pitch when such reproduction implicates the public fisc through welfare programs" (1996, 341). In the 1990s, when most of the family caps were passed, legislators frequently appealed to the idea that the poor were irresponsible procreators.[24] This type of discourse and policies like the family cap lead Solinger to ask, "Do Americans want motherhood to be a class privilege? A life experience only available to middle class women?" (2001, 223).[25]

The myth of the welfare queen, which was especially pervasive in the 1980s and 1990s, played on these anxieties about welfare spending to cast indigent single women, especially African American women, as privileging their own greedy interests above all else.[26] In doing so, it characterized such women's reproduction as profoundly irresponsible. The myth also enabled broad social ills like poverty to be framed in terms of the bad decisions of individuals. Solinger explains that "economic dependency, caused by bad choices and leading to more of the same, was now seen as the core problem of poor, unemployed mothers, not racism or sexism or the effects of deindustrialization, or even the absence of a husband, all of which create powerful constraints on the opportunities of poor women" (2001, 195). The welfare mother trope became a powerful symbol of the dependencies and poor decision making that public subsidies supposedly encourage. Proponents of slashing welfare spending argued that withholding government support of those who reproduced irresponsibly would push such women to make better decisions.

When poverty intersects with race, marital status, and/or disability, the message not to procreate is intensified. In the case of race, Dorothy Roberts argues that since "class distinctions are racialized, race and class are inextricably linked in the development of welfare policy" (1998, 110).

Because of this, it is not a stretch to view former Louisiana state representative David Duke's family cap proposal as an extension of his earlier plan as president of the National Association for the Advancement of White People to give cash payments to welfare recipients for undergoing sterilization (Saletan 2004, 206). Because women of color are presumed to be more irresponsible and more likely to depend on the state, it is likely that Duke meant to target the procreation of women of color.

Roberts has also examined the ways punishment of drug-addicted pregnant women disproportionately targets black women, even though rates of substance abuse vary little across race and socioeconomic lines. The disparate impact of such policies is due in part to the fact that government agents judge that poor black women fail to meet the image of the ideal mother. Roberts argues that "in addition to legitimizing fetal rights enforcement, the prosecution of drug-addicted mothers diverts attention from social ills such as poverty, racism, and a misguided national health policy and implies instead that shamefully high black infant death rates are caused by the bad acts of individual mothers" (1991, 1436). Women who are in danger of being prosecuted for drug use while pregnant have one reasonable option to avoid punishment: abortion. Such discriminatory punishment, then, may coerce those most in danger of prosecution—poor black women—into having abortions. From this perspective, women may be punished for choosing to have a baby rather than an abortion (1991).[27]

The reproduction of women with disabilities is also socially devalued and generally understood as irresponsible, in part because of the commonly held notions that disabilities are inherited and that life with a disability is a life of misery. As Marsha Saxton notes of disabled parents she knows, "a common reaction they hear is that the child they are with could not have been their own and 'should they really be babysitting in their condition?'" (1984, 304). Medical professionals may even presume that women who are disabled will be unable to care for their children. In fact, some physicians counsel women with disabilities not to have children, often with little or no evidence that the woman's disability would pose a problem in pregnancy or childbirth (Kaplan 1989). When even reproductive rights advocates play on stereotypes about disability in their arguments for allowing women to abort "deformed" fetuses, it is not surprising that experts and large segments of society condemn disabled women's procreation (Finger 1984, 281–97). Because there is a nexus between poverty and disability—which results both from the fact that poverty increases risk of disability and the fact that disability is a risk factor for poverty—many women with disabilities who are also poor will experience heightened condemnation of their reproduction (Elwan 1999).

Even though some women's reproduction would be stigmatized in the absence of the right to abortion, when combined with the right, such stigmatization complicates the situation and can change a woman's own evaluation of her action. For example, an option creates the potential for pressure to make a "responsible" decision (see Velleman 2007, 7–8). While there is little evidence that women are directly pressured to abort, an option can also affect a decision about abortion in a more subtle way. Even if no one actively exerts pressure on her, a woman may—knowing that her status as a responsible, autonomous agent depends upon it— choose as others would have her choose. Others' moral evaluations of her action change because they perceive her to have a choice; in turn, how others evaluate her choice may affect her own evaluation of her options.[28] She may thus decide differently than she would have in the absence of the stigmatization of her reproduction and discourses of responsible procreation.

These judgments coexist with opposing pressures and policies, such as those resulting from the line of cases that decline to impose any positive obligation on states to fund or otherwise provide support for indigent women to obtain abortions.[29] The right to abortion cannot be equated with the actual option to abort. Decreasing numbers of abortion providers, persistent harassment of women obtaining abortions, increasingly restrictive state regulations, and the sometimes violent intimidation of doctors create significant impediments to abortion access despite the legal right to abort.[30]

Despite these impediments to abortion, the right to abortion does open up the option of abortion for many women. Moreover, and regardless of actual impediments, others may still assume that because abortion is legal a woman can avail herself of the option to abort if she desires. Therefore, these barriers to obtaining abortion do not necessarily protect women from judgments about procreative responsibility. Rather, many such barriers have resulted from judgments about women's roles and decisions. These judgments are used to justify limiting, controlling, and coercing individual behavior and decisions. As explored in the next chapter, recent legal restrictions on abortion, such as ultrasound mandates, demonstrate how increased options, provided through rights, can enable increased governance of how we exercise those rights.

We might characterize this situation of abortion regulation and judgments of women's procreative decisions as a paradox of personal responsibility. Women, especially those on the margins, are called on to be responsible agents and decision makers at the same time that state actors and others assume they are incapable of being responsible. In other words, regulatory apparatuses and cultural discourses call on them to be autonomous, but also judge them to be incapable of properly governing themselves. This inability then justifies shaping, manipulating, or otherwise interfering in individual actions to promote proper choice making.

The Right to Abortion and Autonomy as Critique

As I have shown, the existence of the right to abortion enables individuals to be governed in accord with "proper" self-legislation. Despite the governance that the right to abortion enables, from the perspective of autonomy as critique and transformation, the denial of the right to abortion would be worse. The absence of the right would enforce childbearing on women and reinforce limiting identities. I have shown how such a limitation emerges in the logic of *Carhart*. Another example will help illustrate the diverse contexts in which this equation of woman and mother occurs and its dangers.

A movement has recently emerged that exploits the history of eugenics and asserts the existence of coercive abortion practices to argue that abortion among African Americans and Latinos is a form of race genocide. In 2011 the pro-life organizations Life Always and the Radiance Foundation put up billboards in cities across the country that proclaimed things such as "The most dangerous place for an African American is in the womb" and "Black Children are an Endangered Species" (Guenther 2012). Latino Partnership for Conservative Principles later displayed billboards that targeted the message to Latinos (Solomon 2011). The billboards are part of a broader movement to portray abortion as a legacy of eugenics. Arizona has even enacted a law that prohibits "race-selective abortion." A similar ban has been introduced in the U.S. Congress and several other states (Jesudason and Baruch 2011).

The abortion as genocide campaign is yet another example of how social and legal discourse often frames women's bodies as primarily reproductive bodies and as sites for the reproduction of the community and society. Loretta Ross, former national coordinator of SisterSong Women of Color Reproductive Justice Collective, says of the abortion as eugenics campaign, "It is about re-enslaving Black women by making us breeders for someone else's cause" (2008). The pressure to bear children that this campaign exerts coexists with the pressures outlined above to act "responsibly" by not having children. Like the discourses that take marginalized women to task for being "irresponsible" procreators when they have children, the abortion as genocide campaign casts women of color as making poor decisions when they have abortions. The campaign would deny women the ability to make a decision for themselves. Furthermore, as happens in *Carhart*, coercion is posited in order to justify taking away control of women's bodies from women. The organizations behind the billboards cast Planned Parenthood as a villain and primary proponent of genocide through abortion (Jesudason and Baruch 2011).

To deny women the right to abortion is to reinscribe, as Cornell puts it, "the identity of women with the maternal function" (1995, 64) that underpins the billboard campaigns as well as the woman-protective antiabortion argument. The denial of abortion is both a way of re-entrenching the social identification of woman and mother and a way of imposing a particular understanding of pregnancy, the female body, and identity on women. Cornell argues that the "denial of the right to abortion enforces the kind of splitting that inevitably and continuously undermines a woman's sense of self. Her womb and body are no longer hers to imagine. They have been turned over to the imagination of others, and those imaginings are then allowed to reign over her body as law" (1995, 47).

Yet reformulating the right to abortion "can play an important role in the re-symbolization of pregnancy in a way that would neither deny the power of maternity nor define a woman only through her reproductive capacity" (Cornell 1995, 64). This is why we must examine other possible interpretations of the right. In her dissent in *Gonzales v. Carhart*,

Justice Ginsburg offers a compelling analysis of the right that echoes Cornell's thinking. Quoting *Casey*, Ginsburg notes, "The destiny of the woman must be shaped . . . on her own conception of her spiritual imperatives and her place in society."[31] She critiques Kennedy's reliance on women's presumed regret following an abortion by noting that the majority's "way of thinking reflects ancient notions about women's place in the family and under the Constitution—ideas that have long since been discredited."[32] Citing Siegel, Ginsburg argues that "legal challenges to undue restrictions on abortion procedures . . . center on a woman's autonomy to determine her life's course, and thus to enjoy equal citizenship stature."[33]

In the vein of Siegel's antidiscrimination argument, Ginsburg's dissent recognizes that abortion restrictions hinder women's autonomy and rely on problematic generalizations about women's identity and destiny. Though focused on challenging the Court's turn away from protecting women's health, the dissent explains the discriminatory impact of the Partial Birth Abortion Ban Act and the way it hinders reproductive autonomy.[34] This is a promising line of reasoning for abortion jurisprudence, as it captures well the ways abortion restrictions limit women's autonomy and identity. Ginsburg also makes an explicit connection between autonomy and equality. For doctrinal reasons, the Equal Protection Clause is probably a more promising basis for the right to abortion than substantive due process, which is the constitutional location of liberty rights. The latter has consistently been interpreted narrowly in terms of negative liberty such that, as mentioned above, states have no positive obligation to ensure the accessibility of abortion.[35] However, this does not mean that locating the right to abortion in the Equal Protection Clause means rejecting liberty or autonomy claims. As Ginsburg argues, the denial of reproductive autonomy to women is a form of discrimination that violates constitutional principles of equality.

Despite the promising aspects of Ginsburg's approach, she does not fully spell out the connection between women's autonomy and social transformation. In other words, she does not clearly articulate that the denial of the right to abortion, with its consequent forcing of motherhood upon women, impedes the project of disrupting the givenness of motherhood and maternal desire. That may partly be due to the paucity of existing legal doctrine that conceives of autonomy in this way.

Moreover, legal reforms and the framing of rights, while important, are not the primary means of achieving social transformation. If the goal is such transformation, we should be concerned when legal approaches—like the antisubordination argument—are at odds with this goal, even if they would protect an important right and rest on established legal precedents. I am arguing that an antidiscrimination interpretation of equal protection, which also has doctrinal grounding, is at least not in tension with a broader, critical understanding of autonomy.

Emphasizing the creative and transformative potential of autonomy means that autonomy is valued in part because it allows for greater room to maneuver and hence be involved in ongoing productive processes. This room to maneuver can further challenge hegemonic forces in a way that can increase autonomy. The relation between autonomy and constructionism, then, is circular. For example, the right to abortion allows women to delay or avoid motherhood in a way that challenges the identification of women with mothers. Not only does the right have the potential to increase an individual's autonomy, in doing so it also affords women more modes by which they can be involved in the ongoing constitution of gender and motherhood.

This evokes Foucault's notion of counter-conduct and Mill's argument about the value of eccentricity and diversity. Counter-conduct is valuable because it can be a way of opening up alternative cultural forms. Eccentric, counter-majoritarian conduct is necessary so as to challenge and avoid the identification of the customary with the natural in a way that renders it unquestionable. Recall Mill's argument: "In this age, the mere example of non-conformity, the mere refusal to bend the knee to custom, is itself a service. Precisely because the tyranny of opinion is such as to make eccentricity a reproach, it is desirable, in order to break through that tyranny, that people should be eccentric" (1998, 74). The right to abortion opens up more room to challenge the dominant production of women as maternal. In doing so, the right to abortion has the potential to disrupt the tyranny of dominant norms in a way that would allow for other understandings of gender and reproduction. In addition to challenging the state's regulation of women's bodies, these disruptions can engender a context in which the identification of women with reproductive capacity and the givenness of maternal desire are brought into crisis. This crisis may foment reflection on maternal desire and expose its contingency.[36] The disruption of the discourse that defines women by reference to maternal capacity and nature will lay the foundation for future generations to have increased possibilities. Members of this generation will have desires that are no less constructed, but they may be a product of a less hegemonic process.

In contrast to the transformation that Ginsburg's dissent presages for abortion access, Kennedy's opinion, though arguably transformative, does not contribute to women's autonomy. As I have shown, Kennedy's opinion builds on antiabortion discourses about women's nature and "post-abortion syndrome." In doing so, the majority opinion in *Carhart* arguably plays a role in transforming larger cultural understandings of gender and reproduction. This transformation, though, is at odds with the transformation promoted by the alternative tradition of autonomy I am advancing. It is instead consistent with autonomy as proper self-legislation. As discussed in the previous chapter with regard to the value of subversion or eccentricity, transformation should be valued when it creates more room for agency. Kennedy's opinion, though, reflects and reinforces the idea that there is a single proper role for women and that women who would abort are not properly self-governing. This thinking would thus constrain the ability to be self-governing. Even if understanding women as essentially maternal could be understood as a form of counter-conduct that resisted an antiessentialist understanding of gender and identity, such conduct would not promote autonomy in the critical sense in that it would restrict women's identity and constrain women's actions. In contrast, recognizing the discriminatory aspects of abortion restrictions as Ginsburg does can be a step toward transformation that opens up greater room for autonomy.

The Double Binds of Autonomy and the Potential of Autonomy as Transformation

Emancipatory feminist efforts often lead to a paradox. On the one hand, the state may hold women to a masculine ideal of the autonomous liberal subject that ignores the ways women's ability to be self-governing is constrained and sometimes justifies punishment when women diverge from that ideal. On the other hand, the state and the law may treat women as special in a process that re-entrenches difference, subjugation, and the presumption that women are incapable of proper self-governance.[37] As Mary Poovey writes, "[U]sing the language of rights exacts its price, for the language of rights coincides with a set of assumptions about the nature of the individual who is possessed of those rights, which is, in turn, intimately bound to a set of assumptions about gender" (1992, 241). This paradox manifests in the tension that attends antisubordination rationales: rights assume the existence of a liberal individual with an abstract ability to be self-governing, but basing a right on a subordinated status entails avowing an imperfect liberal personhood status. This difficulty of concurrently recognizing and overcoming past injustices confounds emancipatory feminist efforts.

The circular and paradoxical relationship of capacity and opportunities for autonomy is related to this paradox and is implicit in the preceding discussion. When the Kantian conception of the autonomous person as one who transcends the world of objects and acts on the basis of reason is rejected and the autonomous subject is recast as produced, the way the availability of options and the context of their availability can constitute the self is revealed. If an actor is not presumed to have the capacity for autonomy, then the state and its regulatory apparatus often restrict her options. However, not to afford an actor options is to constitute her as nonautonomous, which then further justifies the state's restriction of her options. Another way to put this is that ascribing autonomy to women is necessary for women to become autonomous, but this very act of ascription risks neglecting the ways women have been treated and constituted as nonautonomous.[38] I have further complicated this picture by arguing that we can be governed through choice. Beyond illuminating the range and complexity of the interactions among modes of power, this suggests that we must be careful in assessing the emancipatory potential of law and policy. Moreover, we must recognize the limitations of legal reform. Part of what I'm advocating is a shift in the cultural understanding of autonomy and its value that is not confined to or even fully expressed in the law.

Another related tension in the preceding discussion is that between the way the choice to abort results in heightened responsibility and the way women's reconstruction as victims insulates women from responsibility. The extent to which these tensions are truly at odds largely depends upon what follows from the heightened responsibility that attends choice. Choice may increase pressure on women to choose in the way society would have them choose. However, this pressure is effective precisely because when women do not choose according to social expectations, political and cultural discourses often frame women as irrational and incapable of self-governance. This judgment tends to mitigate responsibility and justify paternalistic practices. Sometimes, however, when women do not decide as society would have them, the result is punishment, not paternalism.[39] Connected to this is the fact that what gets socially coded as a choice is contingent on context and circumstance. Others will sometimes judge women on welfare as though they are fully autonomous, choosing subjects and sometimes as though they are so oppressed that whatever they do will be deemed involuntary.

The notion of autonomy as a law one gives to oneself to limit and manage oneself plays out in the context of abortion law in the following way. Autonomy with regard to abortion is to be granted to subjects who, by getting themselves into the situation in which abortion is an appealing choice, have called into question their capacity for self-governance. Others, including state actors, may judge them as being unable to constrain and govern their sexual desires and reproductive capacity properly. There are two common responses to this situation. The standard pro-life position is that women must bear the consequences of their failure to self-manage. Those who are against abortion but defend rape and incest exceptions illustrate this position vividly. The justification for the exceptions appears to be that women who become pregnant through rape and incest were coerced and so their pregnancy is not the result of their failure to govern themselves adequately.[40]

Another common evaluation of women seeking abortions goes something like this: women who try to obtain an abortion should be allowed to abort because women are in the best position to know whether they can adequately fulfill the maternal role and whether they are in a position to be able to make the kinds of sacrifices necessary to performing that role. Some proponents of legalized abortion argue that many women who seek abortions lack the emotional or financial resources to fulfill their maternal responsibilities adequately. Abortion is therefore a rational option. On this view, the decision to abort is evidence of the subject's ability to govern herself appropriately because it reflects a woman's reasonable assessment of her situation.

Kristin Luker has described the differing worldviews that lead to these two different assessments of procreative responsibility (1985). On the pro-life worldview, parenthood is a consequence that those who engage in sex must be willing to accept. Not doing so is an expression of procreative irresponsibility. On the pro-choice worldview, people act responsibly with regard to procreation when they delay parenthood until they are financially and emotionally ready. While what Luker calls the pro-choice worldview does not represent the view of all advocates of legal abortion, it does capture a pervasive strain of thought. The growing movement for reproductive justice, which calls attention to barriers to reproducing and the social context that fails to support the reproduction of those on the margins, stands in contrast to Luker's characterization of the pro-choice worldview.[41]

In fact, the reproductive justice movement is one response to this dichotomous understanding of autonomy, responsibility, and procreation. It reorients the discussion of reproduction around a more inclusive set of concerns and issues than the mere defense of the right to abortion.[42] SisterSong Women of Color Reproductive Justice Collective, which has been at the forefront of the reproductive justice movement, explains its framework: "The intersectional theory of Reproductive Justice is described as the complete physical, mental, spiritual, political, social, environmental and economic well-being of women and girls, based on the full achievement and protection of women's human rights" (Ross 2006).[43] The impetus to reframe reproductive autonomy as an issue not of proper self-governance, but of critique and transformation arises from the kinds of concerns that have led to the reproductive justice movement. Promoting reproductive autonomy understood as counter-conduct that may promote reflection and transformation would entail challenging many of the restrictive and discriminatory judgments and norms that currently undermine reproductive justice.

Conclusion

While the social construction of the subject invites questions about the production of individual preferences, the law is not the place to override women's reproductive decisions. As Mill warned, when the law manages decisions, it frequently does so in a way that reinforces oppressive social forces and reflects dominant norms. Often this is not simply a disingenuous way of expressing concern for autonomy so much as it is a direct outgrowth of the idea that autonomy should be afforded only to those who have the capacity for autonomy. Unsurprisingly, judgments of who has the proper capacity for autonomy reflect gendered, raced, and classed assumptions about who should reproduce and what it means to reproduce responsibly. The state and its regulatory apparatus tend to view those whose behavior does not comport with these norms as lacking an adequate capacity for autonomy, and so they must be guided in their decisions. This tendency within the law and other fields of expertise interferes with individual liberty by imposing ways of life and thereby impedes the transformation of norms and cultural forms.

Emphasis on autonomy as transformation means, as Cornell puts it, "that as a matter of right we should not impose any model of sexual life." Instead, "people should be allowed to craft their own. To give people this freedom does not mean that they have to use it in any particular way" (1995, 181). Furthermore, the abortion right rests on the equal intrinsic value of individuals and the resulting requirement that individuals "be valued as beings who can constantly contest and re-evaluate their own self-images in an endless process of recreation" (1995, 64). In other words, the right to abortion is best understood in terms of autonomy as transformation, because doing so not only protects against unjust imposition of ideas about identity and reproduction, but also points the way toward larger cultural change.

Emphasizing the critical and transformative aspects of reproductive autonomy also allows for a complex understanding of reproduction because it does not rely on generalizations of experiences of pregnancy and motherhood. Again, this is an important element of reproductive justice as articulated, for example, by Evelyn Shen in a SisterSong publication:

> Reproductive Justice stresses both individuality and group rights. We all have the same human rights, but may need different things to achieve them based on our intersectional location in life—our race, class, gender, sexual orientation and immigration status. The ability of a woman to determine her reproductive destiny is directly tied to conditions in her community. The emphasis is on individuality without sacrificing collective or group identity. (2006, 3)[44]

Precisely because autonomy as counter-conduct joins individual conduct to politics and collective social processes, upholding autonomy does not risk re-entrenching or ignoring subordinating social forces in the way that many legal formulations of abortion do. Focusing on autonomy as transformation diverts attention from a narrow consideration of an individual's choice to the social context that constitutes the self and within which the choice operates. Autonomy as critique involves assessing the social context and the implications of individual conduct for emancipatory social transformation. It thus enlarges rather than shrinks the scope of politics. The primary goal is not redress of injury but more radical political change.

This view of reproductive autonomy would thus leave room for and be consistent with advocacy and activism beyond protection of a legal right. Because the importance of abortion is more than escape from oppression on this view, it is not in tension with efforts to transform the social context. Admittedly, legal rights are not *the* path to emancipation, nor does or should advocating for them foreclose other action and conceptualizations of freedom. In fact, legal rights tend to be conservative. As Nivedita Menon argues, "[T]he force of law tends to fix identity in such a manner that it is the dominant and oppressive possibilities that get reinforced" (2004, 50–51). Instituting and calling for rights relies on "the assumption that [they] are self-evident, universally applicable, but some slippage in meaning takes place once they are in the legal arena where diverse discourses of rights converge" (46). The examination here of the jurisprudence of abortion, as well as the upcoming discussions of informed consent laws and sterilization, supports Menon's argument. We have seen how rights can be interpreted to reinforce domination. But they often do this while simultaneously providing actual, even if meager, tools for combating oppression. In fact, Menon does not argue for a complete turning away from the law, but for recognizing the limits of legal reform and engagement in radical political practice as a more promising avenue for transformation (216).

I share Menon's concerns and general assessment, though it is worthwhile to challenge the framings of rights so that they may operate in less exclusionary ways. Defending the right to abortion from a framework of autonomy as transformation mitigates the tendency to reinforce existing power relations, since built within the framework is a continual contestation of subjugating power relations. It does not fix an identity as the basis for a legal right, but asserts the importance of reimagining and contesting identities as a way of opening up future possibilities.[45] I have argued that an antidiscrimination approach to abortion may provide some conceptual tools to combat fixed and essentialized identities. Although recognizing the limitations of rights and the need for broader political activism, I follow Williams, who criticizes arguments that underestimate the power of rights. She argues against the claim that rights lack utility and are harmful. Flawed as they may be, rights have historically provided protection: "For the historically disempowered, the conferring of rights is symbolic of all the denied aspects of their humanity: rights imply a respect that places one in the referential range of self and others, that elevates one's status from human body to social being" (Williams 1991, 153). Even as their liberatory potential is circumscribed upon conferral, rights provide a ground for challenging their flaws and misapplications.

3

Informed Consent Laws

Ultrasound, Surveillance, and Postfeminist Reproductive Rights

In March 2011, two fetuses "testified" before a Ohio House of Representatives committee hearing on a bill that would have criminalized abortion after the point at which a fetal heartbeat can be detected. By 2013, twenty-two states had enacted laws that either require women to receive information on accessing ultrasound or require that an ultrasound be performed prior to an abortion. Early in 2012, Virginia and Alabama legislators went so far as to consider bills that would have required women seeking an abortion to undergo a transvaginal ultrasound rather than the less invasive transabdominal ultrasound. At the state capitol in Virginia in March 2012, state police in riot gear arrested thirty-one participants in a women's rights rally against the proposed ultrasound legislation. Also in 2012, the law student Sandra Fluke was barred from a congressional committee hearing on contraceptive access regarding rules about when religious institutions may exclude contraceptive coverage from insurance plans, leaving only men on the hearing panel. These examples illustrate some important and related trends that characterize American reproductive politics in the early twenty-first century: the fetus is increasingly viewed as an object of public concern, while there is heightened hostility to the inclusion of women's unique concerns in politics. States are also instituting more and increasingly harsh restrictions on women's reproductive health.

Yet the restrictions on women's bodies and health, which often take for granted fetal personhood, are frequently framed in terms of promoting women's autonomy, choice, consent, and rights. They are presented as protecting women from coercion and from making poor decisions in the service of promoting their autonomy. Legislatures often call laws that restrict access to abortion "informed consent" laws. Many of the recent state-level abortion restrictions reflect and can be traced to elements of the woman-protective antiabortion argument examined in the previous chapter. In fact, the decision in *Gonzales v. Carhart* (2007)[1] in many ways laid the groundwork for recent trends in informed consent laws. That opinion, in which the court upheld the congressional Partial Birth Abortion Ban Act, suggests that the alleged regret and anguish women may feel after an abortion stems in part from physicians providing inadequate or misleading information. Justice Kennedy implies that it would be proper for counseling before an abortion to be used to dissuade women from having an abortion (Gold and Nash 2007).

In response, states have instituted progressively stricter and more ideologically driven informed consent provisions. Many of these provisions require abortion providers to give women specific information about the procedure, including alleged risks, as well as information about fetal development. There are three different types of informed consent provisions that I will investigate to varying degrees in this chapter. The first type is the pre-abortion ultrasound mandate. Like the other informed consent provisions, ultrasound mandates claim to protect women from making uninformed decisions about abortions. By 2013, eight states required that ultrasounds be performed before an abortion, while thirteen mandated that under some circumstances a woman must be given the opportunity to view an ultrasound image. The second type of informed consent requirement that I will examine are risk advisories. The extreme South Dakota informed consent law, for example, requires that physicians inform women of the potential psychological and health risks of abortion, including the unsubstantiated claim that abortion is linked to suicide. Eight states require providers to give women information regarding purported negative psychological effects of abortion; five mandate that information about the link between breast cancer and abortion be provided to women, even though medical research does not support such a link. Anti-coercion provisions are the final type of informed consent requirement that this chapter will examine. These provisions, which also arise in the South Dakota law, are aimed at informing women that it is illegal for someone to pressure or force them into an abortion. Fourteen states mandate that women be told that they cannot be coerced into having an abortion (Guttmacher Institute 2013).

No one has yet thoroughly examined the logic and framing of these informed consent requirements. It is crucial that they be examined because, while it is apparent that recent restrictions seek to manage and control women's reproduction and bodies, there is more at stake in the legal framings and justifications of these restrictions than is often thought. They risk, as may be intended, altering or consolidating cultural conceptions of autonomy, rights, gender, and reproduction. As I argue in this chapter, the legal framings of recent state restrictions draw on and reshape the idea that autonomy inheres in proper self-governance or self-management. Postfeminist and neoliberal sensibilities have influenced the laws I investigate in this chapter. As a result, autonomy is being conceived of in terms of risk minimization and a medicalized, though legally controlled, notion of informed consent. In this context, neoliberal and postfeminist perspectives are used to pervert feminist ideas of rights and autonomy. Women are called on to be responsible individuals at the same time that they are subject to heightened oversight. The maternal nature of women is assumed and the view that autonomy is valuable in part for its potential to open up alternative cultural forms and understandings is absent. Autonomy is instead presented as a conservative and weak concept. This permits expert and ideologically driven understandings of risk and security to be used to curb autonomy while claiming to enable it.

This chapter expands on the discussion of reproductive governance discussed in the previous chapter. Although the measures outlined above undermine the right to abortion, the right to abortion as well as the notion that women choose birth or abortion are the preconditions for this increased governance and surveillance of women. Furthermore, sonograms enable some aspects of the discourse of autonomy and reproduction that is examined in this chapter. The fetal personhood and antiabortion movements have used ultrasounds extensively and effectively in order to establish the fetus as a stand-alone object of public concern. Fetal images are also invoked in an effort to facilitate the maternal bonding process between woman and fetus. Ultrasound technology has become key to the management of reproduction that is taken for granted and reinforced in many recent reproductive policies. This chapter takes a close look at how recent state-level ultrasound mandates have employed and interpreted sonograms.

I examine in particular the Texas and South Dakota informed consent laws and the circuit court decisions that upheld them. In *Texas*

Medical Providers v. Lakey (2012),[2] the Fifth Circuit overturned a lower court's preliminary injunction of the Texas version of the pre-abortion ultrasound mandate. In a pair of decisions in 2011 and 2012, the Eighth Circuit upheld South Dakota's informed consent law, which includes anti-coercion provisions and suicide and depression advisories. This chapter argues that the legal discourses embodied in these decisions and laws rely on and reinscribe limiting understandings of gender and autonomy. While Texas and South Dakota have relatively harsh versions of informed consent laws, they are important to investigate because they carry to its logical conclusion the thinking behind many less extreme laws. Moreover, more and more states are adopting informed consent provisions similar to the Texas and South Dakota laws.

The theoretical frameworks of postfeminism, neoliberalism, and biomedicalization—all of which describe and seek to make sense of aspects of the contemporary world—provide context for the chapter's examination of recent state-level abortion restrictions. Those theories help to explain how informed consent laws that manage women's conduct have arisen. They also shed light on why such laws are framed in terms of advancing women's interests and mitigating risk through medical technology. I argue that the legal discourse of informed consent laws reflects aspects of the overlapping frameworks of neoliberalism, postfeminism, and biomedicalization. The chapter thus begins with a discussion of neoliberalism and postfeminism, including their import for the broader terrain of reproductive politics in the United States, some aspects of which were discussed in the previous chapter. After a discussion of how sonograms and medicalization have altered the management of reproductive processes and social understandings of pregnancy and abortion, the chapter turns to an in-depth look at the Texas and South Dakota informed consent to abortion laws, especially as understood in the court opinions upholding them.

Gender, Neoliberalism, and Reproductive Politics

Why has there been such a marked increase in restrictions on women's reproductive health and rights in recent years? Such restrictions can be understood as attempts to shore up traditional gender roles at a moment in which they seem to be quickly eroding. The recent intensification of debates about and policies regarding women's reproductive health may also be tied to the enduring recession that began in 2007 and the seemingly unending wars of this century. Historically, anxiety about economics and poverty has often been displaced onto sexuality and reproduction, thus sometimes fueling fears of overpopulation or population by the "wrong" groups.[3] More generally, as Gayle Rubin argues, at times of social turmoil and angst, conflicts over sexuality "acquire immense symbolic weight. Disputes over sexual behaviour often become the vehicles for displacing social anxieties and discharging their attendant emotional intensity" (1984, 267).

Current reproductive politics can also be placed in the context of other trends in the contemporary United States. The current discourse and anxiety about female reproduction, which are manifest in numerous state laws, can be connected to neoliberalism and postfeminism. Neoliberalism has been described in disparate ways. Dean sums up the different ways neoliberalism has been defined as including "a set of policy assumptions favoring corporations, as inseparable from globalization and imperialism, as a 'project for the restoration of class power,' as a specific form of governmentality, and as a new form of the state" (2009, 51). There are two important facets of these varied views of neoliberalism that are important for my purposes. First is the argument that neoliberalism seeks to redraw public and private lines in an effort to increase corporate power and profit. This neoliberal strategy in turn underpins much of the current social and economic turmoil. Graham Burchell explains that neoliberalism sets itself against the social welfare state, including unemployment benefits, welfare benefits, and state education. The argument that "this governmental apparatus has become an economically and socially costly obstacle to the economic performance upon which it depends and leads inexorably to an uncontrollable growth of the State" is central to neoliberalism (1996, 27).

Second, the related transformation of governance under neoliberalism is important for understanding the way the legal texts discussed later in this chapter refigure and govern reproductive subjects. As opposed to classic liberals, who view autonomous individuals as the foundation or ground of the state, neoliberals view individuals in terms of their reactions to economic incentives (Dean 2009, 51–52). Neoliberal governmentality is concerned with "construct[ing] prudent subjects whose moral quality is based on the fact that they rationally assess the costs and benefits of a certain act as opposed to other alternative acts" (Lemke 2001, 201).[4] As Thomas Lemke explains,

> By means of the notion of governmentality the neo-liberal agenda for the "withdrawal of the state" can be deciphered as a technique for government. The crisis of Keynesianism and the reduction in forms of welfare-state intervention therefore lead less to the state losing powers of regulation and control (in the sense of a zero-sum game) and can instead be construed as a reorganization or restructuring of government techniques, shifting the regulatory competence of the state onto "responsible" and "rational" individuals. Neo-liberalism encourages individuals to give their lives a specific entrepreneurial form. (2001, 201–2)

Instead of framing abortion as only or primarily a moral decision, the laws encourage pregnant women to weigh the costs and benefits of abortion and to make a well-informed and calculated decision. At the same time, the laws present the costs of abortion as overwhelming. This governmentality element of neoliberalism is explored in later sections of this chapter. Here I make some observations regarding the connection between reproductive politics and neoliberal policies to undermine the welfare state.

As Lisa Duggan has persuasively argued, class, race, gender, and sexual hierarchies are key to the establishment and maintenance of neoliberal policies that "aim[] at dismantling the limited U.S. welfare state, in order to enhance corporate profit rates" (2003, x). Taking Duggan's analysis seriously in the context of reproductive politics entails examining how these debates and policies create and maintain gendered hierarchies that bolster neoliberal policies.[5] Although neoliberalism is in many ways characterized by privatization, the state's role in shaping reproductive politics demonstrates that it does not necessarily involve a shrinking of the state. As I explain in further detail below, the recent surge of state-level abortion restrictions also expands state power over medicine and women's bodies. This expansion of state power at the cost of women's sovereignty bears out Inderpal Grewal's point that "for feminists neoliberalism has come to mean new collaborations and dynamism between public and private patriarchies" (2006, 25).

The way the issue of women's reproductive health care became a flash point for the debate over health care reform illustrates that neoliberalism works through establishing and maintaining gendered systems of power. The Affordable Care Act, President Obama's 2010 health care law, is controversial because, even though it keeps health insurance privatized, it regulates private industry and requires that individuals purchase health insurance or pay a penalty. It thus expands the role of the federal government in health care. With the Department of Health and Human Services' announcement in the fall of 2011 that contraceptives would be classified as a preventative health measure and thus not subject to a co-payment, debate over the state's role in providing contraceptive access erupted.

Opponents argued that a government requirement that contraceptives be covered as preventative health care is somehow unjust. Many states have reacted with extreme proposals. In March 2012 Arizona considered a measure that would allow employers to deny employees coverage for birth control that is prescribed for the purpose of preventing pregnancy rather than for the treatment of a health problem. Also in March 2012 the Department of Health and Human Services announced that Texas is losing all federal funding for family planning services because of a Texas law that does not permit Medicaid funds to be used at any Planned Parenthood in the state (Bassett 2012). Although the privatized health care system remains, the contraceptive coverage mandate has come to symbolize what is wrong with health care reform: government interference that benefits individuals who do not deserve it at the expense of corporate autonomy and profit. That it is benefits for *women* that have caused the most controversy exemplifies how gender operates within neoliberal frameworks. It is significant that some opponents of contraceptive coverage defend coverage of Viagra (see Pitney 2008; Belle 2008).

Recognizing the extent to which neoliberalism and gendered power relations are intertwined and the way social and economic anxiety is often displaced onto issues of sexuality and reproduction challenges a common narrative regarding recent battles over women's health care. The common story is that the recent spate of laws and proposals are merely political distractions. Those who say this do not generally contend that these issues are unimportant, but that proposals regarding women's health are simply a way to distract the public from the *real* issues, like economic inequality, corporate power, and war.

This narrative coalesces with the discourse surrounding debates about women's roles more generally. For example, when Hilary Rosen, a Democratic strategist, said in early 2012 that the presidential candidate Mitt Romney's wife, Ann Romney, had "never worked a day in her life," many commentators viewed it as both an attack on stay-at-home mothers and a distraction from more serious issues (Shear and Saulny 2012). While there is truth in that analysis, it is worth considering the extent to which issues ranging from the gendered division of labor to the economic crisis are intertwined with the gendered and class hierarchies that were implicated in Rosen's comment and the responses to it. Consider that in January 2012, Mitt Romney said he believes that mothers on public assistance should be encouraged to have the "dignity of work" (Klein 2012).

As touched on in the last chapter, the vilification of welfare recipients, especially mothers on welfare, has been central to pushing the neoliberal agenda of slashing public assistance. Welfare reform in the 1990s relied on the often-gendered notion of "personal responsibility." The 1996 Personal Responsibility and Work Opportunity Reconciliation Act, which replaced Aid to Families with Dependent Children with Temporary Assistance for Needy Families (TANF), framed single motherhood and nonworking mothers as central to the perpetuation of poverty. It encouraged welfare recipients to work for wages and framed the poverty of women on public assistance as the result of individual irresponsibility rather than wider social injustices (see Luker 1997; Solinger 2001; Smith 2007). Anna Marie Smith points out the "prevalence of neoliberal risk management discourse in TANF policy" (2007, 69) and the way single women on welfare and their children are figured as having an "inherent and unswerving disposition toward high-risk behavior" (71). This framing is used to blame those on assistance for their own situation and justify cuts to public assistance. The vilification of mothers on welfare for not working obscures the fact that capitalism continues to benefit from and rely on the unpaid labor of reproduction and child rearing. Immigrants and women of color perform the bulk of remunerated childcare work, which is poorly compensated and done largely for the benefit of affluent women.

Acting in one's self-interest is often perceived as good or natural in the context of the market. However, when an activity is *framed* as publicly subsidized, which is more likely the more disenfranchised the beneficiaries are, acting in one's self-interest is likely to be maligned and understood as irresponsible.[6] Moreover, since motherhood is culturally presented as a selfless activity, women who act in their self-interest in the context of procreation appear out of place and irresponsible. As Joan Williams argues, though the idea of individuals making self-interested choices is central to American thought, when women make self-interested decisions with regard to abortion, they are denounced as selfish (1991). Aborting for one's own well-being is seen as selfish because women are socially expected to be self-sacrificing maternal caregivers. Furthermore, the market to some extent continues to be defined against the family. Whereas self-interest, individualism, and calculating rationality define the economic realm, the familial realm is one in which selflessness, relationality, and emotion, symbolically embodied in the mother, are supposed to predominate. However, as I argue below, informed consent laws are refiguring the decision to abort as a matter of properly weighing and calculating risks.

This set of expectations of women under neoliberalism causes friction. On the one hand, society expects women, like all individuals, to pursue their self-interest and act selfishly in the market. On the other hand, that behavior is demonized and perceived as irrational in the context of maternity or when women receive certain kinds of government assistance. Postfeminism informs this phenomenon, as well as the gendered character of calls for individual responsibility and blame for the tax burden. The postfeminist perspective is contradictory in that it simultaneously purports to uphold values of autonomy and choice while also increasing interference and surveillance of individuals, especially those society deems to have made "poor" decisions. This perspective is referred to as "postfeminist" because it is informed by but distinct from a feminist perspective. According to Gill, "[W]hat makes a postfeminist sensibility quite different from both prefeminist constructions of gender or feminist ones is that it is clearly a response to feminism. In this sense, postfeminism articulates a distinctively new sensibility. . . . Feminist ideas are both articulated and repudiated, expressed and disavowed" (2008, 442). Feminist ideas of empowerment and agency are employed and valued at the same time they are stripped of their emancipatory meaning and potential (see Gill 2008; McRobbie 2008).

This description of postfeminism captures well some aspects of what is happening today with regard to reproductive politics. As discussed in the previous chapter, the woman-protective antiabortion framework calls on the feminist notions of autonomy and anti-coercion to restrict access to abortion. Moreover, the right to abortion has enabled increased governance of women and their reproductive decisions. As I demonstrate in the coming analysis of informed consent laws, the discourse of autonomy, rights, and consent sits alongside increased surveillance and management of women in that context as well. This is not surprising once it is understood that the very concept of autonomy has often been understood in such a way that only those who are properly self-governing are granted full rights and political subjectivity. Thinkers and state actors have long used autonomy to justify paternalism toward those in danger of making purportedly improper decisions.

The postfeminist perspective, which calls on women to be personally responsible, converges with elements of neoliberalism. Gill describes some of the components of this connection between postfeminism and neoliberalism in the following way:

> First, and most broadly, both appear to be structured by a current of individualism that has almost entirely replaced notions of the social or political, or any idea of the individual as subject to pressures, constraints or influence from outside themselves. Secondly, it is clear that the autonomous, calculating, self-regulating subject of neoliberalism bears a strong resemblance to the active, freely choosing, self-reinventing subject of postfeminism. These two parallels suggest, then, that postfeminism is not simply a response to feminism but also a sensibility that is at least partly constituted through the pervasiveness of neoliberal ideas. (2008, 443)

As discussed above, neoliberalism involves a specific kind of governance in which individuals are called on to self-govern. Burchell explains that "neo-liberalism seeks in its own ways the integration of the self-conduct of the governed into the practices of their government and the promotion of correspondingly appropriate forms of techniques of the self" (1996, 29). The construction of individuals as self-regulating rational actors is now seen as a key element of neoliberalism (see Rose 1990, 1998). More broadly, neoliberal governmentality "increasingly depends upon ways in which individuals are required to assume the status of being the subjects of their lives, . . . upon the ways in which they practise their freedom" (Burchell 1996, 29–30).

Examining the recent trends in state-level abortion laws reveals how postfeminist and neoliberal sensibilities influence and shape those policies. However, this examination also challenges Gill's claim that postfeminism is characterized by a view of individualism that ignores "pressures, constraints or influence" (2008, 443). State reproductive restrictions actually take up feminist concerns about coercion and pressures and turn these concerns against feminist aims. As described in chapter 2 and as will be explained further below, abortion restrictions increasingly rely on the unsubstantiated claim that husbands, boyfriends, and doctors frequently coerce or pressure women into abortion. This formulation is still postfeminist in the sense that it takes up feminist notions and applies them in a way that increases surveillance and paternalism over women, but it does not strictly align with Gill's sketch of postfeminism. The example of state abortion restrictions shows, then, the importance of examining different contexts in which purportedly feminist ideas are employed. It also may suggest a deeper, more insidious version of postfeminism that acknowledges and reframes constraints and influences on actions. This simultaneous acknowledgment and perversion of feminist concerns helps to justify increased surveillance. In fact, the figuring of women as victims—which, as I have shown, is central to certain strands of arguments both for and against legal abortion—along with attention to alleged coercion has contributed to the state's heightened oversight of women and their reproductive decisions.[7]

In its convergence with postfeminism in reproductive discourse, neoliberalism calls on women to be rational, responsible, risk-avoiding procreative actors at the same time that they are subject to increased surveillance. The understanding of autonomy at work in this discourse is similar to the autonomy as proper self-governance tradition, with its expectation of self-legislation and simultaneous intervention in the conduct of those who are not self-regulating appropriately. Postfeminist and neoliberal sensibilities, however, also call on subjects to self-regulate in new ways. The way autonomy operates in the discourse of recent abortion regulations, to which I turn below, demonstrates the danger of depoliticized notions of autonomy that fail to consider the relevance of power relations to self-governance. It also illustrates the potential importance of resignifying autonomy in the realm of reproductive law and politics.

Sonograms and the Medicalized Governance of Reproduction

It does not seem too much to claim that the biomedical, public fetus—given flesh by the high technology of visualization—is a sacred-secular incarnation, the material realization of the promise of life itself. Here is the fusion of art, science and creation. No wonder we look.
—Donna Haraway, "The Virtual Speculum in the New World Order"

While Western societies have long viewed reproduction and sexuality in terms of individual morality and responsibility, individuals in such societies are now expected to fulfill their individual procreative responsibility, not primarily through moral behavior like continence (Gordon 2007), but largely through medical services and knowledge. This is part of a larger trend that the sociologist Adele Clarke and her colleagues call biomedicalization, through which "health becomes an individual goal, a social and moral responsibility, and a site for routine biomedical intervention" (2010, 63). Biomedicalization builds on the existing medicalization of many areas of life. Medicalization refers to the process by which problems such as abortion, formerly seen as under the jurisdiction more or less exclusively of law, come to be conceived of as medical issues under the jurisdiction of the medical profession (Clarke et al. 2010, 50). The medicalization of reproduction tends to displace and undermine women's experiences and perspectives on pregnancy in favor of those of the medical expert. Ultrasounds play an important role in the (bio)medicalization of pregnancy and, as I argue here, enable new forms of governance.

Biomedicalization emerged alongside neoliberal economic policies. In the context of health care, neoliberalism has resulted in shrinking public health services. At the same time, government investment in medical research has expanded and patent rights are increasingly privatized. Public research institutions like universities have also created stronger ties to the medical industry (Clarke et al. 2010, 90–94). The practices and discourses of biomedicalization also converge with neoliberal notions like self-surveillance. As Clarke puts it, key regulatory discourses of biomedicalization include "[p]ersonalized, individualized risk surveillance and management" and "[r]hetorics of choice and knowledge" (2010, 95). Discourses of risk and surveillance have played an important role in how biomedicalization is shaped and carried out. Moreover, risk concerns shape the development of technologies, and technology enables greater surveillance of potential risks. As Clarke explains, "Risk and surveillance are aspects of the medical gaze that is disciplining bodies. . . . They implicate each of us *and* whole populations through constructions of risk factors, elaborated daily life techniques of self-surveillance, and the management of complicated regimens around risk and chronic conditions" (2010, 63–64).

Reproductive practices, like other realms that have come under increased medical and technological control, are increasingly thought of and mediated in terms of risk and surveillance. In the last several decades, ultrasounds have become an important mechanism for managing pregnancy and have allowed for a unique kind of surveillance. Sonograms are now seen as an essential part of prenatal medicine in part because of their use in assessing risk.[8] In addition to their diagnostic function, since the 1980s physicians have considered the emotional potential of ultrasounds. They have been used with the belief that they facilitate bonding between the pregnant woman and her fetus (see Fletcher and Evans 1983).

As the Haraway quote that opens this section suggests, sonograms have also been used to constitute the "public fetus," meaning that fetal imagery has been used to promote bonding between the fetus and the public. The pro-life and fetal personhood movements have relied heavily on fetal images. Rosalind Petchesky notes that the pro-life movement set out "to make fetal personhood a self-fulfilling prophecy by making the fetus a *public presence* . . . [in] a visually oriented culture" (1987, 264). These movements have used fetal imagery from ultrasounds to constitute the fetus as an individual entity in a way that marginalizes and obscures the pregnant woman and the fact that the fetus resides

within her body. Sonograms obscure visually and discursively the ges-
tating body in representations of fetuses and thus further the discursive
and visual separation of woman and fetus.[9] The cultural construction of
fetuses as individuals, which sonograms enable, has in turn resulted in
fetuses becoming a distinct population who encounter risk and should
be surveilled.

It is in part the proliferation of fetal imagery that has contributed to
the destruction of, in Berlant's words, "the world in which pregnancy
could be considered a local event of personal privacy" (1997, 96). The
technology of ultrasound has altered representations and understandings of private and public. The shifts in these understandings are part of
what has enabled neoliberal calls for self-regulation of procreative practices, as well as heightened surveillance of pregnancy and reproduction.
Put in other words, fetal imagery has been intertwined with the expansion of the power of the state to manage pregnancy, which has come at
the expense of women's decision making. Furthermore, fetal figures are
part of the pervasive imagery of what Edelman (2004) calls "reproductive futurity," which asks us to invest in the future by investing in the
figure of the Child. This representation occludes the interests of those
who symbolically stand against the fetus and the future—that is, those
who do not procreate or who abort.[10] The trends in informed consent
to abortion laws, as explained later in the chapter, embody this idea of
reproductive futurity by asking pregnant women to invest in the future
through the fetus.

In many instances, such as in laws that mandate pre-abortion ultrasounds, sonograms are presented as the unmediated truth of pregnancy
and fetuses. In the case of the fetal testimony in Ohio, legislators presumed that it makes sense for a fetus to testify and that the fetus has
something to say. However, the fetal "testimony" consists merely in the
image of the fetus and its faint heartbeat. The image and sounds stand
in for a voice that might tell a layered and contextualized story. There
are no words in the fetus's testimony. Technology makes possible and
mediates the image and heartbeat, although that is obscured when they
are presented as simply revealing reality.

Not only does the recent use of ultrasounds often rely on the notion
that fetal images present the reality of pregnancy, it also shows that different relations of power come into play as more reproductive possibili-

ties are created through developments in reproductive technology. As Foucault argued, power acts when directed at subjects who have some control or choice over how they act. While the possibility of acting in various ways creates the conditions for power, the art of government necessitates the production and management of freedom: "[T]hose who try to control, determine, and limit the freedom of others are themselves free individuals who have at their disposal certain instruments they can use to govern others. Thus, the basis for all this is freedom, the relationship of the self to itself and the relationship to the other" (Foucault 1998, 300). On such an account of governance, power presupposes the subject who is free, and attempts to control the conduct of another mark power relations.

Technological changes, combined with the existence of the right to abortion, create the possibility for the kind of governance of reproduction that is seen in the pre-abortion ultrasound mandates. That is, the expansion of technology, here in the form of ultrasounds, increases the potential sites for legal regulation and creates different opportunities to control conduct. In this instance, a specific representation of medical expertise connects the public rationality of risk management to the governance of allegedly private reproductive decisions. As Macleod and Durrheim note, "It is through expertise that the apparently 'public' issue of rationalities of government are linked in liberalism to the 'private' question of how one should behave, how one 'conducts' one's own conduct" (2002, 53). As discussed in chapter 2, one effect of this kind of governance is that women are called on to be reproductively responsible. As I show below, informed consent laws frequently send the message that bringing a pregnancy to term is the responsible choice. In doing so, such laws play a role in constructing women's understandings of reproduction and responsibility. This encourages a specific kind of self-surveillance and self-governance.[11]

In this way, the use of ultrasound has converged with the postfeminist and neoliberal discourses explored above. Calls to be responsible individuals and manage risk are important aspects of both neoliberalism and postfeminism. In the context of pregnancy, state actors and experts expect self-management to be carried out through medical practices and technology such as ultrasound. The current increase in surveillance and governance of women has been discursively and symbolically intertwined with the use of ultrasound. Ultrasound technology itself has enabled legislators to pass legislation seemingly aimed at protecting fetal life while obscuring the fact that they control women. In the next section, I turn to laws that mandate ultrasound before an abortion, which show the extent to which ultrasounds are being used to surveil and manage the conduct of those who are pregnant.

Pre-Abortion Ultrasound Mandates and the Production of Consent

In 2011 Texas amended its Woman's Right to Know Act, which involved "informed consent to an abortion," by adding a pre-abortion ultrasound mandate to the act.[12] This ultrasound law seeks to shape pregnant women's conduct by encouraging them to bond with the fetus and to view the fetus, as the state does, as a person. Pre-abortion ultrasound mandates also embody the woman-protective perspective of *Carhart* (2007), which upheld the federal Partial Birth Abortion Ban Act and was examined in the previous chapter.

The precursor to many of the ultrasound laws and the *Carhart* opinion came in 2006, when the South Dakota legislature passed an abortion ban. As a proponent of that ban said, "I refuse to show pictures of dead babies" (Davey 2006). Instead, proponents relied heavily on the argument that abortion hurts women and that abortion should be banned in order to protect women. The task force report on abortion commissioned by the South Dakota legislature takes it to be self-evident that women are pressured to abort and asserts that "abortion is a completely unworkable method for a pregnant mother to waive her fundamental right to her relationship with her child" (South Dakota State Legislature 2005, 55). In a reflection of the new pro-life rhetoric, the report claims that

> this method of waiver of the mother's rights expects far too much of the mother. It is so far outside the normal conduct of a mother to implicate herself in the killing of her own child. Either the abortion provider must deceive the mother into thinking the unborn child does not yet exist, and thereby induce her consent without being informed, or the abortion provider must encourage her to defy her very nature as a mother to protect

her child. Either way, this method of waiver denigrates her rights to reach a decision for herself. (56)

This quote exemplifies the pro-life argument that assumes women's maternal nature and uses that fact to make the otherwise unsupported claim that women are pressured to abort. In turn, that alleged pressure to abort violates women's autonomy. We can also see in this quote a turn toward a different configuration of rights with regard to abortion. The crucial right here is posited as a woman's "right to her relationship with her child" (55) instead of a right to abortion. Whereas supporters of legal abortion often claim that the denial of the right to abortion compels motherhood, this argument claims that legal abortion allows "abortion providers" to compel abortion.

Although voters struck down the South Dakota ban in 2006, this legislative report has shaped later South Dakota laws and influenced legislation in other states. For example, in 2008 both Oklahoma and Idaho passed laws concerning coerced abortion. The Oklahoma law, which in 2012 was found in violation of the state constitution, would have "require[d] abortion providers to post notice informing women that coerced abortion is illegal and that they can contact the authorities if necessary." The Idaho legislation "makes it a crime to coerce a woman into having an abortion by either physically harming her or threatening to do so" (Guttmacher Institute 2008). These laws impose requirements on abortion providers to combat women's supposed victimization at their hands.

Crucially, the South Dakota report recommends banning abortion, making it clear that the task force is less concerned with allowing a woman "to reach a decision for herself" than it is with imposing motherhood on women. Recognizing that a ban may not be possible, however, the report recommends a number of other legislative changes, including requiring women to look at ultrasounds, permitting only abstinence-based sex education, and strengthening child support laws. Pre-abortion ultrasound mandates, which appear in state laws like the Texas Woman's Right to Know Act, can thus be traced to the South Dakota report.

The details of the Texas Woman's Right to Know Act merit examination for the peculiar way the law frames consent and creates exceptions to its voluntary and informed consent provisions. I argue that the law produces an ideologically driven notion of consent that claims to enable autonomy and rights while increasing surveillance of reproductive decisions. Furthermore, the law and the court's decision upholding it reinforce and simultaneously reformulate the idea that autonomy consists in proper self-governance. The "informed consent" to abortion laws, of which the Texas law is one example, rework the idea of appropriate self-governance so that it embodies neoliberal ideas of risk management and minimization. Moreover, the law prescribes medical technology as the appropriate means of managing and minimizing risk.

The Texas pre-abortion ultrasound mandate has been upheld in federal court. In response to a challenge to the law brought by physicians and abortion providers, a federal district court issued a preliminary injunction suspending enforcement of the law. In 2012 a panel of the Fifth Circuit overturned the preliminary injunction in *Texas Medical Providers v. Lakey*. The court viewed the ultrasound requirements as furthering informed consent, holding, "The relevance of these disclosures to securing informed consent is sustained by *Casey* and *Gonzales* [*v. Carhart*], because both cases allow the state to regulate medical practice by deciding that information about fetal development is 'relevant' to a woman's decision-making" (578).

According to section 171.012(a) of the act and as the *Lakey* court describes, a woman has provided voluntary and informed consent only if an ultrasound is performed, the sonogram is displayed such that the pregnant woman may view it, and the physician provides a clear explanation of the image, "makes audible the heart auscultation," and provides an explanation of the sound. A later section of the statute makes exceptions to these apparent requirements. Although all women seeking an abortion must undergo the ultrasound, a woman may choose not to view the images and she may choose not to hear the heart auscultation. Informed consent, then, depends on the physician doing certain things, but not on the woman receiving all of the information thus produced.

In cases in which the pregnancy was the result of rape or incest, the fetus has a severe medical condition, or the woman seeking an abortion is a minor who has judicially bypassed parental notification, a woman may avoid hearing the verbal explanation of the ultrasound results. As a matter of statutory definition, then, a woman in such instances does not give informed consent. This is because section 171.012(a), which provides the definition of voluntary and informed consent, includes a requirement that the physician describe the sonogram. As a formal legal matter, even though the law permits exceptions, a woman has not consented unless she fulfills all of these requirements. Consequently, the law will permit abortions to which, by the state's own definition, women have not legally consented. The Fifth Circuit, unlike the district court that first heard the case, saw no vagueness or contradiction in the statute, but merely "a harmonious pair of regulation and exception" (583).

The exceptions in the statute are at odds with one of the apparent goals of the statute, which is to make women bond with the fetus by seeing and hearing it. Since women can opt out of seeing and hearing the fetus—even though they must undergo the ultrasound and, in most instances, hear a description of the fetus—the statute is punitive. Significantly, the state is not, as in older informed consent laws, requiring women to receive standardized information about fetal development and generic fetal images. The state instead is requiring the use of women's bodies to produce images of specific fetuses in the hope that a woman will bond with *her* fetus. They thus require a woman to submit her own body to be used in creating the message the state wants to send (Sanger 2008). In requiring ultrasounds, the state is violating a woman's bodily autonomy and using her body to produce the state's message. When states mandate ultrasounds, their use is not diagnostic and not used to help discover the best way to carry out a woman's decision (Sanger 2008, 380); rather, when states mandate ultrasounds, they impose an understanding of pregnancy on the woman seeking an abortion that is likely in tension with her own view. Such requirements are an exercise of state power that highlights the vulnerability of women's bodies and their control over their own reproductive processes, while asserting the sovereignty of the state. In requiring a procedure that is already common before abortions, though not medically necessary, the state declares its authority to control physician conduct and pregnant women's bodies.

This aspect of the Texas law is a legacy of *Roe v. Wade.* As Poovey (1992) has argued, while *Roe* grants women the right to abortion, it also establishes the state's ability to regulate it. Consider the majority's statement in *Roe* that "a woman's right to terminate her pregnancy is not absolute, and may to some extent be limited by the state's legitimate interests in safeguarding women's health, in maintaining proper medical standards, and in protecting potential human life."[13] The right to abortion has never been framed as absolute. The state's interest in protecting fetal life is to be balanced against the woman's interest in privacy. A consequence of this framing of the right to abortion is that, as Penelope Deutscher explains, "the woman seems to be slyly attributed the status of sinister sovereign, at the mercy of whom the fetus exists in its threshold state. . . . [T]he woman's possible sovereignty may be considered a zone of disputed authority with an alternative sovereign power, the state" (2008, 66).

The text of the Texas Woman's Right to Know Act obscures the fact that the law is an exercise of the state's power at the expense of women. As is typical of laws like this, the ultrasound and heartbeat requirements are framed in terms of a woman's right: a woman has a "right" to view the sonogram and hear the sounds from the heart. In a perversion of feminist ideas and in a reflection of the South Dakota report, this law frames even the most restrictive of abortion measures as a matter of women's rights. This signifies an interesting turn in the conceptualization of rights. Rather than withholding rights from those who are deemed unable to govern themselves, these laws position women as having a right to guidance and intervention in their reproductive decisions. We could say they have a right to make the right choice. Rights themselves are used to shape the conduct of individuals in accordance with legislative and judicial understandings of proper conduct. The appeal to rights here suggests that individuals are free only if they have "full information." There is no acknowledgment of the political, ideological, and cultural manipulation or construction of that information. The right to know is presented as self-evidently facilitating autonomy.

The decision in *Lakey* and the Texas law also conflate autonomy with a medicalized and legalized notion of informed consent. For example, the *Lakey* court reasons, "The point of informed consent laws is to allow the patient to evaluate her condition and render her best decision under difficult circumstances. Denying her up to date medical information is more of an abuse to her ability to decide than providing the information" (579). The court goes on to note that the doctrine of informed consent "itself rests on settled principles of personal autonomy."[14] Rather than acknowledging that the Texas law and the court's decision to uphold it shift the balance between the sovereignty of the state and women's sovereignty in favor of the state, the court reasons that the state is merely enabling women to exercise their sovereignty in a more informed and voluntary way. The rhetoric of informed consent allows the interest of the state and the interest of women to coincide. The decision appears not to be shifting the balance because women's *real* interest is in not hurting the fetus.

Truthful Disclosures and Autonomy as Risk Avoidance

In discussing informed consent in *Lakey*, the court refers to the 2011 *Minnesota v. Rounds*[15] decision (*Rounds I*), in which the Eighth Circuit upheld most parts of a South Dakota law that amended the requirements for informed consent to abortion. The law at issue was passed in 2005 and contains both risk advisories and an anti-coercion provision. The law requires the doctor who is to perform an abortion to give women oral and written advisories in advance of the procedure. The written advisories must include the following information:

(b) That the abortion will terminate the life of a whole, separate, unique, living human being . . . ;
(c) That [the patient] has an existing relationship with that unborn human being and that the relationship enjoys protection under the United States Constitution and under the laws of South Dakota;
(d) That by having an abortion, her existing relationship and her existing constitutional rights with regards to that relationship will be terminated.[16]

In addition, a woman must be provided with a "description of all known medical risks of the procedure and statistically significant risk factors," including "depression and related psychological distress" and "increased risk of suicide ideation and suicide."[17]

In *Rounds I*, a panel of the Eighth Circuit upheld all of the advisories except the suicide advisory. The court held that the other provisions merely inform women that no one can constitutionally force them into having an abortion and that the provisions are meant to respond to the legislature's concern that "people getting abortions . . . feel coercion, they feel pressure, they feel alone" (2011, 668). The *Rounds I* court appealed to *Casey* in upholding the provisions, arguing, "Informed consent requirements 'must be calculated to inform the woman's free choice, not hinder it.' Because an informed consent requirement must 'facilitate[] the wise exercise' of a woman's right to abortion, such a requirement presents an undue burden unless it provides 'truthful and not misleading' information."[18] *Rounds I*, like *Lakey*, demonstrates how informed consent laws manipulate the notion of informed consent to undermine women's knowledge and perspective. The laws simultaneously present themselves as facilitating autonomy understood as making "wise" decisions. The required advisories rest on the presumption that women do not know what it means to be pregnant or what an abortion is. The legislature with its superior knowledge and wisdom needs to shape women's beliefs and choices.

In the 2012 *Minnesota v. Rounds*[19] decision (*Rounds II*), the Eighth Circuit reconsidered *en banc* the legality of the depression and suicide advisories that *Rounds I* had struck down. In *Rounds II*, the court upheld the South Dakota law's requirements that women seeking an abortion be informed of the procedure's alleged risks of depression and suicide. As I argue here, the *Rounds II* court takes up a neoliberal frame focused on risk management through surveillance. The South Dakota informed consent law appeals to autonomy as proper self-governance, yet in this instance what constitutes proper self-governance is that which minimizes certain risks.

Rounds II is fascinating for its detailed analysis of the concept of risk. The challengers to the South Dakota law argued that, as used in the law, "risk" implied a "conclusive causal link between abortion and suicide" (2012, 894). After a lengthy inquiry into the meaning of risk in medicine, the Eighth Circuit concluded that the concept of risk simply implies correlation, not causality. The court also misleadingly relied on the decision in *Carhart* to conclude that, as stipulated in the law, "'depression and related psychological distress' is a 'known medical risk[] of the [abortion] procedure.'" The Eighth Circuit cites the *Carhart* decision for its claim that "[s]evere depression and loss of esteem can follow" an abortion, omitting the sentence that preceded those words: "While we find no reliable data to measure the phenomenon, it seems unexceptionable to conclude some women come to regret their choice to abort the infant life they once created and sustained" (2007, 159).

The *Rounds II* court also dismisses any medical uncertainty regarding these risks, arguing that "the truthful disclosure regarding increased risk cannot be unconstitutionally misleading or irrelevant simply because of some degree of 'medical and scientific uncertainty.'"[20] Quoting the reasoning in *Casey* and *Carhart*, the court held that

> "[m]edical uncertainty does not foreclose the exercise of legislative power in the abortion context any more than it does in other contexts" (quoting *Gonzales v. Carhart*). In particular, "a requirement that a doctor give a woman certain information as part of obtaining her consent to an abortion is, for constitutional purposes, no different from a requirement that a doctor give certain specific information about any medical procedure" (quoting *Casey*). There is no basis in the "non-misleading" and "relevant" requirements of *Casey* for imposing a new, stricter definition of medical risk—a standard that requires certainty of causation—simply because the medical procedure at issue is abortion. (900)

The court here refuses to grant abortion a special status, claiming that it is like any other medical procedure to which physicians must obtain informed consent. The *Rounds II* court ignores the possibility that these provisions are being legislatively mandated only because abortion is a controversial medical procedure. It is difficult to imagine a state legislature enacting a law requiring physicians to disclose risks with inconclusive scientific evidence in any other context.

The legislative preoccupation with risk and the way the *Rounds II* court reasons about risk reflect the contemporary neoliberal and biomedical preoccupation with security and risk. The shift toward prevention of individual ailments and behaviors through assessment and analysis of risk factors characterizes many contemporary medical practices in this era of biomedicalization. In turn, these practices have enabled new kinds of surveillance. As Robert Castel argues, systematic predetection "is a form of surveillance, in the sense that the intended objective is that of anticipating and preventing the emergence of some undesirable event" (1991, 288). Castel goes on to note that, from the perspective of risk and surveillance, the subject disappears and is replaced by a combination of risk factors: "What the new preventive policies primarily address is no longer individuals but factors, statistical correlations of heterogeneous elements" (288). This way of thinking multiplies indefinitely the potential sites for intervention, since all behaviors and situations involve some level of risk. The South Dakota legislature relies on flawed assessments of abortion to conclude that abortion poses substantial risks. In doing so, it exploits the social and medical preoccupation with risk to justify increasing surveillance of women seeking abortions. The primary risk factor the legislature is concerned with is having an abortion.

In *Rounds II*, the related discourses of neoliberalism, postfeminism, and biomedicalization converge. Each of these discourses relies on what Gill describes as the "autonomous, calculating, self-regulating subject of neoliberalism" (2008, 443). This subject is expected to act in such a way that risk is minimized, but this entails increased surveillance to ensure proper self-regulation and risk minimization. This biomedical, neoliberal subject is also postfeminist: in the *Rounds* cases women are presented as simultaneously making informed free choices and requiring state surveillance and disciplinary technology to ensure that the "right" choice is made. The reliance on risk in the advisories recalls the postfeminist, neoliberal subject whose reproductive health decisions are to be carried out through routine medical intervention and are a matter of individual responsibility.

This increased surveillance and use of risk can be connected to the anti-coercion provisions that are now in the informed consent to abortion laws of fourteen states, including South Dakota. These laws require that women be informed that abortion cannot be coerced. Jane Scoular and Maggie O'Neill have examined how British regulations of prostitution have used "increasing evidence of the marginalization, violence and abuse in prostitution" to justify "techniques of risk and responsibilization which operate to control the bodies and subjectivities of women selling sex" (2007, 773). Although abortion anti-coercion provisions have responded to a problem that does not seem to exist, by framing abortion as coerced, states can effectively justify increased intervention and surveillance of women without relying only or primarily on morally or religiously based understandings of fetuses. Presenting women as at risk of coercion makes it easier to implement measures that, though they purport to address coercion and misinformation, actually increase state control of women's bodies.

One important aspect of *Rounds II* is how risk, like rights and autonomy, is conceptualized and used to interfere with individual decisions, while being framed as enabling self-governance. Aside from the skewed information that informed consent to abortion provisions often contain, many of them are worrying for the way they conflate autonomy with the minimization of risk. The presumption of the South Dakota law and *Rounds II* is that the course of action that best serves autonomy is that which minimizes risk. Taken together, the provisions of the South Dakota law suggest that the highest risk comes from women deviating from their supposed maternal nature, although the law also contains a provision that requires pregnant women to be informed of the "statistically significant medical risks associated with carrying her child to term compared to undergoing an induced abortion."[21] The implication of the South Dakota law and *Rounds II* is that the proper way to manage oneself is to take stock of risks and act so as to minimize them. This turn toward risk conflates autonomy and security.

Law and Medicine: The Construction of Pregnancy and Abortion

We must and do apply today's rules as best we can without
hubris and with less sureness than we would prefer, well
aware that the whole jurisprudence of procreation, life and
death cannot escape their large shrouds of mystery, yet, and
perhaps not, to be lifted by advances of science.
—*Texas Medical Providers v. Lakey*, Panel of the Fifth
Circuit, 2012

The law enters into an interesting interaction with science and medicine in the case of informed consent to abortion laws. With regard to pre-abortion ultrasound mandates, the legal realm appeals to medical images and sounds as truthful, even though an expert may be required to explain them. In doing so, the law obscures the ideological aspects of the information provided. In other instances, such as the suicide advisories, legal actors are more dismissive of medical and scientific expertise. In general, court opinions that uphold recent state-level abortion restrictions assert the primacy of legal expertise and manipulate medical knowledge to their own ends.

The analysis in *Lakey* accepts science and images as nonideological per se and neglects the possibility that embedded within the images, sounds, and descriptions is a particular politically and socially constituted understanding of women, reproduction, pregnancy, and fetuses. As the court writes,

> To belabor the obvious and conceded point, the required disclosures of a sonogram, the fetal heartbeat, and their medical descriptions are the epitome of truthful, non-misleading information. They are no different in kind, although more graphic and scientifically up-to-date, than the disclosures discussed in *Casey*—probable gestational age of the fetus and printed material showing a baby's general prenatal development stages.[22]

The court here appeals to and consolidates a certain view of science, technology, and reproduction, yet abortion is an intensely political and ideological issue in which the "truth" is highly contested.

In fact, the debate over abortion, in implicating how the fetus is described and understood, lays bare the construction of reproduction. The statute's requirement that the ultrasound and heart auscultation not only be performed, but also be explained in layperson's terms to the pregnant woman demonstrates that the images and sounds do not "speak" for themselves. This requirement is a tacit admission of the fact that the meaning of sonograms is not objective, transparent, or readily discernible. To achieve the statute's goal, an expert must mediate and interpret such images. Despite the Fifth Circuit's description of these procedures as "inherently truthful and non-misleading," the statute itself suggests that it is a specific interpretation of sonograms and heart auscultations that can provide the true meaning of the procedures. Carol Sanger explains that "[m]andatory ultrasound . . . insist[s] that women take a particular view of fetal existence. That insistence stems not from any innate truth about what an ultrasound picture reveals but from what the visual politics of abortion has taught us to see" (2008, 408).

The way pre-abortion ultrasound laws are written recalls the way physicians in the nineteenth century through the mid-twentieth century successfully rendered abortion an issue to which they had superior knowledge. As Luker (1985) has shown, physicians argued that medical facts and knowledge of which women were ignorant could resolve the issue of abortion. By doing so, they obscured that the debate is in fact about the assessment and moral interpretation of facts. In the current wave of ultrasound laws, legislators are attempting a similar construction of the issue. They are asserting that the debate is simply one of facts, though they are reserving for themselves, rather than physicians, the ability to determine and interpret those facts.

Legislators are moreover suggesting that pregnant women are generally ignorant of what pregnancy and abortion entail. As Sanger puts it, ultrasound requirements "assume[], as many mandatory ultrasound statutes announce outright, that a woman who consents to an abortion does not already understand the nature and consequences of the procedure" (2008, 380). The Woman's Right to Know Act and the *Lakey* opinion take for granted the medicalization of abortion and the centrality of physicians to the abortion decision. The reasoning of this decision is a logical outgrowth of the medicalization of pregnancy, which minimizes the importance of women's independent perception and knowledge of pregnancy and places it under the purview of medicine. As such, the decision privileges the information originating from medical and technological intervention. The veneration of medical experts in this law coincides with the ascendancy of the fetus at the expense of women in the management of reproduction. The privileging of medical expertise and the corresponding derogation of women's perspectives allow the court to ignore that the supposedly "truthful, non-misleading information" is literally in the body of a woman. As Carol Stabile notes of earlier developments in reproductive policy, "the visual and symbolic exclusion of women from reproduction seems . . . yet another strategy for investing power in legal, medical, and other institutional bodies, while ignoring material female bodies" (1992, 194).

The *Lakey* decision, along with other legal decisions upholding the newest phase of abortion restrictions, illustrates that legal expertise is not subservient to medical expertise. In these cases, the legal realm constructs its own understanding of medical expertise and gives that understanding the backing of the law. *Rounds II* further illustrates this point. In upholding the South Dakota suicide and depression advisories, the Eighth Circuit asserted its power to define medical risk and determine the significance of medical knowledge. Recall as well that in *Carhart* the court dismissed medical experts' claims that intact dilations and extractions are sometimes medically indicated to ensure the health and life of pregnant women.

In many instances informed consent laws actually require physicians to speak, convey the state's ideological perspective, and provide misleading information. Physicians have challenged informed consent laws on the basis that they violate physicians' First Amendment right to freedom of speech.[23] This claim was dismissed in both *Rounds II* and *Lakey*. In *Rounds II*, the Eighth Circuit interpreted *Casey* and *Carhart* to conclude, "While the state cannot compel an individual simply to speak the State's ideological message, it can use its regulatory authority to require a physician to provide truthful, non-misleading information relevant to a patient's decision to have an abortion, even if that information might also encourage the patient to choose childbirth over abortion."[24]

These examples demonstrate that abortion is in fact under joint juridico-medical jurisdiction, where the relationship and interactions between law and medicine are complex and dynamic. The control that law wields over, in this case, medical assessments of pregnancy and abortion complicates the notion that abortion has been medicalized. The idea that abortion has been medicalized is used to describe the phenomenon of social problems such as abortion moving away from being primarily under the domain of law and coming increasingly under the purview of medical experts (Clarke et al. 2010). While medical knowledge and expertise are central to reproductive decision making, *Lakey* and the law it upholds, as well as the *Carhart* and *Rounds II* decisions, demonstrate the extent to which the law can and does manipulate medical knowledge and declare its supremacy.

Critiquing Informed Consent

Given the productive power of law, we should consider the legal discourse in this chapter for the messages about ultrasounds, women, and autonomy that it embodies. The legal discourse around ultrasound requirements and informed consent laws more generally reinforces traditional and restrictive understandings of women and reproduction in a way that undermines autonomy as transformation. From the perspective of autonomy as critique and transformation, autonomy is valuable in part because of its potential to create and reshape cultural forms that may shift force relations. Ultrasound requirements and their accompanying legal discourse, on the contrary, further entrench restrictive understandings of reproduction and seek to impose those understandings on pregnant individuals seeking abortions. In particular, ultrasound laws rely on and reinforce a narrow and ideologically driven view of fetuses. This view is wielded to increase surveillance of primarily cisgender women's bodies and to separate discursively the fetus from the pregnant woman. The discourse assumes both that pregnant women's interest is in bringing the pregnancy to term and that the fetus is an individual.

In the cases considered here, courts fail to cite *Casey* for its promising antidiscrimination thread, which is in tension with the surveillance to which that decision opens the door. As Justice Ginsburg puts it in her dissent in *Carhart*, the decision in *Casey* declares that the decision to bear a child is crucial "to a woman's 'dignity and autonomy,' her 'personhood' and 'destiny,' her 'conception of . . . her place in society.'"[25] The attorneys and the Center for Reproductive Rights that challenged the amendments to the Texas Woman's Right to Know Act argued that the changes to the law violate constitutional principles of equal protection. The complaint filed with the district court argues that the revised law "rests upon and perpetuates sex-based stereotypes and imposes 'protections' on women that are not imposed on men." It also "treats women as less competent, less mature, and less informed decision-makers than men" and "seeks to steer women into gender-stereotyped roles in family and society."[26] The complaint furthermore points out the damage that the act forces physicians to inflict on women, including "violating [their] bodily integrity, autonomy and best interests in violation of medical ethics" (36). The complaint, then, has strengths similar to those of the antidiscrimination defense of abortion that I articulated in the previous chapter. Unlike the antisubordination defense of abortion, this antidiscrimination argument highlights the sex stereotypes animating the law but does not base its defense of a stronger abortion right on the intractable subordination of pregnancy and motherhood.

Furthermore, these attorneys' arguments are consonant with the perspective of autonomy as critique and transformation in that the complaint recognizes that the act "perpetuat[es] patronizing and paternalistic stereotypes of women as . . . unable to make medical decisions on their own" (37). The plaintiffs' arguments in *Lakey*, then, acknowledge that the paternalism in the act rests on "the notion that a woman's primary and proper role is that of mother" (37). And that is a problem in part because it limits what women can do and restricts notions of female identity.

Autonomy as critique and transformation would highlight how ultrasound mandates and other informed consent provisions both impose the state's restricted understanding of gender and pregnancy on women and, in doing so, also undermine women's ability to act as eccentric subjects. The complaint filed by the challengers to the Texas law does not go so far as to state explicitly that abortion restrictions prevent women from challenging stereotypes about women's identities and roles in a way that may prompt larger cultural transformation. As noted earlier, there is little doctrinal support for such a legal argument. Nonetheless, the complaint's logic supports that conclusion. In fact, this more social and transformative element of autonomy may be best emphasized within political and social movement arguments rather than legal discourse. However, because of the importance of legal discourse, legal frameworks should not preclude or be in direct tension with the transformative and critical aspects of autonomy, as they are in the *Rounds* cases, *Lakey*, and the antisubordination argument.

In contrast to the alternative tradition of autonomy, the legislative restrictions examined in this chapter depoliticize autonomy. Autonomy is not framed as having important political or social effects. The effects of the conceptualization of autonomy evident in the legal formulations discussed above extend beyond the mere limitation of women's choices and surveillance of women's bodies. These legal formulations reflect and consolidate a conceptualization of autonomy that reinforces women's association with maternal nature and asserts women's inability to make choices without the guidance and scrutiny of experts. Furthermore, the understanding of autonomy at work in this legal discourse uses the language of risk and consent to curb liberty.

Consequently, these laws potentially shape the cultural conception of what it means to be self-governing. In this legal context, autonomy is not about directing one's own life course or about transforming social forms; rather, in neoliberal fashion, the self is called on to engage in rational self-regulation by assessing risk and conducting oneself in a manner that minimizes risk. In these informed consent laws, autonomy embodies a kind of bureaucratic rationality according to which the goals of action go unquestioned, and the means are statistically and rationally assessed in terms of probabilities of risk and benefit. Informed consent provisions are presented merely as requiring the disclosure of "facts." It is significant that in their deployment of risk and medical facts, the above laws and cases disregard the accuracy of the risk assessments and the ideological aspects of scientific knowledge.

The turn to risk and informed consent in the laws discussed above allows the law to appear to escape engagement in substantive discussions about things on which people have deeply held differences of opinion. The decisions discussed in this chapter allow courts to disavow their role in privileging specific subjective values and perspectives. Courts can maintain a thinly veiled stance of neutrality and ignore the way the law is a discourse of power. In other words, in substituting its own judgments of medical knowledge for the judgments of women seeking abortions, the state tries to depoliticize its own message. The state asserts it as neutral scientific fact even as it manipulates medical knowledge.

Informed consent laws make recourse to the self-managing and rational subject of postfeminism and neoliberalism. The state increasingly subjects the pregnant subject to surveillance and medical management to ensure proper self-regulation. As presented in the laws and decisions examined here, this subject is not explicitly tied to the neoliberal agenda of increasing corporate profit and shrinking the social welfare state. Nonetheless, these laws and opinions show how the idea of personal responsibility, which has been wielded to blame poverty on poor individual choices and used to dismantle social welfare programs, has expanded to areas of social policy not explicitly connected to the social welfare state. The discussion in this chapter also shows that the neoliberal subject is gendered. Women's bodies have come under heightened surveillance. Additionally, because women are constructed as maternal, women are called on to be rational and self-managing in specific ways.

As in the long tradition of autonomy as proper self-governance, appeal to principles of self-governance in these informed consent laws results in increased governance of the choosing subject. Once it is taken for granted that guidance or interference in individual decisions can promote autonomy, legal actors can more easily justify legal measures that encourage a particular decision or specific decision-making process. The kinds of informed consent laws I have examined in this chapter are clearly aimed at encouraging birth. They also encourage a decision-making process that entails bonding with the fetus and viewing the fetus as a person. As a result, these laws rely on and constitute an understanding of abortion as traumatic and fraught with psychological risk. In turn, the rejection of abortion is framed as enhancing security or safety and therefore autonomy: the autonomous actor would seek security.

The general appeal to feminist language and women's rights in the context of many of the recent informed consent laws results in the derogation of feminist concerns.[27] Informed consent laws rely on and reshape feminist ideas like coercion, choice, consent, rights, and autonomy. The use of the terms and concepts of autonomy and rights, albeit in ways that obscure rather than bring attention to power relations and social context, indicates that women and their interests cannot simply be ignored in reproductive law. Feminism has succeeded in establishing the connection between reproductive regulation and the regulation of women such that reproductive policies at least have to be framed in terms of women's interests. These laws are examples of a postfeminist use of seemingly feminist ideas to increase surveillance and governance of women. Moreover, presenting women as victims makes it easier to justify surveillance in the name of protecting women.

Understanding the use and manipulation of concepts in these laws reveals that part of what is at stake in them is the meaning of some crucial concepts.[28] The legal discourse examined here not only risks shaping cultural understandings of concepts like autonomy, rights, and consent, it also may affect subjectivity. Subjectivity involves both the process of governing oneself and being governed by another.[29] Informed consent laws hold the potential to affect how women understand and govern themselves in a way that undermines their ability to play a role in cultural constructions and transformations. They attempt to reinforce the state's view of pregnancy as women's proper function and fetuses as persons. Pre-abortion ultrasound mandates, for example, give one understanding of pregnancy the status of law and enforce it on women. It is significant that viewing a sonogram is socially viewed as a woman's first experience of motherhood and marks the beginning of her social constitution as a mother (Sanger 2008, 382). This endorsement of one view of pregnancy is especially troubling considering that these ideologically driven advisories are encoded in the law, which tends to be privileged as neutral and objective. As Cornell would argue, ultrasound laws see women as violable due to their reproductive capacity. Such laws seek to enforce a particular moral and psychic understanding of pregnancy on women, thereby denying women the symbolic space to give their own meaning to their pregnancies.

The problem with this imposition of both a particular moral view and a specific life plan becomes clear if we assume that individuals have equal intrinsic value. As discussed in chapter 1, making such a political claim results in respecting individuals' life plans and allowing them to carry out their plans without undue interference from the state. As Mill argued, the protection of an individual sphere is crucial in order to induce reflection and challenge the customary. As is evident from the example of informed consent laws and as my interpretation of Mill suggests, when the state interferes in individual decision-making processes, it is likely to do so in a way that reinforces common norms. These laws reinforce the idea of women as naturally maternal and seek to reconstruct the fetus into an individual. This intensifies the pressure to act in accord with custom. The state's imposition of these cultural views on women undermines autonomy as transformation. Instead, the law should allow women to make their own valuations that might challenge common cultural forms. Permitting eccentric conduct would enable greater challenges to custom. In the context examined here, acting eccentrically should be privileged as a way of pushing back against the neoliberal, postfeminist, biomedicalized construction of gender, pregnancy, and autonomy that is becoming increasingly customary.

Conclusion

The public viewing of the fetus has reconstituted understandings of pregnancy, in which women's sensory experience used to be primary. Ultrasound allows the public and the pregnant woman to "see" inside and supposedly apprehend the reality of the fetus. As a result, sonograms have enabled the construction of fetuses as stand-alone entities, separated visually and symbolically from the female body.[30] The extreme measures of the early twenty-first century are in some ways an outgrowth of this social, symbolic, and visual separation of the fetus from the pregnant body. The proliferation of sonograms enabled and contributed to this disarticulation. Through the use of ultrasounds, the fetus is presented as independent and as an individual, but also as always under threat and thus requiring protection. This justifies increased surveillance of women's bodies while not appearing to target women.[31] The use of fetal imagery obscures the fact that to surveil a fetus is to surveil the woman in whose body the fetus resides.

Technology has thus played a constitutive role in reproductive politics in a way that supports science and technology studies scholars' argument that science and politics are co-constitutive. The use of images in this debate underscores the importance that images have in today's culture, but those images should not be understood as having an inherent meaning. Fetal imagery may allow for the visual and symbolic separation of fetus and woman, but the image itself does not predetermine that view. It is thus worth examining alternative constructions of pregnancy and reproduction. Two kinds of questions should be asked: What possibilities are there for reframing how ultrasound images are understood? What other kinds of images may be used to shift the terms of the debate over reproductive politics? As will be explored in the next chapter, images of cut or cauterized fallopian tubes could play a role in resignifying the visual politics of reproduction. Other ideas about alternative visual representations should also be explored. JaneMaree Maher has argued that a visual and discursive focus on the placenta could offer an alternative understanding of fetuses and their relation to pregnant bodies (2002).[32] Exploring such possibilities may help to challenge the visual and symbolic separation of fetus and woman that has laid the foundation for some of the recent restrictive laws. It is especially important, at this time of increased state management of women's reproduction and bodies, to seek out alternative images and cultural representations of reproduction.

The implicit appeal to fetal personhood in the ultrasound mandates and other informed consent provisions obscures their insidious effects. In addition, the legislative and judicial recourse to the idea that these laws actually promote informed decisions and personal autonomy conceals the extent of their potential negative effects. I have avoided viewing the legislative and judicial language of informed consent laws as simply

disingenuous. By investigating the logic behind current reproductive restrictions, I have shown that these informed consent laws risk reshaping
our collective understandings of key concepts like autonomy in line with
neoliberal notions of security and a narrow, medicalized understanding
of informed consent. This reveals why it is especially important to consider alternative critical understandings of autonomy that, along with
alternative images, could push back against the recent onslaught of reproductive restrictions and their underlying logic.

4

Sterilization

Self-Governance and the Possibility of Transformation

A young woman with no children reported that when she requested a sterilization, a physician told her, "Go away and come back when you are married" (Campbell 1999, xiv). Medical professionals turned away a friend of mine who had no children when she sought a sterilization in her mid-twenties. The medical establishment did not take her request seriously. In her own words, "After being rebuffed by my family doctor, I contacted the local Planned Parenthood and was unequivocally told that no local doctor, whether associated with Planned Parenthood or not, would perform the operation on a 23-year-old woman who would likely change her mind." After moving to California and after "three 'are you sure' screening interviews," she was finally sterilized (personal communication).

In 2001 doctors told an African American transgender male who was incarcerated in a California prison that he had a fibroid in his uterus and that he needed surgery. No other information or request for consent was provided to him. In a later consultation with a doctor regarding subsequent pain, he could not recall the exact date of the hysterectomy. In response, the doctor said, "how stupid are you not to remember the date of an important event in your life." The incarcerated man described his experience to Justice Now in the following way: "I felt coerced. I didn't understand the procedure. . . . I never planned on having children, but I would have liked that option to be mine" (Levi 2006, 79).

These examples are consonant with an understanding of autonomy as proper self-governance according to which the ability to make one's own decisions is withheld from those who are deemed unable to govern themselves properly. Looking at these practices from the perspective of autonomy as critique and transformation reveals the multiple ways they are an impediment to reproductive autonomy. The simultaneous inaccessibility of female sterilization to some and the imposition of sterilization on others, primarily women of color, limit individuals' ability to carry out their reproductive decisions. Furthermore, impediments to sterilization access limit reproductive autonomy because they both reflect and contribute to what Katherine Franke has called "repronormativity," which is the normative framework that encourages reproduction and takes reproductive desire as a given (2001). Cultural understandings that align female identity with motherhood play a role in producing and reinforcing ideas about the naturalness and inevitability of reproductive desire and thus delimit the range of acceptable reproductive behaviors and desires. At the same time, coerced sterilization contributes to and reflects discriminatory judgments about who is a legitimate reproducer. It contributes to the constitution of classes of people as incapable of proper self-governance and as inappropriate reproducers while taking for granted women's identity as procreators.

Sterilization through the ligation of the fallopian tubes is a common form of contraception in the United States.[1] Of American women who use contraceptives, 27 percent rely on tubal ligation. It is the most common form of birth control among thirty- to thirty-four-year-old women, as well as black and Hispanic women of all ages (Mosher and Bachrach 1996; Mosher and Jones 2010). Before the passage of the Affordable Care Act in 2010, roughly 85–90 percent of private health insurance plans covered sterilization. In January 2012, the Obama administration announced that under the new health care law, health insurance plans would be required to cover female sterilization without a co-payment or deductible. Public funding is also available for sterilization, and the procedure is generally covered as a family planning service under Medicaid (Ranji 2009). However, compared to women with private insurance, women on Medicaid face more barriers to accessing postpartum sterilization because of the thirty-day waiting period between consent and sterilization that is in place to prevent involuntary sterilization.[2] Despite this barrier, in 1990 female sterilization rates were highest for "less-educated, low-income and minority women of all ages" (Mosher and Bachrach 1996).[3]

Because those who have studied the characteristics of women who get sterilized tend to assume that it is a procedure undergone when a woman has *completed* her childbearing, there are no accurate assessments of the numbers and characteristics of women without children who seek sterilization. The limited research that exists, along with journalistic accounts of sterilization, suggests that young women without children, like those quoted above, frequently have difficulty finding a physician willing to ligate their fallopian tubes (Campbell 1999; Lawrence et al. 2011; Zylbergold 2007; Paul 2012). Rates of voluntary childlessness, which may be correlated to sterilization rates, are generally lower among black and Hispanic women than white women, though a 1989 study shows that the disparity in rates between black and white women disappears when class is taken into account (May 1997; Boyd 1989).

The current practice of sterilization cannot be adequately understood apart from the history of eugenics, neo-eugenics, and compulsory sterilization. This chapter begins with a discussion of that history before looking at the contemporary context of both involuntary and voluntary sterilization abuse. I also examine the medical discourse through which women's bodies and reproductive capacity are understood and examine what the contemporary medical discourse and practice surrounding female sterilization reveal about the ongoing production of women, motherhood, and sexual reproduction.[4] Since medical professionals control access to sterilization, this analysis is crucial.

This chapter argues that the identification of female physiology with maternal desire underlies restricted access to voluntary sterilization. Furthermore, both the denial and imposition of sterilization take for granted that women, because of their presumed reproductive function, are appropriate sites for management. The chapter also explores how sterilization itself can help expose procreation as a cultural preference. While the denial and difficulty many women—particularly the young and childfree—experience in obtaining sterilization reflect and reinforce normative ideas about reproduction, the sterilization of such women may disrupt those very norms and their accompanying heteronormativity. As Butler argues, the maternal body can be seen as the "consequence of a system of sexuality in which the female body is required to assume maternity as the essence of its self and the law of its desire" (1990, 92). As such, challenging the maternalizing of the female body may also challenge the system of sexuality that produces it and thereby be a practice of critical autonomy.

I argue that sterilization's techno-medical intervention in the body holds the potential to subvert dominant notions of maternal desire and its connection to women's presumed reproductive capacity. This chapter explores that potential as well as the discursive and regulatory frameworks that enable physicians in the United States to act as gatekeepers to sterilization access. I argue that the regulation of voluntary female sterilization reflects and contributes to the medical and social identification of women with procreative capacity, but that the proliferation of the practice, especially among women without children, could play a role in destabilizing that identity. The disruption of the identification of the female body with reproductive desire holds the potential to loosen the demand to reproduce and thereby enhance reproductive autonomy.

In considering the potential destabilizing effects of voluntary sterilization, the chapter offers an analysis of the practice that relies on a combination of Butler's notion of performativity and Haraway's cyborg theory. I consider sterilization as a performance that has the potential to disrupt associations of womanhood with motherhood. Moreover, I argue that the sterilized body might be read as a cyborg figure that subverts not just the idea of women as inevitably maternal, but also widespread binary notions of woman-man, nature-culture, and organism-machine. Relying on cyborg theory allows for an examination of issues of the body and technology that are often left out of research on nonreproduction, but that are crucial to consider if the identification of women's bodies with reproductive desire is to be challenged. The reading of sterilization offered here leads to an engagement with both the regulative and performative aspects of nonmotherhood, as well as with the materiality of the body. This focus on the body reveals the technological transformation of sterilization as a challenge to the prevailing production of female identity and maternal desire at the level of the body. The relationship between cyborg theory and critical autonomy is explored in more depth in the book's concluding chapter. At this point, though, it is important to note that attention to the ways technology and the body may combine to incapacitate reproductive function is urgent because deep-seated associations of the female body with maternal nature play a role in limiting reproductive autonomy. Moreover, cyborg disruptions can function as a technologically informed form of eccentricity, counter-conduct, or subversion.

Because of the disturbing history of involuntary female sterilization and ongoing sterilization abuses, much scholarship on tubal ligation situates the procedure as a potential violation. A consideration of sterilization that would focus on its disruptive or emancipatory potential has been closed off as a result of this positioning. In other words, sterilization is so often associated with coercion and oppression that the procedure's positive potential has not been thoroughly examined. Placing this analysis of sterilization, which foregrounds the procedure's emancipatory potential, alongside the important scholarship on sterilization abuse[5] adds nuance to understandings of sterilization and better reflects the diversity of individuals' experiences with the procedure.

In analyzing sterilization as a (non)reproductive technology that has the potential to challenge pronatalism and the presumed centrality of maternity and maternal capacity to womanhood, this chapter builds on the literature that examines the complex cultural forces that incentivize reproduction[6] as well as the burgeoning literature on reproduction and technology.[7] While analyses of pronatalism have not engaged in an exploration of the technology of sterilization, which has opened up the possibility of childlessness for an array of women, recent scholarship on reproduction and technology has focused primarily on technologies that enable reproduction, such as in vitro fertilization and surrogacy, or on technology, such as ultrasound and prenatal testing, that is used during pregnancy. Given this focus, scholars have not thoroughly explored the use of technology to foreclose reproduction, which itself may reflect an assumption that the practices that are most interesting and important to study are those that enable reproduction. This chapter challenges that assumption and presents a different perspective on the relation between reproduction and technology by considering how the practice of voluntary sterilization, particularly among childfree women, might challenge pronatalism and help reconstruct motherhood as a preference. In this way, it may serve as the kind of conduct that promotes critical autonomy and cultural transformation.

Eugenics, Neo-Eugenics, and Coerced Sterilization

At the turn of the twentieth century, the eugenics movement—which sought to "better" society by controlling who procreated—took hold in the United States and was tightly linked with the emergence of modern family planning techniques and practices (Roberts 1998, 72–76). For example, the birth control advocate Margaret Sanger wrote in 1919,

"More children from the fit, less from the unfit—that is the chief issue of birth control" (Gordon 1990, 281). The very wealthy often promoted and funded family planning programs at this time. As Thomas Littlewood notes, such funders "fear[ed] that the capitalist system would be threatened by lower-class overpopulation" (1977, 6). Wealthy families like the Carnegies and the Rockefellers funded the numerous eugenic research centers established between 1910 and 1930 (Kluchin 2009, 12).

While wealthy and middle-class women had difficulty accessing contraceptives and were accused of committing "race suicide" when they failed to have enough children, physicians often sterilized women they declared "unfit" against their wills (Kluchin 2009, 14). Laws allowing for forced sterilization of the "socially inadequate" became widespread during the first half of the twentieth century: by 1931, thirty states had enacted such laws (Shapiro 1985). The 1922 "Model Eugenical Sterilization Law," drafted by the influential eugenicist Harry Laughlin and designed to pass constitutional muster, reveals the expansiveness of the category "socially inadequate." His model statute provided for the sterilization of a person who "fail[ed] chronically in comparison with normal persons, to maintain himself or herself as a useful member of the organized social life of the state." The "socially inadequate classes" included the "feeble-minded," the "insane," the "criminalistic," the "diseased," the "deformed," and the "dependent" (Laughlin 1922).

Although eugenic sterilization laws such as Laughlin's model law allowed for the sterilization of both men and women, as fears about women's increasing independence rose in the 1920s, eugenic sterilization efforts increasingly and disproportionately targeted women (Kluchin 2009, 14–17). Officials' determination of whether a woman was inadequate often depended on whether her behavior and lifestyle appeared to conform to ideal norms of femininity and appropriate gender roles. If a woman could convincingly present herself as sufficiently domestic and obedient to male authority, she could avoid sterilization (Schoen 2005). At the same time, officials often took nonmarital sexual activity as sufficient evidence of feeble-mindedness. According to the historian Elaine Tyler May, "In the writings of the eugenic reformers, race, class, sexuality, and ethnicity were all blurred. Nonmarital sexual activity was a code for class and a marker for hereditary inferiority. There is no evidence that middle-class or affluent women were ever labeled feeble-minded or sterilized against their will" (1997, 103). Poor women were also more prone to coming in contact with the social welfare and public health officials who—consistent with the widely held belief at the time that experts could solve social ills—were often charged with determining whether individuals were "socially inadequate" (May 1997, 106).

In the 1927 case of *Buck v. Bell*,[8] the U.S. Supreme Court ruled on the constitutionality of a Virginia eugenic sterilization law that was modeled on Laughlin's. The particulars of the case and the court's reasoning are illustrative of the sterilization practices of the time and beliefs about those practices. The case involved Carrie Buck, an eighteen-year-old white woman. She had been involuntarily admitted to the State Colony for Epileptics and Feeble-Minded when, after a relative of her foster parents raped her, her foster parents discovered she was pregnant (Gould 1985, 15–17). As Stephen Jay Gould writes, Buck was "committed to hide her shame (and her rapist's identity), not because enlightened science had just discovered her true mental status. . . . Her case was never about mental deficiency; it was always a matter of sexual morality and social deviance" (1985, 17).

In an eight-to-one decision, the Court held that the Virginia act fell within the police powers of the state and that the state had instituted sufficient safeguards to protect the due process rights of those being considered for sterilization. Justice Oliver Wendell Holmes, writing for the majority in *Buck v. Bell*, declared,

> We have seen more than once that the public welfare may call upon the best citizens for their lives. It would be strange if it could not call upon those who already sap the strength of the State for these lesser sacrifices, often not felt to be such by those concerned, in order to prevent our being swamped with incompetence. It is better for all the world, if instead of waiting to execute degenerate offspring for crime, or to let them starve for their imbecility, society can prevent those who are manifestly unfit from continuing their kind. The principle that sustains compulsory vaccination is broad enough to cover cutting the Fallopian tubes. Three generations of imbeciles are enough. (1927, 207)

The last line of this quote is a reference to the alleged imbecility of Buck's mother and her daughter. Buck's mother, Emma Buck, had herself borne

Carrie out of wedlock and had, like Carrie, scored in the imbecile range (mental age of six to nine years) of the incipient Stanford-Binet IQ test, in which "normal" corresponded to white middle-class values (May 1997). At the age of seven months, Carrie Buck's daughter, Vivian, had been cursorily assessed by a Red Cross social worker, who attested that "[t]here is a look about it [Vivian] that is not quite normal, but just what it is, I can't tell" (Gould 1985, 17). On the basis of this assessment alone, Vivian was declared a mental defective, and the inheritability of the imbecility that afflicted Carrie and Emma Buck was established. Later assessments revealed that both Carrie and Vivian Buck were of average intelligence (Gould 1985).

Taking sexual deviancy as a proxy for mental deficiency allowed public officials and the court to ignore the will or desires of Buck herself. Buck's personal interest in bearing children is not even mentioned, and it is taken as given that she cannot know what would promote her welfare. That Buck was assumed to be incapable of making her own decisions is clear. In fact, officials and experts widely understood the "feeble-minded" women who were sterilized in this era as irrational and lacking the ability to govern themselves. In a statement reminiscent of Kant's description of people outside the "temperate parts of the world" (1997, 64), E. P. Bicknell, the secretary of the Indiana State Board of Charities, said in 1896, "In the feeble-minded person the animal passions are usually present and are often abnormally developed, while will and reason, which should control and repress them, are absent. The feeble-minded woman, thus lacking the protection which should be her birth-right, falls easily into vice" (quoted in May 1997, 100). As was the case with Buck, what was understood to be in the best interests of those sterilized was also that which best served the interest of society as a whole: sterilization was for the sake of the public good because it was imposed on those who could not exercise proper self-governance.

After World War II, eugenic ideas became less culturally accepted and sterilization organizations and policies started emphasizing "consent."[9] The sterilization strategies that began in the 1950s marked a shift to what Rebecca Kluchin has termed "neo-eugenics." While neo-eugenicists maintained the eugenic preoccupation with "fitness" for reproduction and sterilization of the "unfit," neo-eugenics had distinguishing features. For example, anxieties regarding the dilution of the gene pool by poor, white immigrants primarily motivated early eugenic reformers. In the 1950s, anxieties centered on the reproduction of blacks, especially in the South, and Mexican immigrants. Later, these anxieties were combined with fears of global overpopulation and worries over expanding welfare programs. Also, eugenics was a formal movement with established research centers and conferences; by contrast, neo-eugenics was a more diffuse and informal movement (Kluchin 2009).

Despite these differences, neo-eugenicists continued the eugenicists' project. They promoted and even coerced those whom experts deemed unfit into sterilization. Many physicians made medical care such as delivery and abortion contingent upon the patient's agreement to sterilization or, in some cases, did not even attempt to obtain consent. Women in institutions were at times given the "choice" to undergo sterilization in exchange for being released from the institution in which they were being held. Other physicians threatened women with the revocation of welfare benefits if they did not consent to sterilization (May 1997). There is much evidence that sterilization abuses continued throughout the 1960s and 1970s (Gordon 1990; Petchesky 1981; Shapiro 1985). During this time the link between family planning and control of the reproduction of the poor continued. Plans to create a federally funded family planning program gained support due to the belief that such programs would reduce the numbers of the poor and dependent (King and Meyer 1997, 12). The desire to keep the welfare rolls down provided a rationale for the nonconsensual sterilization of women of color in particular. The sterilization abuse of Native American women was especially egregious: by one estimate, more than 25 percent of Native American women were sterilized without their consent in the mid-1970s (May 1997, 119).

Sterilization in the Contemporary United States

Coerced Sterilization

The patterns that have characterized the practice of sterilization since its inception continue today. Notably, the Court has never explicitly overturned *Buck v. Bell*. However, in a case that concerned a male prisoner, the Supreme Court ruled that an Oklahoma act that imposed sterilization as punishment for only some categories of felonies violates equal protection.[10] The Court has also increasingly protected the right to "bear or beget a child."[11] To protect against sterilization abuses, courts have required that additional procedural safeguards be followed (Blank and Merrick 1995, 16). These procedural safeguards have been insufficient to prevent wrongdoing. Women who come in contact with the criminal justice system are especially likely to be victims of sterilization abuse (Silver 2004, 863).

A 2008 human rights report on abuses in prisons in California found that medical professionals at prison facilities tend to recommend hysterectomy for inmates for medical conditions that either the patient does not have or that could be treated by less aggressive means that would preserve the prisoner's reproductive capacity. The women who are thus sterilized often do not have full information about the procedure and sometimes do not consent (Lee, Levi, and Sok 2008, 16). A governmental prison advisory committee in California "considered evaluating the cost effectiveness of doing 'voluntary sterilizations' on people in prison who have recently given birth and installing IUDs in women in prison" (Lee, Levi, and Sok 2008, 17). As a result, in 2006 the Gender Responsive Strategies Commission in California recommended that postpartum sterilization or sterilization at the time of a caesarean section be considered "medically necessary" rather than elective, thus allowing the California Department of Corrections, which does not provide elective surgeries, to perform sterilizations. The commission recommended that the change be made in a way that avoided the need for legislative approval. In a reflection of neoliberal concern for economic efficiency above other values, the commission also "discussed the cost effectiveness of elective sterilization" (Scraton and McCulloch 2008, 151). Justice Now points out that since "women of color are imprisoned at rates 3 to 5 times higher than white women," the Department of Corrections "has effectively defined the sterilization of imprisoned, pregnant women of color as 'medically necessary'" (2012, 5). Since the committee recommendation, more than 150 people in women's prisons have been sterilized during labor (Justice Now 2012).

The change reflected existing policies in California prisons. Justice Now has documented the ongoing uninformed and coerced sterilizations of women and at least one transgender male in the state's prisons. The organization collaborates with individuals incarcerated in California women's prisons to document human rights abuses. Robin

Levi explains that "the focus on women of color, the words used, and the fact that the tactics are so similar [to previous ones] suggests these sterilization[s] are the next step in the historic reproductive oppression of women of color" (Levi 2006, 77). There is evidence that similar abuses occur in other states as well (Lee, Levi, and Sok 2008, 16).

Additionally, prosecutors and judges sometimes pressure women into accepting sterilization by making it a condition of receiving a lighter sentence. For example, in 2005 a Georgia woman who had been charged with killing her infant daughter consented to sterilization in order to avoid prison (Volz 2006, 203). Judges may also issue general no-procreation orders. Rachel Roth has shown that women are more likely than men to receive such orders (2004). Many of the old eugenic rationales regarding the irresponsibility of women of color, who make up a disproportionately high percentage of incarcerated women, are cited as reasons for sterilizing them (Lee, Levi, and Sok 2008, 16).[12] But, as Jeanne Flavin notes, "contemporary proponents of sterilization and no-procreation orders . . . couch them in terms of 'personal responsibility' and cost savings" (2009, 41). Such rationales are consistent with the neoliberal framework discussed in the previous chapter and provide another example of how cutting public spending is linked to the maintenance of gender and race hierarchies.

The recommendation of aggressive therapeutic procedures that result in sterility occurs outside prisons as well. Sue Fisher has demonstrated that the course of treatment medical professionals recommend to women with abnormal Pap smear results is connected to their race, socioeconomic status, and number of children. In particular, "older women who had their families, poor women, minority women, women who were on welfare, women who had had multiple abortions, and women who had had several children without being married seemed more likely to have hysterectomies recommended" (1988, 32). Fisher reports that a young, married, Mexican American woman who had three children was initially counseled to undergo a hysterectomy upon receiving abnormal Pap smear results. She subsequently had a tubal ligation, after which the doctor retracted the hysterectomy recommendation, opting instead to freeze the abnormal cells (1988, 49–50).

Other doctors continue simply to sterilize women without their consent. For example, a Massachusetts woman alleged that in 2006 she was sterilized without her consent after giving birth. The woman, who is the mother of nine children, is on public assistance and is disabled due to non-Hodgkin's lymphoma (Harding 2010). This woman and others for whom therapeutic hysterectomy is aggressively recommended are situated as illegitimate reproducers, a category that is intimately tied to their presumed inability to govern themselves adequately. Their sterilization thus comports with neo-eugenic ideas (Day 2007, 82). Because they are viewed as irrational, intervening in their bodies and decisions is not thought to hinder their autonomy.

Roberts has linked the history of nonconsensual and coerced sterilization to more recent policies that "degrade Black women's reproductive decisions" (1998, 7). Most relevant were plans in the 1990s to distribute Norplant—an implant that releases a synthetic hormone and prevents pregnancy for up to five years—to black communities, those on public assistance, and low-income women who are ineligible for welfare benefits (Roberts 1998, 106–12). Norplant is so effective and long-lasting that Roberts calls it "a form of temporary sterilization" (1998, 106). Since only a doctor can remove Norplant, it is one of only a few contraceptive methods that women do not control. Its implantation and removal are dependent on the willingness of physicians to perform the requested procedure and thus give "doctors and other health care workers the opportunity to impose their own judgments upon poor minority patients by refusing to remove the device" (1998, 129). Roberts shows that many women were coerced into getting Norplant implanted and that trying to get the device removed was often extremely difficult. A Native American woman who wanted Norplant taken out was told that it would be removed only if she submitted to a tubal ligation (1998, 128–33).

Additionally, some organizations have started offering women who are addicted to drugs cash incentives to undergo sterilization or use long-term birth control like Norplant or the IUD. Project Prevention, which was previously named Children Requiring a Caring Kommunity (CRACK), is a private organization that makes such offers, although state and federal governments often pay for the sterilizations (Kluchin 2009, 222–23). Kluchin notes that this organization presumes a right to interfere in women's decisions for the sake of society when "the women in question have 'demonstrated' their lack of reproductive fitness through their poverty, illegitimacy, and /or criminality" (2009, 223).

Physicians also take this attitude and presume they are better decision makers than their patients.

At the same time that these pressures are put on marginalized women to curb their reproduction, the recent effort to cast abortion among African Americans and Latinos as a form of genocide appeals to the history of eugenics. As discussed in chapter 2, in 2011 various pro-life organizations placed billboards in cities across the country that proclaimed, among other things, "The most dangerous place for an African American is in the womb" (Guenther 2012). Later billboards targeted the message to Latinos (Solomon 2011). Both the billboards, which are part of a larger movement to manipulate the history of eugenics to curb abortion rights, and coercive sterilization policies cast women of color as essentially reproducers and as vessels to carry on the race. In either case, African American and Latina women's reproduction must be managed for the sake of the larger social good, though the content of the social good differs.

Voluntary Sterilization and the Childfree

Although there is relatively little research on voluntary sterilization, that which exists shows that many middle- and upper-class women who sought sterilization from the early 1900s onward were unable to access sterilization because physicians were generally unwilling to sterilize "socially adequate" women. However, some women succeeded in getting their tubes tied by presenting themselves as poor or sexually deviant to officials who then deemed them good candidates for "compulsory" sterilization (Schoen 2005, 5).

In the postwar era, even as neo-eugenicists continued to sterilize some women against their wills, emerging rules governing sterilization barred other women from the procedure. One such rule was the "120 rule," which restricted sterilization to those women whose age multiplied by their number of children totaled at least 120. The American College of Obstetricians and Gynecologists (ACOG) promoted this rule until 1969. More generally, physicians at this time were reluctant to perform sterilizations on privileged individuals (May 1997, 113–20). A woman who tried to get sterilized in 1970 noted, "Just like women who are sterilized without consent, we're treated as objects of population policy" (May 1997, 113).

ACOG no longer promulgates guidelines regarding how old a woman must be or how many children she should have in order to qualify for a tubal ligation; nonetheless, as many anecdotes reveal, some doctors refuse to sterilize women under thirty or women without children (Zyl-bergold 2007; Paul 2012). Although little has been written about current impediments to sterilization procedures, research suggests that young, childfree, middle-class women have the greatest difficulty finding a phy-sician willing to ligate their fallopian tubes (Campbell 1999). Despite the presumptive status of sterilization as a right (which will be discussed at greater length below), physicians are generally guaranteed the ability to choose their patients.[13] They are thus free to limit access to sterilization based on their idea of a patient's "best interest"—an idea that medical research and professional norms heavily inform (Fisher 1988).

That women without children have difficulty accessing sterilization is significant since rates of voluntary childlessness, and presumably of childfree women seeking sterilization, have been increasing since the baby boom era. Although childlessness for women born in the first de-cade of the twentieth century was 20 percent, that rate was cut to below 10 percent for women born in the 1920s and 1930s. Women in the latter category were in their childbearing years in the baby boom era. Rates of childlessness have been increasing since that era, and the increase appears to be due mostly to the increase in rates of voluntary childless-ness (May 1997, 12, 182). According to May, "In 1990, . . . 25 percent of all women aged thirty to thirty-four were childless, compared to only 16 percent in 1976" (1997, 182).

Since the voluntary sterilization of women without children is more disruptive to dominant understandings of women than the steriliza-tion of mothers, it is worth surveying the "childfree movement" and the attendant phenomenon of increasing rates of childlessness. May has characterized this movement as partially "a function of feminism, environmentalism, and the increasing tolerance for alternatives to the nuclear family" and partially "as a reaction to the intense pronatalism of the baby-boom years" (1997, 183). Women who remain childfree cite a number of reasons for their decision, including their aversion to the physical changes of pregnancy, concerns about overpopulation, wanting to increase their standard of living, and their rejection of motherhood and the primacy of children to many women's lives (May 1997, 196–207; Campbell 1999, 168–69; Gillespie 2003, 123). Childfree women who seek sterilization generally say that they have never wanted to procreate and that the only way for them to represent accurately their chosen lifestyle is to be sterilized. If performed correctly, sterilization has few to no significant side effects and frees them from monthly scares and continual anxieties (Campbell 1999, 158).

Heterosexual women without children are frequently called on to justify or explain their decision not to have children, whereas mothers whose reproduction is socially encouraged are rarely asked to explain or justify their decision to have children (Morell 1994, 49). This is true despite the fact that, as one childfree woman noted, the decision to have a child is one that "affect[s] many more people with far more widespread consequences" than not having a child (Campbell 1999, 123). Just as in the medical context discussed below, in society more broadly, reproduction is conceived of as women's default desire and thus requires no explanation.

The assumption that reproduction is woman's natural or default desire is reflected in some of the labels—such as "intentionally childless" or merely "childless"—used to refer to those without children. Many nonparents reject those terms because they emphasize an absence or lack. In addition, "intentionally childless" or "childless by choice" perpetuates the idea that it is nonparenthood that must be chosen, thereby (re)constructing the idea that parenting or motherhood is the default that does not need to be justified and is not necessarily characterized as a choice. As a result, nonparents tend to prefer the more positively framed term "childfree," which emphasizes the unburdened character of not being a parent (Campbell 1999).[14] Since women without children challenge the idea of reproduction as woman's default desire, there are many cultural assumptions about childfree women that tend to undermine the subversive potential of childlessness. In her study of women without children, Carolyn Morell outlines three primary cultural assumptions about such women: that they do not like children and are anti-family (where children are taken to define family), that they are self-absorbed, and that they had unhappy childhoods. Since wanting to be a mother is seen as natural, the presumption is that "only women who are morally suspect or flawed by events beyond their control would reject motherhood" (1994, 77). Nonmothers, then, are viewed as morally or psychologically deficient and are presumed to suffer for not having children (Morell 1994, 97; Gillespie 2003, 124). Both the explanation of deficiency and the frequent characterization of childlessness as a "lifestyle choice" depoliticize the issue (Morell 1994, xv).

It is important to note here that, especially compared to the literature on eugenics, there is relatively little research on the childfree movement. In particular, little is known about the numbers and characteristics of women who seek and are turned away from sterilization. In any case and given the paucity of research, I want to resist making easy assumptions about who professionals are turning away from sterilization procedures. At the same time, though, a discussion of sterilization cannot get away from the historical and ongoing appropriate/inappropriate reproducer divide. This divide and the assumption that voluntary sterilization is an issue of concern only to those in the former category leave me open to the charge that this is a "luxury" issue that affects only privileged women. Even if that were the case, the relatively unexplored impediments to voluntary sterilization warrant analysis. Also, as the subsequent analysis demonstrates, juxtaposing a discussion of voluntary sterilization alongside sterilization abuses illuminates both practices and the way they interact to maintain the fit/unfit dichotomy. In fact, the maintenance of the category of the "fit" depends on an exclusion of and thereby the maintenance of the category of the "unfit."

Moreover, I show how each form of regulating women's bodies both relies on an understanding of proper self-governance and impedes critical autonomy. Taken together, contemporary modes of sterilization regulation provide a compelling example of how the discourse of proper self-governance is deeply racialized. Although I spend slightly more time on the question of voluntary sterilization, the following analysis demonstrates the importance of thinking through the two modes of sterilization injustice together. Moreover, as I argue, the proliferation of voluntary sterilization may help disrupt the notion that women are essentially maternal, which underlies a range of practices of reproductive injustice, including both the denial and imposition of sterilization. As such, it holds the potential to transform cultural understandings and enhance autonomy as critique and transformation.

The Medical Production of Woman-Mother

The social view of women as naturally maternal is connected to medical notions of women's bodies and their function. Given the intense medicalization of contemporary American society, in which social issues are increasingly conceptualized in terms of medicine and health, medical discourse plays an important role in the constitution of the "normal" subject (Lupton 1997, 100). With reference to historical and sociological research, I demonstrate here that the identification of the female body with reproduction is a key element of the current medical paradigm. Because of this identification, the sterilization of women without children is rendered suspicious and abnormal in a way that affects the treatment of such women when they seek sterilization. Although important and partially successful social movements have opened up nonmaternal identities for women, the medical treatment of reproduction, especially with regard to sterilization, remains restrictive in its ascription of female identity and thus severely hinders reproductive autonomy understood in terms of critique and transformation. Additionally, the medical regulation of sterilization relies on and reinforces the idea that women without children who seek sterilization are not making a proper decision, which warrants paternalistic oversight.

Key to the argument in this section is the philosopher and historian of science Thomas Kuhn's concept of a paradigm (1970). In Kuhn's lexicon, a paradigm is a shared body of theoretical assumptions, techniques, and beliefs, which remain unquestioned in normal, everyday scientific practice. Adoption of a paradigm and its accompanying conceptual apparatus profoundly affects how scientists perceive phenomena. For example, a pre-Copernican scientist "saw" a planet when observing the moon, whereas after the Copernican revolution, astronomers "see" a satellite when looking at the moon. As Kuhn argues in general about science, medical practice and research occur within the confines of a paradigm.

With regard to reproductive medicine, women's bodies have not always been viewed in the way they currently are. The Western biomedical characterization of female bodies as essentially different from male bodies has a relatively recent history. Until the eighteenth century, biomedical science in the West understood male and female bodies as fundamentally similar, with the one key difference between male and female bodies being that genitals on the female were inside the body. This framework of bodily similarity gave way in the eighteenth century to a framework that took the female body as profoundly different from the male body. This shift in perspective led to the isolation of the study of women's bodies from men's and to the emergence of gynecology as a distinct field of medicine in the late nineteenth century. Because the male body was understood as representative of the human body, the male body was not set apart as a discrete focus of study (Laqueur 1990). Nelly Oudshoorn argues further that gynecology "established a discursive practice in which sex and reproduction became considered 'more fundamental to Woman's than Man's nature'" (1996, 153). That reproductive function is seen as peripheral to man's nature and body explains why andrology—the medical study of men's reproduction—is a minor branch of medicine (153).

The convergence of medical thought on the idea of bodily difference is tied up with medical education. Scientific training, according to Kuhn, is central to the dominance of a given paradigm: "[N]ormal research, even the best of it, is a highly convergent activity based firmly upon a settled consensus acquired from scientific education and reinforced by subsequent life in the profession" (1991, 140). A textbook-driven pedagogy and a "rigid education in exclusive paradigms" (142) characterize this education, which he argues distinguishes science from other academic disciplines. Assigned reading for students, even at the graduate level, comes almost exclusively from textbooks. These textbooks may discuss different subjects but not different approaches to a given subject: they are all written from within the dominant scientific paradigm and so do not differ in overall approach or perspective. Students of science are not asked to read collections of scientific work or historical classics of their fields—"works in which they might discover other ways of regarding the problems discussed in their textbooks" (141).

Textbooks dominate medical education. The sociologist Suzanne Day has analyzed the treatment of voluntary sterilization in medical textbooks and contraceptive guides published between 1987 and 2007. Her research shows the extent to which the belief that reproductive capacity is fundamental to women's bodies and identity characterizes the prevailing medical paradigm. For example, Day demonstrates that medical literature characterizes the appropriate sterilization candidate as a woman who has completed her childbearing. The texts she examines do not consider the possibility of a childless woman or a woman who is a parent through adoption seeking sterilization. Also, the timing of sterilization is discussed in relation to a woman's most recent pregnancy (2007, 60–61). Since an identification of the female body with the maternal body marks the medical paradigm, the possibility of a woman without children seeking sterilization does not even occur to the authors of these texts.

The textbooks Day analyzes also warn that a woman's stated reasons for sterilization may not be trusted and that emotional instability may be causing her to seek the surgery. The doctor has the responsibility to ensure that the patient is making a rational decision (Day 2007, 62). One textbook even suggests that physicians tell single, childless patients that the right man "might just turn up tomorrow" (63). Unsurprisingly, these same texts discuss the consequences of tubal ligation in terms of "loss, regret, and dysfunction: a loss of identity that was rooted in a woman's reproductive capacity, a regret at the inability to fulfill a woman's 'primary desire' to reproduce, and a dysfunctional body responding to the medical intervention in woman's 'natural' state of reproduction" (73). In fact, medical texts and some sterilized women themselves discuss the potential for post-sterilization regret, as well as other adverse emotional and physical consequences of sterilization, in terms of "post-tubal ligation syndrome" (Day 2007, 72; Post-tubal Coalition 2006). Like "post-abortion syndrome" discussed in chapter 2, "post-sterilization syndrome" conflates women and reproductive capacity and links contraceptive sterilization to both mental and physical dysfunction. The language of syndrome casts the sterilized body as abnormal and inadequate.

The discourse of regret and loss also appears in biomedical research on sterilization outcomes, much of which focuses on the issue of post-sterilization regret. These studies tend to show that women who are sterilized under the age of thirty have higher rates of regret than older women, although the regret rates for all women, especially those under thirty, are probably inflated.[15] What is most revealing about the medical paradigm, though, are the research questions that are not posed.

For example, there is a dearth of research on and discussion of post-vasectomy regret. The only American studies I found that examined men's post-vasectomy regret looked at regret of both husbands and wives after one of them had been sterilized (Miller, Shain, and Pasta 1991, 1993).[16] A pamphlet published by the American College of Obstetricians and Gynecologists in 2005, titled "Sterilization for Women and Men," only mentioned regret with regard to tubal ligation, although in the organization's most recent publication on the topic, regret is not mentioned at all (2012). The lack of attention to post-vasectomy regret may reflect the presumption that men know their minds, as well as a difference in the way men's reproductive capacity is linked to their identity. Although ideas of masculinity and fertility vary widely across cultures, virility and potency are sometimes tied to understandings of male identity. In the United States, masculinity is often identified with fertility and responsible fatherhood.[17] Nevertheless, as the medical literature shows, male bodies tend not to be viewed primarily as reproductive bodies. Since men are not medically understood by reference to their procreative potential, a loss of that potential is not discursively linked to a crisis of identity as it is for women. Given the assumptions of the dominant medical paradigm, neither post-vasectomy regret nor post-pregnancy regret present themselves as objects of study.[18]

In investigating medical discourse, it is important to note that medical contexts do not merely reflect an independent reality regarding sterilization regret. Not only do norms governing motherhood and women—which are tied to medicine's paradigmatic assumptions regarding women—render post-sterilization "syndrome" and regret possible objects of medical study, these very studies set up an expectation of regret and contribute to the construction of those norms. This is not to say that post-sterilization regret is a fiction or that a medical practitioner should not discuss the possibility of regret with patients; it is to say that the discursive context of sterilization and regret must be critically examined, especially since fear of a patient's future regret is likely to contribute to doctors' reluctance to perform tubal ligations on certain women. Moreover, denying sterilization on the basis of potential regret functions to keep women's bodies in line with dominant assumptions about women's reproductive essence.

The medical conflation of woman and mother is also evident in the way medical literature conceives of women who are involuntarily infertile. The discourse surrounding involuntary infertility supports the conflation of woman and mother insofar as infertility is rendered a pathology (Ikemoto 1996). Even menopause is sometimes conceptualized as a disease or pathology.[19] Viewing infertility as a disorder is consistent with the idea that the medical paradigm takes reproductive function as central to female bodies. Such a view supports the idea of reproductive function as woman's natural and appropriate state.

Another significant aspect of the research on sterilization is that studies frame sterilization as an option for couples and focus on the use of sterilization among married women (Godecker, Thomson, and Bumpass 2001). Medical research, then, reinforces not only the identification of women with reproductive capacity, but also heteronormative ideals regarding the proper site for procreative decision making. Such studies ignore, perhaps because the paradigm prevents them from seeing, the possibility of a single woman seeking out and obtaining a sterilization.

Foucault argues that much medical research uses "comprehensive measures" and "statistical assessments" to determine what is normal or deviant for a given population. In turn, these assessments inform clinical practice. In the sterilization consultation, the doctor examines the body as well as a woman's motives for seeking sterilization and applies expert knowledge gained from the comprehensive study of tubal ligation (Foucault 1978, 1977). Women who try to obtain sterilizations report that medical professionals treat them like children and that practitioners tend to dismiss or trivialize their reasons for requesting sterilization. Such treatment is no doubt connected to research that constitutes the sterilized body as deviant and dysfunctional (Campbell 1999, 119). Given the notion that women have an innate desire to reproduce, physicians are especially reluctant to sterilize childfree women; one such woman reported that a physician told her to return when she was married with children (Campbell 1999, 114).

A 1985 study on sterilization suggested that men who seek sterilization are not treated as paternalistically as women who seek the operation in part because they are expected and trusted to know their minds
(Campbell 1999, 134). Also, given the differing ways reproductive function is linked to women's and men's identities and bodies, men's decisions to get sterilized are treated as less momentous since, even if they
do not know their minds, they are not violating their nature by getting
sterilized. There is a connection, then, between how physicians treat
women during consultations and how medical literature depicts women.
The physician is trained and the research is conducted from within the
prevailing medical paradigm that closely identifies women with reproductive capacity.

The link between the paternalism women encounter when they seek
sterilization and the view of the female body as maternal is also evident
in discussions of the reversibility of tubal ligations. While women presumably seek out sterilization precisely because of its permanence, some
of the medical literature Day examined presents the more difficult-to-
reverse procedures—which are also more effective—as negative precisely
because of their permanence. One book advises against performing the
most difficult-to-reverse tubal ligations, such as the electrocauteriza-
tion of the fallopian tubes, on women under twenty-five and those with
few children. Day argues that such texts situate the decisions of young
women with few children as untrustworthy (2007, 66). It is to be expected that a woman's default, innate desire to reproduce will overcome
her current, misguided decision to be sterilized, and doctors are there
to manage such decisions. Such women are not trusted to be properly
self-governing. Even though physicians inform patients on the irrevers-
ibility of the tubal ligation, medical textbooks focus on the potential of
reversibility with regard to young women with few children.[20] It is un-
surprising, then, that medical literature characterizes the ideal female
sterilization patient as one who does not want any *additional* children
(Day 2007, 60).

The alignment of the female body with reproductive function is also
evident in discussions of the ethics of performing a difficult-to-reverse
tubal ligation on a young woman with relatively few children (Benn and
Lupton 2005; Berger 2007). One British medical ethics article begins

with the question, "Is it ethical to sterilise a young woman who is determined she never wants children, even if there are no strong medical reasons to avoid pregnancy?" (Benn and Lupton 2005, 1323). This article and others like it ask whether respecting an adult's desire regarding her own fertility is unethical. The point of departure for these authors is the ethical status of sterilization, not the ethical status of not respecting the wishes of the patient. Although other forms of elective surgery may be framed in a similar way, a sterilization operation performed at a woman's behest is likely to seem potentially unethical if her desires are discounted in favor of a potential and allegedly likely future desire. One of the articles concludes by stating that "it is morally defensible" to sterilize such a woman as long as the physician does not think it is contrary to the best interest of the patient, although there is no discussion of how the physician might come to know what is in the best interest of the patient or why the patient's best interest might depart from her expressed wishes (Benn and Lupton 2005). The authors thus assume that women seeking sterilization in this circumstance will not necessarily govern themselves properly. Physicians must provide paternalistic oversight to ensure that women are making the "right" decisions for themselves.

The trends found in the medical literature surveyed here comport with the research about and stories of young women who seek sterilization. Annily Campbell (1999) documented the stories of many childfree and sterilized women in Britain who faced physician resistance to their sterilization requests. Additionally, a 1988 study in the United States found that "physicians were most willing to sterilize older, postpartum, parous, black, married, poor, or well-educated women" (Harrison and Cooke 1988, 565). A 2010 follow-up to that study surveyed physicians about how they would react to women's sterilization requests, but did not inquire into how race would affect their reactions. The study also only asked physicians to respond to scenarios that involved women who were married and already had at least one child, which reflects the presumption that only women with children are appropriate sterilization candidates. Nonetheless, this study is insightful for its finding that in the United States, ob/gyn physicians reported that they would be more likely to dissuade younger patients with fewer children from surgical sterilization (Lawrence et al. 2011).

The medical literature discussed here suggests that physicians' understanding of patient best interest and who is an appropriate sterilization candidate are closely associated with medical understandings of the female body, female identity, and reproductive capacity. While this literature characterizes women in general in terms of reproductive capacity and rarely discusses the race or class of women seeking sterilization, women of color and low-income women are frequently understood as "too fertile."[21] As discussed above, involuntary sterilization continues to take place in the United States. Although the female body is understood in terms of reproductive capacity, the medical profession disciplines the female body differently based on discriminatory ideas of fitness for reproduction.

Through the regulation of sterilization, the population is controlled at the same time the body is disciplined. The regulation and management of reproduction can be considered a form of what Foucault called biopower, which refers to the exercise of power over life. In contrast to forms of power that dealt "simply with legal subjects over whom the ultimate dominion was death," biopower deals with "living beings" and the exercise of power "at the level of life itself" (1978, 142–43). Biopower is concerned with the optimization of the body and its functions, as well as the regulation of the population. The population—"with its specific phenomena and its peculiar variables: birth and death rates, life expectancy, fertility, state of health, frequency of illness, patterns of diet and habitation"—has emerged as a political and social problem to be managed (Foucault 1978, 25). Biopower joins the management of the population and its attendant technologies of normalization with the optimization of the body and its functions.

Thus, the body itself becomes an important site of governance, which accounts for the increased importance of medicine and the study of health in contemporary American society. Under biopower, reproduction and reproductive capacity emerge as sites in which power might act to manage and improve life and the population. Reproductive bodies—which have become synonymous in many ways with women's bodies—have become a site in which the state, as well as medical and social science experts, may intervene. When women are deemed to have failed or be close to failing at properly managing or governing their own reproduction, expert intervention is justified, both for the sake of the governed and for the sake of society. Judgments about who is fit to reproduce—which are themselves informed by racial, gendered, and class biases—reflect expert assessments that some women's sterilization is necessary while the sterilization of others is problematic.

As I argue below, sterilization can be understood as a form of counter-conduct with political effects for how we conceive of reproduction and gender. However, this discussion of the pathologization of voluntary sterilization among many women who do not have children is significant in part because of its potential to undermine the political efficacy of sterilization as counter-conduct. Davidson argues that "[t]he appearance of a type of conduct within the conceptual space of the normal and the pathological often has the effect of weakening the ethical and political force of this conduct" (2011, 34). This observation highlights how the normalization and pathologization of behavior pose a danger for cultural transformation. It also suggests the importance of challenging the process of medical normalization.

Sterilization as Performance

Experts have relied on the idea that autonomy should be afforded only to those subjects who have proven themselves to be properly self-governing in order to justify intervention in individuals' reproductive lives and capacities. In contrast, a different framework for autonomy—one that emphasizes critique and transformation—may have more emancipatory potential. In this section, I examine how sterilization enacts a material transformation of the body that often both prompts and is preceded by a critique of the association of women with maternity, as well as women's bodies and maternal capacity. In this way, it may be understood as the kind of eccentric behavior or counter-conduct that is part of the autonomy as critique and transformation tradition.

The medical regulation of the female body can be thought of as, in Butler's words, a "mechanism for the compulsory cultural construction of the female body *as* a maternal body" (1990, 90). On Butler's understanding of performativity, it is through our very performance of gendered norms regarding, for example, reproduction that we come into being as gendered subjects. Gender is brought into being by the very performances—which consist in the reiteration of norms—that are taken to be its result. While the production of maternal desire as natural to womanhood and as located in the female body masks its very production, Butler argues that the maternal body could "be understood . . . as an effect or consequence of a system of sexuality in which the female body is required to assume maternity as the essence of its self and the law of its desire" (1990, 92).

To the extent that the female body is understood as an essentially maternal body, the childless woman presents a potentially radical challenge to the ontology of gender (Hird 2003, 16). As Myra J. Hird argues, although reproduction is taken as essential to women's bodies and femininity, childless women challenge this association, along with the more specific associations of "women's bodies and children, women's desire and proclivity for children, men's bodies and the lack of maternal function and men's lack of desire for children" (2003, 15). Relying on Butler's theory of performativity, Hird argues that childless women present transformative potential in that they may "parody gender, to reveal the 'arbitrary' relation between various acts taken to be inimical to gender identity" (15). Nonmotherhood, then, is one way of challenging the maternal gendering of women that the medical literature discussed above reflects and perpetuates.

Consequently, and as the women in the early 1900s who defended voluntary childlessness argued, childlessness among women has the potential to challenge the identification of womanhood with motherhood (Gordon 2007, 94–95). Because norms such as motherhood require our performance to be sustained, in our performance lies the possibility of subversion of those norms. Since childless women challenge prevailing norms, they may appear as "developmental failures or logical impossibilities. . . . Their persistence and proliferation, however, provide critical opportunities to expose the limits and regulatory aims of that domain of intelligibility and, hence, to open up within the very terms of that matrix of intelligibility rival and subversive matrices of gender disorder" (Butler 1990, 17). Although Butler focuses on disrupting "heterosexuality's claim on naturalness" (1993, 125), childlessness, when it is chosen, challenges the accompanying presumed naturalness of maternity in a way that expresses autonomy as critique and transformation.

While voluntary childlessness challenges the maternal gendering of the female body and its attendant heteronormativity, the specific technologies that some heterosexual women use to remain childfree may be seen as subversive as well. Since many childfree women seek out sterilization to express their commitment to being childfree, it is worth exploring that technology even if it is not always used in a disruptive manner. Although women who are and want to remain childfree often seek sterilization, women who already have children also use sterilization. Important, too, is that a woman without children who gets sterilized is not precluded from becoming a mother through adoption. Moreover, given ongoing sterilization abuses and the prevalence of neo-eugenic ideas regarding who should and should not reproduce, not every sterilization has transformative potential. Forcing sterilization on a woman serves more to impose hegemonic notions of responsible reproduction than it does to disrupt the constitution of woman-mother. The idea that a woman would choose infertility is important to this analysis of the destabilizing effects of sterilization.

Although in many instances the subversiveness of a performance does not turn on the intent of the agent, in this context the choice to be sterilized affects the discursive understanding of the act in an important way. In some sense, as will be discussed below, the sterilized female body is itself a challenge to prevailing understandings of the female body. However, the imposition of sterilization is more likely to be understood as an action that further confirms the natural maternity of the female body. Experts may view the imposition of sterilization as a necessary intervention precisely because they presume the maternal nature of the female body and identity.

Nevertheless, the possibility of the permanent foreclosure of sexual reproduction arguably presents a greater challenge to "repronormativity" (Franke 2001) and the gender binary than the nonsterilized, heterosexual childfree woman. The latter woman can much more easily forgo contraception, and even if she is deeply committed to remaining childfree, her situation will more readily conform to normalizing discourses. Although she may be just as committed to being childfree and may have good reasons for not seeking sterilization, others may presume she will change her mind, perhaps when the "right man comes along." Even though these normalizing discourses are precisely the ones that childless women will encounter in trying to obtain a sterilization, such women's subsequent sterilized bodies (and even their attempts to be sterilized) present a potentially more severe disruption to the ontology of gender than the presumably fertile childfree woman.

In its transformation of the female body, sterilization can be seen as a performance that challenges the naturalness and inevitability of maternity in a way that may prompt reflection on and transformation of cultural norms. In so doing, such action can be an expression of autonomy as critique and transformation. However, sterilization does more than enable the performance of childlessness for sexually active heterosexual women. The technology changes the female body. Turning attention to the technology of sterilization allows for an analysis of the sterilized body as a union of technology and organism—as a cyborg. This analysis complements the Butlerian analysis of the practice in that, in its material transformation of the body, sterilization parodies gender and thereby reveals the contingency of the female body's association with maternity.

Cyborg Disruptions

Haraway first discussed a cyborg world in her 1985 article "A Manifesto for Cyborgs," in which she defines a cyborg as "a cybernetic organism, a hybrid of machine and organism, a creature of social reality as well as a creature of fiction" (1991, 149). She intends the figure of the cyborg as both a "tool and myth, instrument and concept" (154) and argues that in our time we are all "theorized and fabricated hybrids of machine and organism: in short, we are cyborgs" (160). By this she means that technology so pervades our world that the distinction between organism and machine is unclear. We both produce and are produced by technology. Interweaving and overlapping developments in fields such as medicine, technology, pharmaceuticals, and communication since the mid-twentieth century have led to the profound entanglement of machine and organism. The cyborg represents this entanglement. The diffusion of technology and machines in society gives rise to a connected and networked world. The cyborg world is not a world of individuals constructed outside society or technology, but a world of connectivity and networks. Humans are immersed in networks and, together "with each other and with objects," we produce "what it means to be human" (1996).

Haraway introduced the cyborg in the midst of the Cold War, and with it she countered the tendency to see technology as necessarily a mode of domination. Instead Haraway sees possibility in the hybridity that marks cyborg culture: "My cyborg myth is about transgressed boundaries, potent fusions, and dangerous possibilities which progressive people might explore as one part of needed political work" (1991, 154). She argues that viewing technology as domination or as a perverting influence on the human is to "recall us to an imagined organic body," thereby re-entrenching prominent dualisms of nature/culture and organism/machine (153–54). Of principal concern to Haraway are precisely these dualisms—which also include mind/body, animal/human, public/private, man/woman, and primitive/civilized—that underpin much historic and contemporary oppression. With the cyborg as instrument and concept, she blurs the distinctions between and generally disrupts these dichotomies.

The cyborg is a figure that undermines "the certainty of what counts as nature" (1991, 152) and is thus an embodied form of eccentricity or subversion. It may challenge accepted norms and ways of being and thus prompt critique and social transformation. The cyborg is simultaneously a tool to destabilize boundaries and a figure that can suggest "some very fruitful couplings." The cyborg mirrors political and technological transformations and also provides a means to project political possibilities borne out of these transformations. Since modern medicine is a realm that is "full of cyborgs, of couplings between organism and machine," it is also a realm in which we might find potent fusions that challenge the status quo (150).

Although the first tubal ligation in the United States was performed in 1880 (Zurawin 2009), the development of fiber optics, which Cold War military interests fueled (Hecht 1999), transformed the process of ligating the fallopian tubes and allowed for the proliferation of female sterilizations. Laparoscopy, or the use of fiber optics to view the body's interior, allows a physician to clip, cut, tie, or burn the fallopian tubes with only a few small abdominal incisions (Zurawin 2009). Laparoscopic tubal ligations, which are less invasive, safer, and faster than previous methods, have multiplied since the 1960s. While tubal ligation remains the most common form of female sterilization in the United States, and thus my analysis is focused on that procedure, there are now other sterilization practices and options. For example, the recently developed Essure device has further simplified the sterilization process. In a procedure that requires no anesthesia, the device—which is composed of "polyethylene terephthalate (PET) fibers wrapped around a stainless steel core, surrounded by 24 coils of nickel-titanium alloy"—is inserted into the fallopian tubes through a catheter that passes through the vagina. The design of the device induces the formation of scar tissue around the implant, and a few months after the procedure, the tubes are fully occluded (Zurawin 2009). Emerging technologies therefore continue to simplify the actual process of ligating the fallopian tubes, even as the technology becomes more and more complex.

The cyborg is meant to be used as a tool for thinking imaginatively about the entanglements of technology and culture that are transforming society, even though Haraway's focus was often on organism-machine hybrids that are self-regulating in a way that distinguishes them from merely modified bodies. The cyborg draws attention to these entanglements to think through "the social relations of science and technology" (1991, 163). Although the sterilized body does not self-regulate in the way that Haraway emphasizes in discussing machine-organism hybrids, the cyborg is nonetheless a useful figure for examining sterilization. In fact, Haraway encourages using the cyborg for its "imaginative resources" (150). High-tech medicine, whether or not it results in self-regulating machine-body hybrids, changes bodily possibilities and challenges ideas of essence and nature. Rather than faithfully employing some pure notion of what a cyborg is, I am "thinking within the frame of the cyborg" (Butler 2004, 13) to explore the entanglements of technology and culture, and their attendant disruptions, with regard to reproduction in general (as will be discussed more in chapter 5) and sterilization practices in particular.[22]

Performativity and cyborg theory serve complementary functions in this analysis of modern sterilization practices. While performativity involves an analysis of norms, analyzing sterilization in terms of cyborg theory allows for an accounting of the complexity and mutability of the corporeal body. Since sterilization is a bodily transformation that challenges gender norms, it requires attention both to norms and to the corporeality of the body. Importantly, the shifting techno-bodily configurations of a cyborg world can be taken as "crucial political ingredients" such that technological transformation adds another dimension to the politics of reproduction. The figure of the cyborg is important for a discussion of tubal ligation because not only does the sterilized nonmother disrupt the identification of women with motherhood via her dissension from procreative norms—as does any childless woman—the sterilized body itself provokes awareness of the mutability of the body. Through bodily change, the sterilized woman challenges the prevailing production of women and women's bodies at the level of the body. Since the association of female identity with maternity is itself maintained through the maternal gendering of the female body, sterilization can be thought of as a performance that challenges that gendering through the modification of the body. This challenge occurs not only via performance or discourse, but also via the material, fleshy body. The very body of the sterilized woman is a potential challenge to the construction of that body as made for reproduction.

This bringing together of performativity and cyborg theory allows for a deeper engagement with the body. A number of feminist scholars have called for this engagement (Bordo 1997; Davis 1997; Grosz 2005; Davis 1983). Susan Bordo writes that "the study of cultural representations alone, divorced from consideration of their relation to the practical lives of bodies, can obscure and mislead" (1997, 104). McNay argues that Butler's "discursive paradigm does not provide the conceptual resources to elaborate certain crucial aspects of agency pertaining to its embodied context" (2008, 169). In contrast, the cyborg directs attention to the agency of the body. Approaching sterilization from the perspective of cyborg theory allows for an examination of the materiality of the sterilized body in a way that does not merely presuppose matter. In other words, cyborg theory does not efface the dynamic character of materiality.[23]

Cyborg analysis also challenges prominent understandings of technology as something that humans wield in the service of their wills. As Haraway says of high-tech culture, "It is not clear who makes and who is made in the relation between human and machine" (1991, 177). In the context of sterilization, humans may make the technology that allows for the proliferation of sterilization, but that technology in turn allows for the remaking of the human. Rather than viewing technology and medicine, and the procedure of tubal ligation specifically, as merely mechanisms of domination or of negative constructions of the feminine, we can view technology as a co-constructor of alternatives. Medicine can be used to modify—indeed, to change irrevocably—the "natural" female body. Even as medicine constructs the female body by reference to reproductive function, its techniques may be used to break that connection and thereby promote autonomy as critique and transformation.

This use of the expert-driven and often normalizing practice of medicine for subversive ends occurs in other contexts, such as trans surgery and assisted reproductive technologies. In the case of assisted reproductive technology, the techno-medical management of bodies enables some people who would not otherwise be able to reproduce and whose reproduction may be subversive, to procreate. As Jana Sawicki has argued, "At the same time that these new technologies create new subjects—that is, fit mothers, unfit mothers, infertile women, and so forth—they create the possibility of new sites of resistance. Lesbians and single women can challenge these norms by demanding access to infertility treatments" (1991, 84). Despite this potential, Charis Thompson has shown that patients and doctors often reaffirm traditional gender roles as a way of normalizing the assisted reproductive technology that threatens to disrupt the gender binary (2005). This does not mean that the technology has no subversive effects, but that the context and discourses within which it operates need to be considered. Like the technology Sawicki is considering, sterilization creates new subjects and opens up new sites of resistance. However, the kind of resistance that sterilization technology enables is notably different, as it incapacitates reproductive function. Assisted reproductive technology can be seen as correcting abnormalities or pathologies that result in infertility, whereas sterilization creates sterility.

Such sterility destabilizes prevailing constructions of women and may contribute to an opening up of greater possibilities. The sterilized body as cyborg blurs the boundaries of machine/organism and culture/nature. To the extent female is coterminous with reproductive capacity, such a body also potentially disrupts the male/female binary. The nonreproductive female body may challenge the idea that the female body has an inherent meaning by revealing the mutability, not just of ideas about the body, but also of the body itself. This, however, is only a potentiality: the cyborg is dangerous if vision becomes unitary and if the cyborg ceases to be a site of contestation. In the context of sterilization, there is no necessary way the sterilized body will be understood, and thus attention to norms and discourse is crucial as well.

This analysis of the destabilizing potential of sterilization raises the question, How might the procedure of sterilization—the effects of which are internal, quite in the body's interior—have such politically disruptive effects? First, the marking of sterilization, especially with the aid of laparoscopy, is quite visible to the physician who performs the procedure. Because of medical understandings of the female body and identity as well as the role of the medical profession in maintaining reproductive norms, the doctor's perception is key. Second, the existence of a sterilized body is as visible or public as a person decides to make it. My friend who is childfree and sterilized had a "no baby shower" and passed around pictures of her cauterized fallopian tubes in a way that mimicked the display and rituals around pregnancy and birth and that also had the effect of publicizing her sterilization. The very technology that enabled the doctor to cauterize her fallopian tubes also allowed her to make the effects of her internal surgery public and visible. Despite the internal character of sterilization, the procedure may disrupt the production of women as mothers and challenge the ontology of gender.

In fact, reproduction has become an area in which cultural perceptions of reproduction increasingly depend on visual technology and representations. As discussed in the previous chapter, images of fetuses have proliferated and played a crucial role in the constitution of fetuses as separately embodied entities. Perhaps alternative visualizations of women's interior could play a role in countering the dominance of fetal images in the politics of visualizing (non)reproduction.

Although I have argued that sterilization has the potential to transform larger cultural meanings regarding reproduction, the disruptive potential of sterilization needs to be considered alongside its potential conservatism. To take sterilization as subverting a maternal gendering of the female body may be read as a way of confirming the identification of female physiology with maternity. The necessity of the apparently dramatic and seemingly extreme intervention of sterilization to combat that gendering may appear to essentialize the female body as the basis of that identification and thus of maternal gendering. The notion that sterilization is a dramatic intervention, however, relies already on the identification of female physiology and maternity. Sterilization appears dramatic and extreme when the equation of female physiology and maternity is presupposed. Although there is a potentially conservative element to sterilization, it nonetheless reveals the mutability of the body. Attention to the body is important precisely because female physiology is discursively and normatively linked to maternity. To disrupt that link and promote critical autonomy, we must engage with the female body. The approach to sterilization advanced here, which combines performativity and cyborg theory, allows for such an engagement but resists essentializing the female body.

The Regulation of Sterilization

While the proliferation of (childfree) sterilized women may undermine the woman-mother identification in a way that increases autonomy, the medical paradigm discussed above and the accompanying legal framework both hinder access to tubal ligation and shore up existing hierarchies. Although the Supreme Court has never explicitly ruled on whether there is a right to sterilization, many lower courts have extended the court's reasoning in other cases to find such a right.[24] As the First Circuit Court of Appeals has noted, "While *Roe* and *Doe* dealt with a woman's decision whether or not to terminate a particular pregnancy, a decision to terminate the possibility of any future pregnancy would seem to embrace all of the factors deemed important by the court in *Roe* in finding a fundamental interest, but in magnified form."[25] Just as with abortion, though, the right to sterilization does not guarantee access to the procedure, and doctors serve as gatekeepers to the exercise of the right. In fact, the very existence of sterilization creates the possibility for women to be governed through the option. In other words, it creates the opportunity to be managed through the provision of sterilization surgery. In addition, despite the presumptive status of sterilization as a right, the regulation of medical sterilization is geared toward protection from sterilization abuse. In part because of the successful advocacy of anti-sterilization abuse activists, the regulation of sterilization situates the procedure primarily as a violation of the right to bear children and not as a means to reproductive autonomy (Scott 1991). That is, the possibility that some women would experience the *withholding* of sterilization as a violation is not considered.

In the 1970s, women who had been sterilized against their will brought numerous lawsuits to recover damages for their loss of fertility. These lawsuits failed overwhelmingly, but the sterilization abuse movement was nonetheless successful in changing sterilization policy.[26] Following the publicity of the case of the young African American sisters Minnie Lee and Mary Alice Relf—who were sterilized using federal funds without their knowledge or consent in Montgomery, Alabama, in 1973—officials paid serious attention to reforming federal sterilization policies (Kluchin 2009). Against the wishes of physicians and some liberal feminists, the Department of Health, Education, and Welfare eventually promulgated guidelines for federally funded sterilizations. These guidelines forbade the sterilization of individuals under twenty-one years, required a thirty-day waiting period between consent and surgery, increased regulations governing the sterilization of individuals in institutions, and provided for regular audits of physicians who performed sterilizations (Kluchin 2009; May 1997).

Anti–forced sterilization advocates were also successful in getting courts and legislatures to increase procedural safeguards. As Elizabeth Scott notes, following a Washington Supreme Court case, most sterilization reform laws came to "embody strict procedural and substantive requirements that create a strong presumption against sterilization" in cases of people determined mentally incompetent (2002, 391). Scott concludes that laws tend to "treat sterilization as an infringement of the right to procreate rather than as a means of exercising the right not to procreate" (420). That law tends to treat sterilization as a violation is also evident in state laws that protect doctors from liability if a woman changes her mind, but not from liability if they refuse to perform a sterilization.[27]

At the same time that advocates were pushing for stricter safeguards to prevent involuntary sterilization, some activists fought for greater access to sterilization. Their efforts were partially successful. In the 1970s, such activists overturned numerous hospital policies that, for example, required spousal consent to obtain sterilization, restricted sterilization based on a woman's age and/or parity, or required that more than one doctor approve a sterilization. The Association for Voluntary Sterilization, the American Civil Liberties Union, and Zero Population Growth, which was an organization with a history of eugenics advocacy, jointly undertook this advocacy effort. This advocacy failed, however, with regard to conscience clauses (Kluchin 2009, 115–47). These clauses—which include the federal "Church Amendment"—allow physicians or private hospitals to refuse to perform sterilizations or abortions. They were more difficult to overturn in part because they set women's rights "against hospitals' and individuals' religious freedom" (Kluchin 2009, 147).

Even as sterilization is primarily seen as a violation in part because of the success of efforts to prevent coerced sterilization, anti–sterilization abuse procedures have been inadequate. The framework that policy makers have set up to protect against sterilization abuses has contributed to the significant decrease in forced sterilization rates, but it has nonetheless failed to prevent abuses completely. That abuses have not been fully prevented reflects the inadequacy of changes in formal law to effect change in practice. Requiring consent forms, for example, does not guarantee that a woman has been fully informed about the procedure. More broadly, changes in law have not precluded other coercive practices, the continuation of which reflects the endurance of neo-eugenic ideas that deny decision-making authority to those perceived as unable to regulate and manage themselves properly.

Another reason abuses have not been fully prevented is that the law continues to privilege experts' interests and rights over those of their patients. Significantly, both the legal and policy contexts surrounding access to sterilization and protection from sterilization abuse often emphasize doctors' interests and opinions over the interests of their patients. In deciding the cases that were brought to redress the injury of forced sterilization, courts "privileged physicians' judgment over patients' rights" (Kluchin 2009, 176). For example, in 1977 a court ruled in favor of Dr. Clovis Pierce, who required pregnant women on Medicaid with two or more children to submit to sterilization as a condition of delivering their babies. Because he was the only obstetrician in his county in South Carolina who would serve women on Medicaid, such women had little choice but to accept his conditions (Kluchin 2009, 161–67). The court that heard the case, however, pointed to the existence of signed consent forms and concluded, "We perceive no reason why Dr. Pierce could not establish and pursue the policy he has publicly and freely announced" (Kluchin 2009, 164). Similarly, in determining the validity of conscience clauses that restrict access to sterilization, courts have privileged doctors' interests. In both cases the presumption is that it is worse to force physicians to act against their judgments than it is for women to be forced to conform to physicians' judgments. In other words, because physicians are generally trusted to govern themselves and often others, their autonomy is respected over and above that of women who are represented as lacking good judgment and the capacity for autonomy.

The regulation of sterilization is thus notably different from the contemporary trends in abortion regulation discussed in the previous chapter. In that context, the trend is to compel physicians to deliver the state's ideological message in an effort to undermine women's decisions and decision-making authority. In the case of sterilization, the state privileges and trusts physicians' judgments. Though the relationship between legal and medical authority differs in these two contexts, in each instance the result is less concern and respect for women's decision-making authority. In fact, in each case the lack of respect for women's self-governance is premised upon women's presumed inability to govern themselves properly without adequate guidance and intervention.

Just as framing abortion in terms of risk management depoliticizes the issue, framing the issue of sterilization in terms of physicians' rights to act on the basis of their personal and professional judgment depoliticizes the topics of access and abuse. The physician's opinion and how it was formed are placed outside the realm of inquiry; this authorizes the expert not only to question a woman's opinion or motivation but to control her access to medical services. As Haraway writes of experts,

> Who, within the myth of modernity, is less biased by competing interests or polluted by excessive closeness than the expert, especially the scientist? . . . Whether he be a male or a female, his passionless distance is his greatest virtue; this discursively constituted, structurally gendered distance legitimates his professional privilege, which in these cases, again, is the power to testify about the right to life and death. (2004, 88)

It is precisely this false distance that is at work in the legal context. As Haraway argues, the object of study simultaneously legitimates the expert's career and is constituted by expert practice (88). In obstetrics and gynecology, "truths" about the female body legitimate the expert's opinion, even as medical practice constitutes the female body. Medicine and its paradigm play a role in constructing the maternal nature of women, which it understands as an independent reality.

Autonomy, Law, and Medicine

Supporters of forced sterilization and the denial of sterilization have each justified these practices in terms of their supposed benefit to individual women and also to society at large. In both cases, law and policy regulate women's individual bodies for the betterment of society. Foregrounding autonomy as critique and transformation could serve as a corrective to the continually oppressive context of sterilization.

By privileging women's autonomy, I do not set up an essential tension between autonomy and a notion of the social good. Rather, I problematize the epistemic basis of an expert assessment of the social good. Privileging autonomy as transformation can counter expert determinations of the social good. As the persistence of neo-eugenic thinking that permeates sterilization practice reveals, expert assessments of the social good often derogate women's reproductive interests. Moreover, this knowledge is assumed to be universal and without perspective. When this expert knowledge is permitted to reign over the body in the form of law, an individual's own knowledge is disparaged. A better approach to knowledge, as discussed in chapter 1, would be to view knowledge as situated. Knowledge emanates from a perspective. The goal should be to engender a context of critical reflection upon partial perspectives without permitting the expert's partial perspective to reign over others in the form of law.

In the context of sterilization, we must examine how women, maternity, and autonomy are rendered in medical and legal discourse. We should begin to politicize the expert and his practice, including the way the discourse of self-governance operates in that practice. Both Haraway's critique of expertise and Mill's critique of society's imposition of the customary on individuals call for such an examination. Haraway shows how power and expertise are intertwined, while Mill provides an important defense against coercing individuals to act in accord with customs that reflect power relations in society. Giving the expert's perspective the status of law is likely to shore up existing customs and prevent eccentric conduct that might challenge the customary. Expert assessments often invoke the idea of autonomy as proper self-governance and compromise an individual's ability to be an eccentric cyborg.

Because decisions about one's reproductive capacities are significant matters that deeply affect how one's life is lived, it is crucial that those decisions ultimately rest with the individual. In the context of reproductive regulation in the United States, it is vital to foreground autonomy, but also to resist interpretations of it that would justify regulations that take decision-making authority away from the individual and allow experts to impose their own judgments. Such an imposition constrains autonomy as transformation. This resonates with Cornell's observation that

> our sense of freedom is intimately tied to the renewal of the imagination as we come to terms with who we are and who we wish to be as sexuate beings. . . . [I]t demands that no one be forced to have another's imaginary imposed upon herself or himself in such a way as to rob him or her of respect for his or her sexuate being. (1995, 8)

To allow the expert's determination of the often conflated individual and social good to reign over the individual in the form of coerced sterilization or refusal of voluntary sterilization is to restrict the imaginary and to disrespect the individual. In Cornell's words, it is to degrade or to fail to "be treated as worthy of the right to pursue sexual happiness" (1995, 11). Paradoxically, this imposition of another's will is often justified in terms of autonomy, where autonomy is understood as the capacity for proper self-governance.

One way of moving beyond the rule of medical expertise in the context of sterilization is to recognize that the law, itself a field of expert knowledge, is not powerless with regard to medical expertise. Carole Smith argues that, as opposed to Foucault's understanding that "law is fated to justify its operations by 'perpetual reference to something other than itself,'" such as nonlegal expert knowledge, the law has the power to constrain the practice of experts and hold them to account for their actions. Through the examination of British cases dealing with caesarean sections and sterilization, Smith argues that "law and the juridical field operate to manipulate and control expert knowledge to their own ends" (2000, 283). Indeed, comparing the judicial treatments of the informed consent to abortion laws examined in the previous chapter to the regulations discussed here illustrates this vividly. In that context, the law at times dismisses medical expertise and at times requires physicians to speak the state's ideological message. In the case of sterilization, the law gives the doctor more power and privileges the doctor over the patient.

Furthermore, the paternalism that marks physician consultations over sterilization and medical literature on tubal ligations treats and plays a role in (re)producing women as irrational and incapable of proper self-governance. Even when a woman succeeds in obtaining a sterilization from a doctor who is hostile to the idea, she may be treated paternalistically. She may also feel pressure to present her reasons for wanting sterilization in a way that comports with dominant, normalized discourses of womanhood and reproduction. One childfree woman assured her practitioner that she would adopt if she later decided she wanted children even though she was certain she never would.[28] Similar in some ways to the pressures transgender individuals who seek surgery face,[29] women seeking sterilization must conform to normalizing discourses about gender in order to access a procedure that would transform the body. In both cases, medical professionals perform a gatekeeping function.

Since the refusal or reluctance of the physician to perform a tubal ligation emanates from the idea that reproductive capacity is fundamental to women's bodies and identity, the denial of sterilization reinforces the notion of women-mothers. Rendering maternity fundamental to the female body and identity contributes to and obscures the processes by which the production of that body and identity occurs. Moreover, in denying a (childfree) woman the ability to ligate her fallopian tubes, medical professionals deny her one significant avenue by which she can resist the identification of women with motherhood. They deny her the ability to be a cyborg boundary figure and in doing so limit the ways she can participate in the ongoing reiteration of norms regarding gender and reproductive function. Being denied sterilization both compels women to continue being potential reproducers and denies women seeking sterilization an opportunity to disrupt or subvert, through their bodily performance, the identification of women with reproductive function. This thus undermines their participation in autonomy as transformation.

I am not suggesting that voluntary sterilization is inherently subversive. In fact, a single act can be an instance of both resistance and conformity. For example, a woman's childlessness could be understood as resistant to dominant gender ideologies and also as conforming to a consumerist ideology. One reason some women cite for being childfree is their desire to have more money to spend on themselves rather than children (May 1997, 196–207). Also, there is a similar strand of Malthusian discourse in both (neo)eugenics and the childfree movement. A woman's voluntary sterilization may be read as and explicitly joined with a call to others to do the morally responsible thing by getting sterilized as well. A request for sterilization from a woman without children might also reinforce sexist notions about mothers' self-sacrificing nature. In any case, discursive analysis remains important because it provides a way of assessing both the destabilizing and reifying effects of the cyborg.

Regardless of these complications, a better legal approach to sterilization would put primary emphasis on allowing patients to carry out their interests. Waiting periods and requirements that women receive written information on the details of tubal ligation are still necessary to ensure that patients have the ability to carry out their wishes, although more empirical research is needed to find out how these requirements operate in practice. While similar measures could be considered paternalistic and an imposition of the state's conceptualization of pregnancy on women in the context of abortion, given the history and ongoing existence of sterilization abuses, such measures are crucial for women who are at risk for coerced sterilization. Furthermore, sterilization is a less time-sensitive procedure than abortion, which makes waiting periods less onerous.

Just like the women who cannot access sterilization, the women who have it forced on them are subject to the will of doctors who think they know what is best. Women who are forcibly sterilized are also understood as incapable of properly deciding for themselves. Moreover, the doctor's decision to sterilize a woman without her full knowledge or consent is rooted in the idea that she is overly fertile. The woman who is coerced into sterilization is viewed in terms of reproductive capacity, although her reproduction is viewed as dangerous and irresponsible.

Instead of abolishing safeguards, then, guidelines should place a strong presumption in favor of carrying out a patient's desire. Although medical research informs a doctor's opinion, this research assumes and is part of what establishes maternal desire as normal. Rather than placing the burden on a woman to justify her decision to get sterilized, the burden should be on the doctor who would deny her that option. A physician who would deny a woman a sterilization would have to put forth strong reasons for denying the procedure: simply pointing to the possibility of future regret or to her childlessness would not suffice.

Crucially, this formulation does not protect individuals from future regret and rejects the idea that the interests of the woman who comes to regret her tubal ligation would have been better served had she not had the surgery. Such a view assumes that such a woman's later inclination is somehow better or more authentic than her preference at the time of sterilization. Like some of the justifications given for recent abortion restrictions, it is assumed that women regret taking actions that are opposed to their supposed maternal nature and thus they must be protected from doing so. Moreover, the view that would privilege a woman's potential future desire not to be sterilized not only emphasizes protection from regret, it also singles out infertility as that which should be feared. This understanding ignores that, like sterilization, having a child is irreversible and forecloses future possibilities. The fact that childbearing is taken as the default preference and as normal for women conceals the regret some experience after pregnancy and parenthood. To prevent or discourage a woman from undergoing sterilization because she may regret it presents lack of fertility as the chief reproductive outcome to be feared and further normalizes reproduction.

Conclusion

Reading sterilization as a performance and the sterilized female body as a "potent fusion" of cybernetics and organism is a particularly fruitful way of understanding the practice of sterilization and provides a distinctive perspective on a practice often associated with coercion and violation. Even though the young and childfree experience the most difficulty in obtaining sterilization, their very requests for sterilization could help disrupt the naturalization of maternity that marks medical discourse. Although the medical paradigm understands sterilization in terms of loss and dysfunction, this does not foreclose the possibility of a

5

Autonomy, Technology, and the Politics of Reproduction

This book has illustrated how understandings of autonomy and motherhood function in American reproductive law and politics. I have examined current issues in reproductive law through the framework of autonomy both to deepen our understanding of how reproduction is currently regulated and to reveal how the notion of autonomy plays a crucial role in that regulation. The book has furthermore examined how technology constitutes ideas about reproduction and what it means to exercise reproductive autonomy. The book has not only provided these critical feminist insights into reproductive politics, but also presented an alternative tradition of autonomy. In doing so, the book serves as a call to feminists and political theorists to rethink the notion of autonomy and consider its emancipatory potential, especially in the context of reproductive politics.

In this final chapter I trace some of the implications of these arguments and explore in further depth some of the book's themes. The chapter looks first at how autonomy as proper self-governance intersects with notions of the public and the private to increase management of the female body. I then explore the connection between autonomy and justice. I argue that, as applied to reproduction, the alternative tradition of autonomy is consistent with and can help advance reproductive justice. The conclusion thereby examines the promise of the autonomy as critique and transformation tradition. It also presents an overview of my analyses of the policy areas examined in the book. I join that discussion with an elaboration of the role of law in reinforcing existing social relations and bringing about transformative social change. Finally, the chapter turns to a discussion of the role of technology in creating reproductive norms and opportunities for transformation. I examine the resonances between cyborg theory and the alternative autonomy tradition. I argue that the cyborg models a technologically informed kind of eccentricity or subversion that can point the way toward alternative understandings and social transformation. Its focus on the role of technology adds an important element to our understanding of how critical autonomy may be practiced.

Public and Private Autonomy

Examining the autonomy as proper self-governance tradition reveals that current trends in reproductive law are drawing on and refiguring this tradition, which I traced in chapter 1 to Rousseau and Kant. Neoliberalism, the medicalization of reproduction, and postfeminism have converged in recent reproductive law and politics to heighten the demands put on individuals, especially women, to be self-governing with regard to their reproduction. As a result, the perceived failure to self-govern properly has resulted in more severe judgments. Moreover, those who are perceived to fail at governing themselves suffer a loss of their alleged privacy.

The autonomy as proper self-governance tradition thus intersects with and informs the constitution of the public and private realms in reproductive law. In some instances women are presented as autonomous agents with control over their private realm and who, therefore, should be held responsible for their decisions. This representation results in women being blamed for their reproductive decisions with little attention to the broader social context. The other side of privacy and placing reproductive responsibility on women is that public interference is warranted when experts or others perceive women to be in danger of acting irresponsibly. A putative privacy coexists with the representation of women's bodies as sites for public regulation. Because women's bodies are viewed as maternal bodies and therefore as essential to the social future and social order, they are often viewed as public spaces. This representation is apparent in the fact that incarcerated women and women in poverty face greater surveillance of their reproduction. It is also apparent in efforts to coerce women to reproduce by denying them sterilization or abortion. In all of these instances, women's bodies are to some extent viewed as public spaces.

At times an appeal to victimization justifies public intervention in the putatively private realm of reproduction. For example, as in *Gonzales v. Carhart*, legal discourse increasingly presents women seeking abortions as the victims of doctors' manipulations or boyfriends' intimidations. Recent efforts to cast abortion among black and Latina women as genocide figure Planned Parenthood as the victimizer. In these cases such victimization is presented as hindering women's autonomy, and so intervention is needed to protect women and guide them toward proper self-governance. State intervention in what might be thought of as the private sphere is justified to address alleged private domination. In such cases, then, legal actors and activists take up feminist calls for intervention in private domination because "the personal is political," not to address actual domination or violence, but to provide more opportunities to manage women's decisions.[1]

When abortion is posited as a woman's private decision, a woman may be opened up to punishment and shaming for that decision. Presenting abortion as properly a matter of public concern—because of victimization in the private realm or because women's reproductive capacity is key to the social future—provides grounds for intervention in a woman's reproductive decisions. In any case a woman is not governing herself "properly." All such cases are premised on claims to know what is best for women. Importantly, such claims are claims to power. As Barbara Cruikshank says in a different context, "any claim to know what is best for poor people, to know what it takes to get out of poverty and what needs must be met in order to be fully human, is also a claim to power" (1999, 38). A similar statement holds in this context: any claim to know what is best for women with regard to their procreation is a claim to power. In this context, such claims undermine women's control over their reproduction in the name of promoting their autonomy.

The example of reproductive politics demonstrates how slippery the division between public and private can be. In fact, women's bodies are rarely seen strictly as either private or public, but more often both at once, blurring the division between the two realms. Despite the framework of privacy in *Roe*, the female reproductive body is subject to intense public scrutiny and intervention. While procreating "properly" may provide a modicum of privacy, the very fact that outsiders are given standing to determine who is making rational reproductive decisions means that a woman's putatively private reproductive practices are always potentially subject to outside scrutiny. Put in other words, the framework of proper self-governance opens the door to public scrutiny and state surveillance to determine who is acting improperly. This dynamic is heightened for the reproductive body because the law does not conceive of a woman's body, especially during pregnancy, as fully her own. For example, Justice White's concurrence in *Roe* declares that "[t]he pregnant woman cannot be isolated in her privacy. She carries an embryo and, later, a fetus."[2]

It is also important to note how the notion of autonomy as proper self-governance is being refigured under neoliberalism and the consequences of that refiguring for understandings of the public and private. The neoliberal governmentality that I have argued is present in much reproductive law and politics further complicates the traditional division between public and private. As Lemke argues in his analysis of neoliberalism, "[T]he dividing line the liberals draw between the public and private spheres . . . itself becomes an object of study. In other words, with reference to the issues of government these differentiations are no longer treated as the basis and the limit of governmental practice, but as its instrument and effect" (2001, 201). The state develops techniques for managing women's reproduction while simultaneously placing primary responsibility on women and expecting them to bear the full consequences of their actions. It is inaccurate to see this shift as simply a withdrawal of the state that increases privacy. Rather, neoliberal governmentality "aspires to construct prudent subjects whose moral quality is based on the fact that they rationally assess the costs and benefits of a certain act as opposed to other alternative acts" (Lemke 2001, 201). Reproductive laws and policies increasingly frame autonomy as a matter of managing oneself according to cost-benefit analysis. As I showed in chapter 3, informed consent laws present and construct notions of abortion's risks and present the decision to abort as a matter of weighing various risks.

This examination of the tradition and shifting understandings of self-governance, as well as the ways these understandings intersect with discourses of public and private, helps us understand how and why autonomy has been such a contested concept. Feminists have long strived to get the state to deem women autonomous. These efforts have often seemed crucial, but also not especially transformative. Liberal feminists, for example, explicitly invoke the tradition of autonomy and rights, seeking to extend their potential protections to women. In doing so, they implicitly acknowledge the power of the state to determine who is autonomous and thereby decide who has privacy and under what conditions. When the use of autonomy to shore up existing hierarchies is not challenged, those who invoke autonomy and merely seek to expand its ambit risk reproducing and legitimating its exclusionary function. Although not always acknowledged, the exclusionary function plays a key role in many debates about using liberal notions like autonomy for feminist ends.

In addition, recognizing autonomy's exclusionary and paternalistic function allows us to understand how it has easily converged with postfeminism. In many ways, an emphasis on and valuation of autonomy has long sat alongside state and expert oversight of how that autonomy is exercised. This is because thinkers and state actors have frequently understood autonomy in terms of proper or rational self-governance. Current legal frameworks are reshaping that tradition, but these frameworks retain an emphasis on making the right kinds of decisions. The recent turn toward understanding autonomy as a matter of rational calculation of costs and benefits, for example, shows how autonomy continues to operate to justify the state's management of reproduction. It also illustrates why it is so important to undertake a critical inquiry of autonomy.

Autonomy and Justice

One way to put many of the observations that I have made in this book is to say that a narrow focus on reproductive autonomy understood as proper self-regulation justifies and underlies much reproductive injustice. Understanding that is important to challenging reproductive injustices that both deny women the ability to have or parent children and force them to bear children. As those in the reproductive justice movement make clear, thinking of reproductive rights in terms of simply providing choice ignores the context in which choices are made. Similarly, thinking of autonomy as proper self-governance conceals the politics behind determinations of which choices are proper. The turn toward autonomy as "informed consent" and minimization of risk further obscures the politics and values involved in regulating reproductive decisions. Intense management of women's bodies and decisions in ways that shore up existing norms and power relations is shrouded in seemingly neutral and supposedly expert-informed concepts of consent and risk.

Part of what I have shown in this book is how much reproductive rights discourse is mired in the logic of autonomy as proper self-management and corresponding ideas of responsibility. This has the effect of detracting from efforts to transform the social context and makes it easy to blame women and justify paternalistic intervention. When translated into policy and law, the logic of proper self-management and responsibility is applied differentially based on race, class, and gender. Reproductive regulations thus tend to perpetuate injustice in the form of racial, economic, and gendered hierarchies. As Asian Communities for Reproductive Justice (ACRJ) puts it, "[T]he control and exploitation of women's bodies, sexuality and reproduction [is] an effective strategy of controlling women and communities, particularly those of color. . . . Thus, controlling individual women becomes a strategic pathway to regulating entire communities" (ACRJ 2005, 2).[3]

Therefore, trusting women and protecting against government interference in and management of reproductive decisions have important implications for the groups and communities to which women belong. If controlling individual reproduction is a mechanism of control of a population or group, then challenging that control can be a mechanism of resistance. The most promising trends in reproductive advocacy come from the reproductive justice movement because it makes this link between the individual and the community explicit. It is focused on enabling women to make decisions for themselves and addressing the social context of economic domination, racial oppression, and patriarchy. Their focus is on "women's ability to exercise self-determination" and on winning "real individual, community, institutional and societal changes" (ACRJ 2005, 2). In putting forth such simple slogans as "Trust Black Women," organizations like SisterSong challenge the widespread surveillance and management of women of color borne out of distrust and ideas of what "proper" self-management looks like. The movement thus calls into question the dominant logics of proper self-governance and responsibility on which much reproductive injustice relies.

Given how the notion of autonomy can be used in an exclusionary way to justify paternalism and injustice, how does autonomy as critique challenge this use of autonomy? As discussed in chapter 1, the alternative autonomy tradition does not allow for the legal second-guessing of women's reproductive decisions and is more strongly anti-paternalistic in protecting the individual from government interference. I have shown how the understanding of autonomy as proper self-legislation does not provide adequate protection, and the alternative tradition of autonomy is meant to address that lack without representing the personal and the political as two essentially different spheres. Autonomy in its transformative register posits a crucial connection between the individual and society. It provides a strong protection against government interference, but does not characterize the personal sphere as beyond politics.

The personal, nonreproductive practices examined in this book have the potential to undermine the logic that equates woman with mother. As acts of counter-conduct or subversion, they reveal that another understanding of gender and reproduction is possible. They challenge social norms and also may prompt reflection in society at large regarding that which has been taken as customary and natural. This potential for individual conduct to push back against and prompt reflection on custom and norms rests on the connection between the individual and the political. Personal conduct is political due to its ability to call into question that which is assumed to be natural and beyond question. As such, autonomy as transformation reframes the public/private dichotomy that is manipulated in reproductive discourse. For example, my friend's decision to be sterilized is not easily understood as strictly private or public. Autonomy as critique and transformation would protect her ability to take such an eccentric action—noting that in such instances *public* interference would likely shore up existing norms. In that sense, her decision might be understood as private. However, one of the justifications for providing such protection of the personal realm is quite public and political. Such conduct has political effects for cultural forms and ways of life.

I have shown how the discourse of autonomy is variously used to justify interference in the reproductive lives of women and how that interference reinforces and relies on racialized narratives of reproduction. The alternative tradition of autonomy is transformative of these narratives in rejecting the state's authority and interest in deeming individuals capable of proper self-governance. Autonomy is not a concept that is used to sort people into the categories of properly and improperly self-governing and thereby justify political interference in the personal realm of those deemed nonautonomous. Autonomy as critique and transformation involves trusting individuals—whatever their race, class, or sexuality—to make their own reproductive decisions, but also paying attention to the ways those decisions reverberate throughout society.

This book has argued that autonomy can serve as a theoretical underpinning for trusting women with regard to procreation and prompting broader social change. Autonomy as critique and transformation aims to protect the individual from paternalism and promote social transformation. Autonomy in its transformative register, then, demonstrates why a concern for justice does not necessarily entail turning away from the individual. Although critiques of autonomy often argue that its individual focus detracts from context and community, the alternative tradition of autonomy reveals why a focus on and protection of an individual sphere can be important. Such a sphere can provide protection against the imposition of the often discriminatory judgments of others. It also provides the space and opportunity to challenge oppressive power relations and norms through counter-conduct. In other words, this alternative understanding of autonomy can be applied to promote social justice. Group-based oppression often happens along with and through a denial that those in the group have the capacity to self-govern. Autonomy as critique and transformation protects individual self-governance and values social transformation, especially transformation that would challenge subordination.

Thus, despite the exclusionary and conservative interpretation of autonomy, the concept can be used to resist existing hierarchies and move toward justice. Autonomy may hold enduring appeal in American law and politics in part because it is possible to interpret it in so many varied ways. Autonomy is a contested and pliable concept, which makes it especially open to resignification. Instead of rejecting the notion of autonomy, this book has examined how the notion operates in reproductive politics while attending to the ways an alternative understanding of autonomy could be used to shift reproductive norms. Because of technological and legal developments, individuals now have heightened potential for control over their reproduction. This has enabled experts and state actors to apply the notion of autonomy as obedience to appropriate self-given laws more extensively and intensively to reproduction.

At the same time, these technological and legal developments have created the potential for the subversion of the very norms that are reflected in the management of reproduction.

Critique, Subversion, and Policy

The policies described in this book rely on the heteronormative identification of woman with mother. The idea that nonprocreative practices could be fruitfully disruptive does not mean that oppression only comes from being denied access to the means to prevent reproduction. Many women have been denied the right to mother. Coerced sterilization, like coerced childbearing, represents women as essentially the reproducers of society and their fertility as key to the social good. Coerced sterilization is premised on a narrative of excessive fertility and the maternal construction of the female body. As such, the nonreproductive female body may challenge the essential maternity of women on which coerced sterility rests. Nonetheless, in considering the policy implications of the framework advanced in this book, we must consider how best to safeguard against the imposition of childbearing as well as the denial of motherhood.

Applying the framework of autonomy as critique and transformation to the policy areas examined in this book would result in important changes in each area that would both protect the individual and point the way toward larger cultural change and justice. In the context of abortion jurisprudence, I have argued that understanding the right to abortion as promoting autonomy as critique would be more affirmative and emancipatory than existing frames of woman protection or antisubordination. A transformative autonomy take on the right to abortion would entail eschewing the prominent privacy framework and instead focusing on liberty and transformation. Although there is little legal doctrine to support such a fully transformative understanding of autonomy, I argued that it is at least important that legal frameworks not reify traditional understandings of women or preclude cultural transformation.

As a legal matter, I argued that an antidiscrimination defense of abortion, which focuses on how abortion restrictions rely on and reinscribe restrictive female identities, is preferable to an antisubordination defense, which depoliticizes the broader social context. In particular, I demonstrated that the antisubordination approach is in tension with recognizing that many women face harm from the denial of motherhood. The antidiscrimination principle avoids that problem and is consistent with the alternative tradition of autonomy. Autonomy as transformation involves protecting the individual and acknowledging that that protection is important because it guards against normative and often discriminatory impositions on the individual, whether the result is the denial or imposition of motherhood. In either case, trusting women is central.

With regard to informed consent to abortion, I have shown how such laws increase surveillance, violate liberty, and treat women as less-than in denying them the ability to make decisions for themselves. Assuming that individuals have equal intrinsic value results in respecting individuals' life plans and allowing them to carry out those plans without undue interference from the state. Autonomy as critique and transformation relies on this assumption, but the trend in informed consent to abortion laws is to impose the state's ideological message on women and to require the use of ultrasound on women's bodies to create that message. The alternative tradition of autonomy would support only those informed consent provisions that provide women with the ability to construct, without coercion, their own understandings of their pregnancies. Any given provision would have to be analyzed from the perspective of trusting women and respecting their decision making.

In the case of the regulation of sterilization, as in informed consent to abortion laws, primary emphasis should be placed on allowing patients to carry out their interests. Unlike in the case of abortion, coercion is a serious concern in the context of sterilization due to the ongoing existence of involuntary sterilization. I have thus argued that informed consent provisions such as waiting periods should still be required before a sterilization. This does not mean that the state can impose its ideological message; rather, such safeguards are needed to protect against discrimination. These measures should also not amount to a significant bar to sterilization access for those seeking the procedure. In all cases, the law should presume that the patient knows her own goals and interests better than medical professionals. As I have demonstrated, physicians are likely to impose dominant norms that maintain hierarchies because they often hold discriminatory and gender-essentialist ideas. Creating regulatory frameworks that reduce the power of physicians to impose their judgments on women in the context of sterilization is important.

The existing policies in each of these areas share a paternalistic frame. In each case, thinking of autonomy as critique and transformation would protect against that paternalism because it recognizes that in these contexts paternalism and corresponding notions of proper self-governance preserve the status quo and function as instruments of oppression. Autonomy as critique and transformation offers personal protection alongside the recognition that doing so can be part of larger cultural transformation. The idea of autonomy as protection from interference is too important an idea to abandon to the tradition that uses it in exclusionary and discriminatory ways. Reproductive law and policies in the areas this book has examined demand an alternative interpretation of autonomy that would protect the individual's decisions and combat social and legal exclusion and discrimination. I have argued that autonomy as critique and transformation is such an alternative.

I have approached autonomy from a distinct angle in order to call into question how the notion is often conceived and employed in law. Doing so has shown what is wrong with how reproductive law tends to frame autonomy. It has also allowed for a reorientation of the discussion about autonomy and law. Instead of focusing on who has the requisite capacities for autonomy or whose decisions are the product of oppressive circumstances, the autonomy as critique and transformation tradition focuses on protecting individual self-governance for the purposes of transforming the social context.

My critique of autonomy as proper self-management, combined with my demonstration of how it operates in reproductive law, shows why it is not a good idea to focus, especially for legal purposes, on how oppression affects the capacity for autonomy. I sideline concerns about what constitutes a capacity for autonomy because, as I have shown, biased judgments about who has the proper capacity for autonomy provide the foundation of many reproductive injustices and exclusionary practices. Similarly, Menon counsels from a feminist perspective that the law is not the place to address the problems of free will raised by an oppressive social context (2004, 216). She argues that the *production of oppression* as natural, fulfilling, and so on, escapes constitutional and legal logic. When we try to address this . . . through the language of constitutionalism, we are in effect, mobilising the coercive force of the state to *prevent* the operation of free will—a free will operating in a manner we believe to be antithetical to our vision. (2004, 213)

For example, claiming that a woman cannot make a decision about her pregnancy with sufficiently free will because of the overarching influences of patriarchy would open her up to legal judgments of what is proper for her body and her future. Such legal judgments are likely to shore up, rather than challenge, existing hierarchies and norms. As Scoular explains, the "law . . . remains a vital process through which modern power relations operate" (2010, 28). As a legal matter, then, it is best to provide protection from interference in individual reproductive decisions, even though women may make those decisions in oppressive circumstances.

Because of the way law tends to operate as an expression and reification of power relations in society, it is important to recognize both that the legal changes I advocate here will be difficult to implement and that legal change is by itself inadequate to enact broader transformations. I have argued that law can undermine such efforts and thus that attention to the juridical is critical and can be important to promoting transformation. Although they should not be the sole focus of political struggles, rights and legal changes can play a significant role in challenging the status quo. However, the promise of autonomy in its transformative register extends beyond legal reform. In fact, it has implications for how we think about politics more broadly. This observation explains the book's primary focus on autonomy, not rights.

Technology and Cyborg Critique

This book has demonstrated that technology affects reproductive law and politics in multiple ways. Humans and medical technology are increasingly perceived as controlling reproduction, and the importance of medical expertise has expanded. This expertise is often used in conjunction with the law to reinforce existing norms, as is the case with sterilization access and pre-abortion ultrasound mandates.

Developments in reproductive technology have also subtly changed understandings of reproductive autonomy, as they have allowed for the perception of increased control of reproduction, even as access to technology is limited and managed. Technological innovations have opened the door for the judgment that individuals are hyper-responsible for their reproduction. In addition, the development of ultrasound has enabled the construction of the fetus as a stand-alone person. Taken together, these examples demonstrate how technological changes are constitutive of ideas about what it means to exercise reproductive autonomy.

Cyborg theory highlights how such technology creates possibilities for liberation as well as oppression. It is thus important to consider how medical and technological practices have enabled not just new forms of control and management of reproduction, but also new forms of resistance. As I have suggested, reproductive technologies serve as potential tools of critique and transformation. I have discussed in particular the potential of voluntary sterilization, abortion, and alternative images of pregnancy that would foreground the placenta and so the connection between woman and fetus. These practices can be framed as challenges to what has come to be perceived as "natural"—both the woman-mother link and increasingly the view of the fetus as an individual person.

The medicalization and technologization of reproduction have two important implications. In many instances technology has created possibilities for challenging the naturalness of female maternity, which I have argued is a good thing. However, there is another side to this medicalization. Increased use of medical technology allows for more expert intervention in women's bodily processes. Reproduction has become so medicalized that women's own understandings and knowledge of their bodies are often displaced in favor of expert judgments. This tension between the possibilities that technology creates and the increased management of individual bodies that technology often enables is one of the core tensions explored in this book. Trusting individuals' decision making and creating laws that protect it can help challenge the paternalism and displacement of women's knowledge that often accompany medicalization.

Cyborg theory not only invites us to investigate the liberatory potential of technology, as this book has done, it also pushes further some of the insights regarding the importance of critique and transformation

explored in this book. The figure of the cyborg has important resonances with and implications for autonomy as critique and transformation as applied to reproductive policy. Recall that the critical tradition
of autonomy would provide protection against interference with personal decisions in order to preserve the ability to engage in conduct that
may challenge norms, customs, and that which is taken to be "natural." Cyborg theory complements this take on autonomy well since, like
counter-conduct, it calls into question the "natural." Indeed, the cyborg
makes explicit the fact that the "natural" is always constructed, but it
does so by emphasizing how *technology* raises questions about what is
natural.

The figure of the cyborg is in fact a kind of "eccentric subject" (Haraway 2004, 60) that can point the way toward alternative understandings
of humanity, technology, nature, reproduction, and gender. The cyborg
is a figure that represents "potent fusions" that challenge accepted understandings. Just as Foucault, Butler, and Mill theorize, respectively,
resistance, subversion, and eccentricity as ways of countering received
customs and ideas of "the natural," Haraway theorizes the cyborg to
challenge received ideas about "the natural," especially as that category
is set against "the cultural." In this way, the cyborg converges easily with
the alternative autonomy tradition. The cyborg is a figure, like the eccentric or subversive subject, that can prompt reflection on norms and
that which is taken to be natural.

Haraway adds a focus on the potential for technological transformation to disrupt categories such as the natural and cultural to the afore-
mentioned theorists' understandings of power and transformation.
Whereas Foucault, Butler, and Mill are all concerned with conduct, none
of them explores or theorizes how technology can be used to open up
critical reflection on dominant norms and understandings of the natural. Since, as this book has demonstrated, reproductive politics and law
are deeply intertwined with reproductive technology, the turn to cyborg
theory is crucial because it draws attention to how that technology constitutes and may reconstitute reproduction.

Furthermore, in assigning agency to technology and machines, cyborg theory complements the poststructuralist take on the self and
autonomy on which autonomy as critique and transformation relies.
Cyborg theory offers an understanding of technology that does not see

humans as simply creating and wielding technology for our own uses. Technology becomes a force itself, something that is involved in shaping what it is to be human rather than something that stands apart from society or humanity. In this way, the co-constitutive relationship between humanity and technology parallels the relationship between the individual and society.

The self on which cyborg theory relies also parallels the self of critical autonomy. Haraway describes the cyborg as "a kind of disassembled and reassembled, post-modern collective and personal self" (2004, 23). This, she says, "is the self feminists must code" (23). In many ways, autonomy as critique and transformation thinks of the self in this way, as both "collective and personal." On this understanding, the self transforms and disrupts received binaries—especially perhaps the public/private dichotomy—owing to this tension of being at once both collective and personal. Julia Martin notes that the cyborg "represents (if ironically) a kind of affirmation—not of solid, inherent 'identity,' a 'self' in opposition to 'nature,' but of a networking life that is polymorphous, changing and so potentially more liberated" (1996, 108). This is partly why the cyborg fits so well with autonomy as critique and transformation—both are affirmative and seek out positive transformations of the complex and dynamic world.

Conclusion

Reproduction turns out to be an especially interesting and important area in which to think about autonomy and the production of the self. The state and experts have often appealed to maternal capacity to provide grounds for women's subordination and alleged inability to self-govern. Because understandings and ascriptions of autonomy are gendered and tied to women's reproductive capacity, it is especially crucial to pull apart and think critically about the discourse of autonomy in reproductive law and politics. The traditional rendering of women as unable to self-govern properly arises in new ways in the recent jurisprudence of abortion: women are presented as ignorant, vulnerable, and subject to the pathologies of denying their maternal nature while simultaneously being called on to self-manage their reproduction through the use of technology, medical expertise, and risk minimization. As I have argued in this book, the notion of autonomy frequently plays a limiting, status quo–enforcing role in twenty-first-century reproductive law and politics in the United States. In accord with historic understandings of autonomy as proper self-governance, the intervention in the self-governance of those who are judged to be in danger of improperly governing themselves—where these judgments reflect gender, race, and class biases—is justified often for the sake of both the governed and society. In this schema, the construction of the autonomous subject and the formation of understandings about what constitutes autonomy fall outside the realm of concern. In other words, the fact that autonomy inheres in proper decision making is taken for granted.

Understanding that the notion of autonomy employed in much reproductive rights discourse has a long history helps to explain why recent restrictions on women resonate with legislators, judges, and even voters. It also helps to explain how appeal to autonomy and choice can corrode projects for reproductive rights and justice. The autonomy as proper governance tradition directs attention toward how to govern those deemed incapable of governing themselves. Whether in the medical discourse of female sterilization, the rationales for ultrasound laws, or woman-protective arguments for abortion restrictions, the notion of autonomy is employed to justify keeping reproductive decisions in line with certain norms. As such, autonomy as proper self-regulation plays a crucial role in current reproductive regulation. Yet there is room for transformation, and the possibility of transformation is what gives autonomy its potentially critical and justice-oriented edge. The alternative tradition of autonomy can be used to challenge the norms and hierarchies that are reinforced in recent reproductive regulations. It is thus crucial to consider what transformative possibilities the new forms of governance have enabled.

NOTES

1 See the Guttmacher Institute reports at guttmacher.org for a comprehensive overview of state restrictions.

2 See, e.g., Joel Feinberg (1989, 28).

3 For a nice summary of feminist critiques to mainstream ethics and some feminist responses, see Samantha Brennan (1999). For the origin of this critique, see Carol Gilligan (1982). This critique is also closely related to the communitarian critique of liberalism. Communitarians see the individual as partially constituted by society, family, and community and thus resist the atomistic individualism of liberalism. See, e.g., Michael Sandel (1998, ix–xiv), though Sandel himself rejects the label "communitarian."

4 Jennifer Nedelsky (1989) and Marilyn Friedman (2003, 82–87) provide good summaries of critiques of this kind. See also Iris Marion Young (1995). She argues that self-sufficiency and autonomy should be theoretically untangled.

5 In contrast, Nancy Hirschmann (2003) prefers freedom to autonomy because she believes that autonomy ultimately relies on a notion of an authentic or true self who governs. Freedom, which on her account primarily includes "the ability to make choices and act on them," is thus a necessary prerequisite to autonomy (2003, 30).

6 My approach differs from McNay's (2000) in that I see this potential for creativity and autonomy in the works of Foucault and Butler, whereas McNay sees those theorists as exemplars of the negative paradigm of subjectification and agency.

7 Paul Benson (1990, 1994), however, focuses instead on "free agency."

8 This example comes from Hirschmann (2003).

9 It may be useful to contrast my perspective with Nancy Hirschmann's since she prefers the notion of freedom to autonomy. She states that "the ability to make choices and act on them is the basic condition of freedom," but "that choice needs to be understood in terms of the desiring subject, of her preferences, her will, and identity" (2003, 30). Her resistance to the notion of autonomy lies in this claim. She holds that autonomy, unlike freedom, ultimately relies on a notion of an authentic or true self who must do the choosing and governing. She argues that freedom from patriarchal construction of the self and its concomitant barriers is necessary before we can ever achieve autonomy. I disagree with Hirschmann's characterization of freedom as a prerequisite of autonomy. I instead view

autonomy as an instantiation of freedom—as one way to understand, or give content to, the broader idea of freedom.

10 Critical race theory has offered a sustained critique of rights and law reform. See, for example, Bell (1980) and Crenshaw (1991). Dean Spade (2011) draws on critical race theory to offer an analysis of the limits of law in the context of trans politics.

11 See Hartouni (1997). She discusses the implications of some reproductive technologies.

12 Whereas *trans* is a Latin prefix meaning "across" or "over," *cis* is the term for "on the same side." Kristen Schilt and Laurel Westbrook describe cisgender as referring to "individuals who have a match between the gender they were assigned at birth, their bodies, and their personal identity" (2009, 461).

13 See, for example, Braidotti (1997), D'Adamo and Baruch (1986), Ikemoto (1996), and Shultz (1990). Also, Elizabeth Sourbut's work (1996) on gynogenesis uses Haraway's cyborg theory as a tool for exploring the potential of emerging or potential technologies to transform motherhood.

14 This investment in reproduction and the future provides context for understanding why, although queer bodies are stigmatized as nonreproductive, elements of the gay political movement have become increasingly invested in the nuclear family ideals of marriage and parenthood.

15 Muñoz describes pragmatic gay politics as against his utopian queer thinking in the following way:

> Seeing queerness as horizon rescues and emboldens concepts such as freedom that have been withered by the touch of neoliberal thought and gay assimilationist politics. Pragmatic gay politics present themselves as rational and ultimately more doable. Such politics and their proponents often attempt to describe themselves as not being ideological, yet they are extremely ideological and, more precisely, are representative of a decayed ideological institution known as marriage. (2009, 32)

16 *Gonzales v. Carhart*, 550 U.S. 124 (2007).

CHAPTER 1. AUTONOMY

1 This is the case whether the noumenal and phenomenal represent ontologically separate worlds (Guyer 2000), or whether they are understood epistemologically, as two different ways of apprehending an object (Allison 2004).

2 For this reason, and also because of the relation between autonomy and self-limitation I identified in Rousseau's thought, I often use self-limitation as a way of describing the autonomy as proper self-governance tradition.

3 Diana Tietjens Meyers (1999) and Edwina Barvosa-Carter (2007) provide an interesting critique of the view of the self underlying much autonomy theory. Each has brought together autonomy and intersectional identity to critique the common reliance on a unitary, static self as the basis of autonomy. They emphasize multiplicity of identity and highlight the complexity and dynamic character of individuals. These intersectional approaches understand individuals as often

having deeply conflicting desires and commitments but decline to attribute nonautonomy categorically to subjects so conceived. Both Meyers and Barvosa-Carter argue that being socially subordinated does not necessarily lead to impaired reflective abilities and could even be a boon to those abilities. Their accounts reveal previous accounts of autonomy as overly exclusionary insofar as they are based on the kind of reflection expected of those in privileged positions. Barvosa-Carter and Meyers both reveal as unjustified the assumption that oppressive socialization is a hindrance to reflection and autonomy.

4 Process and substance are intertwined. For example, the substance of one's commitments may shape the process by which one determines one's plans or preferences. If an agent is committed to living a life that comports with religious dictates, the process by which she decides on a course of action will look quite different from the process of an agent who is committed to living a life of pleasure. Furthermore, as Marilyn Friedman argues, to require that the substance of one's values accord with autonomy is to require that a person value the *process* of coming to autonomous decisions (2003, 21). Regardless of how the distinction between procedural and substantive autonomy is conceived, each is concerned with ascribing autonomy to agents.

5 This point is similar to a question Judith Butler poses: "[W]hat kinds of agency are foreclosed through the positing of an epistemological subject precisely because the rules and practices that govern the invocation of that subject and regulate its agency in advance are ruled out as sites of analysis and critical intervention?" (1990, 144).

6 As Mary Poovey puts it, from this masking it "has seemed to follow not only that mother-love emanates from the body, in the form of maternal instinct but also that the desire to be a mother motivates and lies at the heart of all female desire" (1992, 243).

7 Rasmussen (2011) refers to this as the autonomy as creativity tradition.

8 Jana Sawicki has similarly noted that freedom for Foucault "lies in our capacity to discover the historical links between certain modes of self-understanding and modes of domination, and to resist the ways in which we have already been classified and identified by dominant discourses" (1991, 43). Bevir makes a similar observation. Although Bevir uses the term "agency" to mean something similar to what I mean by autonomy as critique, he also locates the importance of critique for freedom within Foucault's later work. According to Bevir, "We are agents, but we exercise our agency properly only when we resist the pressures of normalization by challenging a morality through our personal, ethical conduct. . . . As agents, we can draw on the resources society makes available to us to question received norms" (1999, 76–77).

9 Cornell and Stephen D. Seely have gone further and argued that Foucault should be considered a revolutionary thinker. In their words, "Foucault's project of seeking new arrangements of bodies and pleasures should be read as an attempt to articulate new forms of individual and collective conduct, or, in other words,

an attempt to produce revolutionary bodies and minds" (2014, 15). Davidson (2011) also argues that Foucaultian conduct and counter-conduct are political.

10 Bruce Baum (2000) has also suggested the similarity of aspects of Millian and Foucaultian thought, especially regarding their theories of power.

11 Similarly, Hirschmann (2003) argues that "Mill valorizes the 'eccentric' not because of individualism per se but rather because difference is so vital to the productive confluence and interaction of ideas, an interaction which in turn stimulates individual mental processes" (63–64).

12 For a discussion of the phrase "room to maneuver," see Schultz (1989) and Coombe (1989).

13 As Nancy Fraser asks of Butler, "Why is resignification good? Can't there be bad (oppressive, reactionary) resignifications?" (1995, 68). Similarly, Amy Allen queries, "But why should we resignify these norms? Why expose them as unnatural? Why denaturalize sex?" (1998, 466). Another related question that is often posed to Butler is whether agency is ever precluded. Butler at times suggests an all-encompassing notion of agency, while at other times she privileges the transgressive or subversive. For example, she writes in *Psychic Life of Power* that "agency is the assumption of a purpose *unintended* by power, one that could not have been derived logically or historically, that operates in a relation of contingency and reversal to the power that makes it possible, to which it nevertheless belongs" (1998, 15). Here Butler seemingly excludes from agency that which is intended or would reinforce power such that agency appears only as that which is unintended by and acts as a *reversal* of power. For a discussion of Butler's preference for subversive agency, see Saba Mahmood (2005).

CHAPTER 2. ABORTION AND THE JURIDICAL

1 Francois Ewald examines the emergence of "social law"—the joining of normalization and the law (1990). For a further discussion of the relation between norms, law, and governmentality, see Rose (1998).

2 Snitow (1992) has provided an overview of relationships between feminism and motherhood at different stages since the 1960s.

3 In Foucault's explanation of Greek ethics, the practice of freedom is understood as itself an ethical issue: "Freedom is the ontological condition of ethics. But ethics is the considered form that freedom takes when it is informed by reflection" (1998, 284).

4 As Siegel reports, the pro-life activist David Reardon urged activists to embrace a woman-centered approach in order to reframe the political debate in a way that would be more favorable for the pro-life movement (2007, 1019).

5 *Gonzales v. Carhart*, 550 U.S. 124 (2007).

6 *Planned Parenthood v. Casey*, 505 U.S. 833 (1992).

7 The Court uses the fact that the Partial Birth Abortion Ban Act will not "prohibit the vast majority of D&E abortions" as support for its claim that the act does not impose an undue burden on women obtaining abortions. *Gonzales v. Carhart*, 156.

8 Justice Ginsburg dissenting, *Gonzales v. Carhart*, 184.

9 See, for instance, U.S. Congress, *U.S. Code* 18, §1531(b)(1)(A).

10 For example, Kennedy writes that "the former occurs when the fetus is partially outside the mother." *Gonzales v. Carhart*, 160. See also *Carhart*, 159.

11 For example, the pro-life advocate David Reardon argues that "from a natural law perspective, we can know in advance that abortion is inherently harmful to women. It is simply impossible to rip a child from the womb of a mother without tearing out a part of the woman herself—a part of her heart, a part of her joy, a part of her maternity" (Reardon 1996, 5–6, quoted in Siegel 2007, 1019). Similarly, the report of the South Dakota Task Force to Study Abortion states, "Either the abortion provider must deceive the mother into thinking the unborn child does not yet exist, and thereby induce her consent without being informed, or the abortion provider must encourage her to defy her very nature as a mother to protect her child" (South Dakota State Legislature 2005, 56). Moreover, in the woman-protective frame, the essence of the mother-child relationship is closely connected in the woman-protective frame with women's biology (52–55).

12 Kennedy uses the term "unborn child" in *Carhart*. See, e.g., *Carhart*, 134.

13 The South Dakota Legislature's task force report on abortion, which is discussed in the next chapter, illustrates this well. See South Dakota State Legislature (2005, 52–55).

14 Ludlow discusses how pro-choice emphasis on "traumatic" abortions—such as those involving women who were raped or live with violence—covers over the mundane reasons women have abortions and in the process contributes to the stigma and grief constructed around such everyday experiences of abortion (2008, 30–32).

15 Reardon was quoted in Siegel (2007, 1019).

16 *Roe v. Wade*, 410 U.S. 113 (1973). Examples of antisubordination abortion rights arguments include Siegel (1992), Law (1984), and Allen (1995).

17 Siegel is quoting *Mississippi University for Women v. Hogan*, 458 U.S. 718 (1982), 725.

18 Here Siegel expresses a sentiment similar to that of Catharine MacKinnon, who argues, "However difficult an abortion decision may be for an individual woman, it provides a moment of power in a life otherwise led under unequal conditions that preclude choice in ways she cannot control" (2005, 141).

19 For a critical approach to experience, see Scott (1991).

20 This does not exclude the possibility that they could be subordinated via lack of access as well.

21 See Dworkin (1982). He argues that with choice comes heightened responsibility for the consequences of one's decision.

22 Kimberlé Crenshaw, for example, has critiqued the application of antidiscrimination law for the ways judges have failed to grapple adequately with discrimination arising from both race and sex (1989).

23 The devaluation of such women's reproduction is discussed in Roberts (1998), Solinger (2001), Saxton (1984), Finger (1984), and Flavin (2009).

24 See Anna Marie Smith (2007) for a comprehensive analysis of sexual regulation and welfare reform, including the family cap. She argues, among other things, that family caps have borrowed from facets of the pro-choice movement in presenting women as "approach[ing] pregnancy and childbirth in a consumerist manner" (148).

25 I would add that making the decision to bear a child a choice—which is prompted not only by the existence of the option to abort but also by pro-choice, reproductive rights rhetoric—gives the state greater discretion over whether to support children. Supporting children comes to be seen more as a state's choice and less like its responsibility.

26 Roberts discusses how the myth of the welfare queen works and how it casts black women as poor decision makers (1998, 17–19).

27 For a more recent discussion of the ways women may be punished for having children, see Flavin (2009).

28 For a discussion of a similar dynamic in the context of euthanasia, see Velleman (2007).

29 For example, the Court has upheld the Hyde Amendment's restrictions on federal funding of abortions in *Harris v. McRae*, 448 U.S. 297 (1980); has held that the state need not fund nontherapeutic abortions for the poor in *Maher v. Roe*, 432 U.S. 464 (1977); and has held both that a state may prohibit the use of public facilities for abortions and that a state may prohibit public employees from performing abortions in *Webster v. Reproductive Health Services*, 492 U.S. 490 (1989).

30 Information on trends in abortion access can be found in Jones et al. (2008) and Henshaw and Finer (2003).

31 Justice Ginsburg dissenting, *Gonzales v. Carhart*, 185 (quoting *Planned Parenthood v. Casey*, 852).

32 Justice Ginsburg dissenting, *Gonzales v. Carhart*, 185. Ginsburg cites the following cases that prohibit legislating on the basis of ancient notions about women: "*United States v. Virginia*, 518 U.S. 515, 533, 542, n. 12 (1996) (State may not rely on 'overbroad generalizations' about the 'talents, capacities, or preferences' of women; '[s]uch judgments have . . . impeded . . . women's progress toward full citizenship stature throughout our Nation's history'); *Califano v. Goldfarb*, 430 U.S. 199, 207 (1977) (gender-based Social Security classification rejected because it rested on 'archaic and overbroad generalizations' 'such as assumptions as to [women's] dependency.')"

33 The National Women's Law Center filed an amicus brief in *Carhart* that makes some similar points. It argues, for example, that "the act impermissibly imposes one moral viewpoint on women, denying them personal dignity and equality." It also points out that the congressional act has ramifications for autonomy because it does not allow women to make freely an "intensely personal decision[]."

Amicus Brief (2006), National Women's Law Center, filed in *Gonzales v. Carhart*, 19, 21.

34 For example, Ginsburg quotes *Casey* in declaring that the decision to bear a child is crucial "to a woman's 'dignity and autonomy,' her 'personhood' and 'destiny,' her 'conception of . . . her place in society.'" Justice Ginsburg dissenting, *Gonzales v. Carhart*, 170 (quoting *Planned Parenthood v. Casey*, 505 U.S., 851–52).

35 For example, *Harris v. McRae*, 448 U.S. 297 (1980); *Maher v. Roe*, 432 U.S. 464 (1977); and *Webster v. Reproductive Health Services*, 492 U.S. 490 (1989) all illustrate the limitations of the current framing of abortion. Each decision declines to impose a positive obligation on the state to ensure abortion access. Eileen L. McDonagh (1996) has proposed an interesting alternative framing of the right to abortion based on a woman's right to bodily integrity and consent that she argues would entail a more positive government role in ensuring abortion access.

36 Another way to understand this argument is by reference to Butler's understanding of subversion. The "persistence and proliferation [of gender identities that fail to conform to the norms of cultural intelligibility] provide critical opportunities to expose the limits and regulatory aims of that domain of intelligibility and, hence, to open up within the very terms of that matrix of intelligibility rival and subversive matrices of gender disorder" (1990, 17). Gender performance is subversive "to the extent that it reflects on the imitative structure by which hegemonic gender is itself produced and disputes heterosexuality's claim on naturalness" (1993, 125).

37 This paradox evokes Carole Pateman's analysis of the paradox of social contract theory in which women are left out of the originary contract and thus subordinated yet also assumed to be free in entering the marriage contract (1988).

38 See LaVaque-Manty (2006, 383–87) and Ben-Ishai (2010). Ben-Ishai provides an interesting account of aspirational recognition, according to which the act of ascribing autonomy could be put to subversive ends.

39 For a thorough examination of how women are punished for their reproductive decisions in contemporary reproductive law, see Flavin (2009).

40 Some antiabortion advocates go so far as to argue that it is highly unlikely that women will get pregnant as a result of rape. This is the view of Missouri Representative Todd Akin, who said in 2012, "It seems to be, first of all, from what I understand from doctors, it's really rare. If it's a legitimate rape, the female body has ways to try to shut the whole thing down" (Moore 2012).

41 Insofar as the reproductive justice movement is a response to the perspective that sees procreative responsibility as a matter of having children only when one is "ready," while minimizing the importance of the social forces that constrain choices and shape procreative judgments, it illustrates the prominence of that view.

42 For discussions of the reproductive justice framework, see Zakiya Luna (2009) and Kimala Price (2010). Luna describes the movement as "represent[ing] a shift

for women advocating for control of their bodies, from a narrow focus on legal access and individual choice . . . to a broader analysis of structural constraints on agency" (2009, 350).

43 Other groups that have organized for reproductive justice include Asian Communities for Reproductive Justice, Generations Ahead, Justice Now, California Latinas for Reproductive Justice, African American Women for Reproductive Freedom, Native American Women's Health Education Resource Center, and the National Women's Health Organization. For a thorough account of the organizing of women of color for reproductive justice, see Silliman et al. (2004).

44 Quoted in Luna (2009, 358).

45 In the defense of her understanding of the right to abortion, Cornell makes a similar argument: "Our right to our imaginary domain . . . is a right to imagine, represent, and symbolize the meaning of the material constituents of sex and gender as we lead our lives as sexuate beings" (1998, 179).

CHAPTER 3. INFORMED CONSENT LAWS

1 *Gonzales v. Carhart*, 550 U.S. 124 (2007).

2 *Texas Medical Providers v. Lakey*, 667 F.3d 570 (5th Cir. 2012).

3 Kluchin (2009) discusses this phenomenon with regard to the eugenics and neo-eugenics movements; also see Luker (1997) and Solinger (2001) for discussions of this phenomenon with regard to the rhetoric, respectively, on teen pregnancy and the "welfare queen."

4 Brown similarly argues that "neo-liberalism is not simply a set of economic policies; it is not only about facilitating free trade, maximizing corporate profits, and challenging welfarism. Rather, neo-liberalism carries a social analysis which, when deployed as a form of governmentality, reaches from the soul of the citizen-subject to education policy to practices of empire" (2005, 39).

5 Margaret Thornton also argues that it is important for feminist scholars to investigate "the insidious workings of the anti-feminist neoliberal state" (2006, 165). This chapter takes up her call in examining recent reproductive restrictions in the context of neoliberalism.

6 Schneider and Ingram, for example, argue that "the social construction of target populations has a powerful influence on public officials and shapes both the policy agenda and the actual design of policy" (1993, 334).

7 As Dean writes, "[T]he political trajectory that follows from the complaints of victims enhances surveillance and control, policing and security" (2009, 7).

8 See Kurjak et al. (2000) for a medical discussion of the diagnostic function of sonography. See also Palmer (2009) for a discussion of the use of various kinds of sonography.

9 See the following for feminist analyses of ultrasound: Franklin (1991), Duden (1993), Sandelowski (1994), Stabile (1994), Taylor (1998), Mehaffy (2000). For

background on the history of fetal rights and its negative consequences for women, see Roth (2003).

10 As Edelman goes on to explain, reproductive futurism is often tied to "the fetishization of the Child at the expense of whatever such fetishization must inescapably queer" (2004, 29).

11 Macleod and Durrheim note that "surveillance becomes powerful by extending itself to self-reflection and self-consciousness" (2002, 48).

12 Texas House Bill 15, 82nd Leg. Reg. Sess. (Tex. 2011).

13 *Roe v. Wade*, 410 U.S. 113 (1973).

14 *Texas Medical Providers v. Lakey*, 667 F.3d 570, 585 (5th Cir. 2012).

15 *Planned Parenthood Minn., N.D., S.D. v. Rounds*, 653 F.3d 662 (8th Cir. 2011).

16 South Dakota Codified Law, §34–23A-10.1, http://legis.sd.gov/Statutes/Codified_Laws/DisplayStatute.aspx?Type=Statute&Statute=34–23A-10.1 (accessed June 19, 2014).

17 South Dakota Codified Law, §34–23A-10.1.

18 *Planned Parenthood Minn., N.D., S.D. v. Rounds*, 653 F.3d 662, 669 (8th Cir. 2011), quoting *Planned Parenthood v. Casey*, 505 U.S. 833 (1992).

19 *Planned Parenthood Minn., N.D., S.D. v. Rounds*, 686 F.3d 889, 893–94 (8th Cir. 2012).

20 *Rounds*, 686 F.3d 889, 900 (8th Cir. 2012), quoting *Gonzales v. Carhart*.

21 South Dakota Codified Law, §34–23A-10.1, http://legis.state.sd.us/statutes/DisplayStatute.aspx?Type=Statute&Statute=34–23A-10.1 (accessed June 19, 2014). The Texas law is similar, stating that women must be informed of the "medical risks associated with carrying the child to term." Texas Health and Safety Code, Title 2, Subtitle H, §171.012, http://www.statutes.legis.state.tx.us/Docs/HS/htm/HS.171.htm (accessed November 12, 2013). There are twenty-nine states that require women seeking an abortion to be provided with information regarding the health risks of pregnancy (Guttmacher Institute 2013).

22 *Texas Medical Providers v. Lakey*, 667 F.3d 570 (5th Cir. 2012).

23 See Post (2007) as well as Gaylord and Molony (2013) for First Amendment analyses of informed consent laws.

24 *Planned Parenthood Minn., N.D., S.D. v. Rounds*, 686 F.3d 889 (8th Cir. 2012).

25 Justice Ginsburg dissenting, *Gonzales v. Carhart*, 170 (quoting *Planned Parenthood v. Casey*, 505 U.S., 851–52).

26 Amended Class Action Complaint: Texas Medical Providers Performing Abortion Services v. Lakey, filed July 21, 2011, in U.S. District Court for Western District of Texas, p. 25. Available at http://reproductiverights.org/en/document/amended-class-action-complaint-texas-medical-providers-performing-abortion-services-v-lakey (accessed October 11, 2013).

27 Similarly, Jeannie Suk has argued that the legal discourse of post-abortion syndrome is tied to feminist treatments of women's experiences of sexual and bodily trauma (2010). The antiabortion discourse of trauma appeals to and

manipulates apparently feminist concerns originating in the feminist discourse of trauma.

28 Vanessa Munro and Jane Scoular (2012) have made a similar point with regard to the concept of vulnerability.

29 Barbara Cruikshank describes Foucault's understanding of subjectivity in the following way: "modern forms of power tie the subjectivity (conscience, identity, self-knowledge) of the individual to that individual's subjection (control by another). The subject is one who is both under the authority of another and the author of her or his own actions" (1999, 21).

30 See Stabile (1992), Hartouni (1997), and Petchesky (1987).

31 Siegel (1992) has made a similar point with regard to abortion restrictive legislation.

32 See also Betterton (2002) for a discussion of potentially disruptive images of pregnancy.

CHAPTER 4. STERILIZATION

1 Tubal ligation is most commonly accomplished through the tying, clipping, or cauterizing of the fallopian tubes. Newer methods of sterilization include the Essure device, described later in the chapter, as well as the controversial quinacrine, which has been used to sterilize women in India, Pakistan, Indonesia, and Vietnam (Subramaniam 1999). Quinacrine is not approved for sterilization in the United States. The analysis in this chapter focuses on sterilization that is accomplished through the more routine tying, clipping, or cauterizing of the fallopian tubes.

2 See the American College of Obstetricians and Gynecologists 2012 report, which recommends changes to the Medicaid requirements.

3 There is no clear explanation for the difference in sterilization rates among different groups. Some explanations posited for why female sterilization rates are lower among more educated, higher-income, and white women include higher rates of male sterilization in partners of such women and reliable access to other forms of contraceptives (Frost and Driscoll 2006). Also, Hispanic women tend to have more children at any given age than other groups, which may account for some of the difference in sterilization rates (Godecker, Thomson, and Bumpass 2001).

4 See Hird (2002) for an account of why the qualifier "sexual" is important. She points to the innumerable processes of reproduction that are continually happening on and in our bodies to urge us to problematize our assumptions regarding the necessity of sex and sexual difference to reproduction.

5 Important works on sterilization abuse include Briggs (2002), Davis (1983), Gordon (1990), Petchesky (1981), Roberts (1998), and Shapiro (1985).

6 See Franke (2001), Gillespie (2003), Hird (2003), Meyers (2001), Sandelowski (1990), and Snitow (1992) for discussions of childlessness and pronatalism.

7 Literature in this expanding field includes the following: Allen (1991), Arditti, Klein, and Minden (1984), Braidotti (1997), Clarke (1998), D'Adamo and Baruch

(1986), Franklin (1997), Ginsburg and Rapp (1995), Hartouni (1997), Ikemoto (1996), Kaplan and Squier (1999), Rapp (2000), Roberts (1998), Rowland (1987), Shultz (1990), Sourbut (1996), Stanworth (1987), and Thompson (2005). For a comprehensive review of the literature on infertility and technology, see Thompson (2005, chap. 2).

8 *Buck v. Bell*, 274 U.S. 200 (1927).

9 The series of name changes undergone by a eugenic organization exemplifies this shift in rhetoric. The organization, which called itself Birthright Inc. in 1943, changed its name to the Human Betterment Association of America in 1950, and then to the Human Betterment Association for Voluntary Sterilization in 1962, before settling on the name Association for Voluntary Sterilization in 1965 (Kluchin 2009, 26–30).

10 *Skinner v. Oklahoma*, 316 U.S. 535 (1942).

11 *Eisenstadt v. Baird*, 405 U.S. 438, 453 (1972).

12 For other examples of sterilization and no-procreation orders, see Flavin (2009, 37–38).

13 See, e.g., American Medical Association, Principle VII (American Medical Association 2001).

14 However, Carolyn Morell, who is herself childless, declines to use the term "childfree" because she thinks it manifests a hostile attitude toward children (1994, 21).

15 The rates are likely inflated because these studies often take women's inquiries about reversal as a proxy for regret, thereby not accounting for the fact that some women who ask about reversal do so as a sop to a new partner's desire for children (Campbell 1999, 148–50). Given that younger women are more likely to have new partners post-sterilization, the reported rates for sterilization regret for women under thirty are probably even more inflated than those for older women. Studies of regret also tend not to isolate women who are childfree. One study discusses sterilization only in relation to women's last pregnancy and thus does not even consider the possibility of women without children getting sterilized (Day 2007, 60). Even a study of childfree women did not consider the possibility of women showing their commitment to being childfree through sterilization (Morell 1994). There is some evidence, however, that sterilized women without children have much lower rates of regret (Campbell 1999, 150; Schmidt et al. 2000; Guttmacher Institute 1999).

16 For a study that looks at post-vasectomy regret among Danish men, see Rungby et al. (1994).

17 President Obama's promotion of responsible fatherhood is part of this trend. For an example of one of Obama's fatherhood messages, see Phillips (2009).

18 It should be noted, though, that vasectomy is both simpler and less costly than tubal ligation. Vasectomy, however, is not necessarily more reversible. For a discussion of the reversibility of different kinds of sterilization procedures, see Hendrix, Chauhan, and Morrison (1999).

19 Woods (1998) examines two different conceptualizations of menopause, one of which understands menopause as a disease. Ferguson and Parry (1998) analyze the pathologization and medicalization of menopause. Goodman (1980) discusses the methodology that contributed to the classification of menopause as a disease.

20 Some methods of ligating the fallopian tubes are more reversible than others, although guides suggest that physicians tell women to regard the procedure, no matter how performed, as irreversible (Day 2007, 66).

21 This term comes from Lisa Ikemoto (1996). For a recent study demonstrating the link between cultural understandings of low-income women and abundant fertility, see Bell (2009).

22 Thus, the question of which sterilization processes are really cyborg—and whether the Essure device is more cyborg than other practices—is not a crucial question. I am not primarily concerned with the degree of automation of entanglements of machine and organism so much as I am interested in the blurred boundaries and disruptive bodies that sterilization technology enables.

23 This has similarities to Elizabeth Grosz's argument that "the biological, the natural, and the material remain active and crucial political ingredients precisely because they too, and not culture alone, are continually subjected to transformation, to becoming, to unfolding over time" (2005, 79). Although Grosz is thinking about processes like evolution, cyborg theory reveals that technology can also transform the material.

24 *In re Grady*, 85 N.J. 235 (N.J., 1981); *Matter of Guardianship of Eberhardy*, 102 Wis. 2d 539 (Wis., 1981); *Ponter v. Ponter*, 134 N.J. Super. 50 (N.J. Super. App., 1975); *Morris v. Sanchez*, 746 P.2d 184 (Okla., 1987).

25 *Hathaway v. Worcester City Hospital*, 475 F.2d 701 (1st Cir. 1973).

26 Rebecca Kluchin (2009, 148–61) has analyzed all such lawsuits and notes that only one out of thirty-three cases filed by victims of forced sterilization was marginally successful. She argues that this discrepancy can be attributed to the fact that the "Operation Lawsuit" cases—as the suits aimed at overturning restrictive sterilization policies were called—were able to draw upon a growing precedent regarding women's reproductive rights, particularly access to abortion. Because this law was concerned with access to reproductive health services, it was not easily applied to cases of forced sterilization.

27 For example, both Delaware and Tennessee protect doctors from liability via statute (Del. Code, Title 16, Ch. 57., Section 5715 (2010); Ten. Code, Title 68, Ch. 34, Section 109 (2007)).

28 A British study showed that the process of obtaining a sterilization compromised many women's integrity and sense of self (Campbell 1999, 142–43).

29 See Spade (2006) and Stone (2006) for accounts of the medical profession's normalizing role in transgender surgery.

CHAPTER 5. AUTONOMY, TECHNOLOGY, AND THE POLITICS OF
REPRODUCTION

1 For a discussion of the public-private dichotomy within feminism, see Menon
(2004, 9–17).

2 *Roe v. Wade*, 410 U.S. 113, 159 (1973).

3 Roberts (1998) makes this argument as well.

REFERENCES

Allen, Amy. 1998. "Power Trouble: Performativity as Critical Theory." *Constellations* 5 (4): 456–71.

———. 2008. *The Politics of Our Selves: Power, Autonomy, and Gender in Contemporary Critical Theory.* New York: Columbia University Press.

Allen, Anita. 1991. "The Socio-Economic Struggle for Equality: The Black Surrogate Mother." *Harvard BlackLetter Journal* 8: 17–31.

———. 1995. "The Proposed Equal Protection Fix for Abortion Law: Reflections on Citizenship, Gender, and the Constitution." *Harvard Journal of Law and Public Policy* 18: 419–55.

Allison, Henry. 2004. *Kant's Transcendental Idealism: An Interpretation and Defense.* New Haven: Yale University Press.

American College of Obstetricians and Gynecologists. 2005. "Sterilization for Women and Men." ACOG Education Pamphlet AP011.

———. 2012. "Women on Medicaid Face Unfair Barriers to Sterilization Requests." ACOG News Releases. http://www.acog.org/About%20ACOG/News%20Room/News%20Releases/2012/Women%20on%20Medicaid%20Face%20Unfair%20Barriers%20to%20Sterilization%20Requests.aspx. Accessed July 21, 2014.

American Medical Association. 2001. "Principles of Medical Ethics." http://www.ama-assn.org/ama/pub/physician-resources/medical-ethics/code-medical-ethics/principles-medical-ethics.shtml. Accessed July 21, 2014.

Arditti, Rita, Renate Duelli Klein, and Shelley Minden, eds. 1984. *Test Tube Women: What Future for Motherhood?* London: Pandora.

Asian Communities for Reproductive Justice. 2005. "A New Vision for Advancing Our Movement for Reproductive Health, Reproductive Rights, and Reproductive Justice." http://strongfamiliesmovement.org/assets/docs/ACRJ-A-New-Vision.pdf. Accessed July 21, 2014.

Bapat, Sheila. 2013. "Repealing Welfare Family Cap Laws a Common Goal for Some Pro- and Anti-Choice Groups." RH Reality Check, August 21. http://rhrc.us/1fwp7jR. Accessed July 21, 2014.

Barvosa-Carter, Edwina. 2007. "Mestiza Autonomy as Relational Autonomy: Ambivalence and the Social Character of Free Will." *Journal of Political Philosophy* 15 (1): 1–21.

Bassett, Laura. 2012. "Texas Loses Entire Women's Health Program over Planned Parenthood Law." *Huffington Post*, March 15. http://www.huffingtonpost.

com/2012/03/15/texas-loses-entire-womens_n_1349431.html?ref=mostpopular. Accessed July 21, 2014.

Baum, Bruce. 2000. *Rereading Power and Freedom in J. S. Mill.* Toronto: University of Toronto Press.

Bell, Ann V. 2009. "It's Way Out of My League: Low-Income Women's Experiences of Medicalized Infertility." *Gender and Society* 23 (5) (October): 688–709.

Bell, Derrick A. 1980. "*Brown v. Board of Education* and the Interest-Convergence Dilemma." *Harvard Law Review* 93: 518–33.

Belle, Nicole. 2008. "Jack Cafferty: Viagra Is for a Medical Condition, Birth Control Is a 'Lifestyle Choice.'" *Crooks and Liars*, July 16. http://crooksandliars. com/2008/07/17/jack-cafferty-viagra-is-for-a-medical-condition-birth-control-is-a-lifestyle-choice. Accessed July 21, 2014.

Benhabib, Seyla. 1995. "Feminism and Postmodernism: Subjectivity, Historiography, and Politics." In *Feminist Contentions: A Philosophical Exchange.* New York: Routledge.

Ben-Ishai, Elizabeth. 2010. "Sexual Politics and Ascriptive Autonomy." *Politics and Gender* 6 (4): 573–600.

———. 2012. *Fostering Autonomy: A Theory of Citizenship, the State, and Social Service Delivery.* University Park: Pennsylvania State University Press.

Benn, Piers, and Martin Lupton. 2005. "Sterilisation of Young, Competent, and Childless Adults." *British Medical Journal* 330 (7503) (June 4): 1323–25.

Benson, Paul. 1990. "Feminist Second Thoughts about Free Agency." *Hypatia* 5 (3) (October 1): 47–64.

———. 1994. "Free Agency and Self-Worth." *Journal of Philosophy* 91 (12) (December): 650–68.

Berger, Gary S. 2007. "Ethics of Tubal Ligation." *Tubal Ligation Reversal Blog*, December 26. http://www.tubal-reversal.net/blog/2007/case-study/tubal-ligation-ethics. html. Accessed July 21, 2014.

Berlant, Lauren. 1997. *The Queen of America Goes to Washington City: Essays on Sex and Citizenship.* Series Q. Durham: Duke University Press.

Betterton, Rosemary. 2002. "Prima Gravida: Reconfiguring the Maternal Body in Visual Representation." *Feminist Theory* 3 (3) (December 1): 255–70.

Bevir, Mark. 1999. "Foucault and Critique: Deploying Agency against Autonomy." *Political Theory* 27: 65–84.

Blank, Robert, and Janna C. Merrick. 1995. *Human Reproduction, Emerging Technologies, and Conflicting Rights.* Washington, DC: Congressional Quarterly Books.

Bordo, Susan. 1997. "The Body and the Reproduction of Femininity." In *Writing on the Body: Female Embodiment and Feminist Theory*, edited by Katie Conboy, Nadia Medina, and Sarah Stanbury. New York: Columbia University Press.

Boyd, Robert L. 1989. "Minority Status and Childlessness." *Sociological Inquiry* 59 (3): 331–42.

Braidotti, Rosi. 1997. "Mothers, Monsters, and Machines." In *Writing on the Body: Female Embodiment and Feminist Theory*, edited by Katie Conboy, Nadia Medina, and Sarah Stanbury. New York: Columbia University Press.

Brennan, Samantha. 1999. "Recent Work in Feminist Ethics." *Ethics* 109 (4) (July 1): 858–93.

Briggs, Laura. 2002. *Reproducing Empire: Race, Sex, Science, and U.S. Imperialism in Puerto Rico*. Berkeley: University of California Press.

Brown, Wendy. 1995. *States of Injury: Power and Freedom in Late Modernity*. Princeton: Princeton University Press.

———. 2005. *Edgework: Critical Essays on Knowledge and Politics*. Princeton: Princeton University Press.

Burchell, Graham. 1996. "Liberal Government and Techniques of the Self." In *Foucault and Political Reason: Liberalism, Neo-Liberalism, and Rationalities of Government*, edited by Andrew Barry, Thomas Osborne, and Nikolas Rose. Chicago: University of Chicago Press.

Butler, Judith. 1990. *Gender Trouble: Feminism and the Subversion of Identity*. New York: Routledge.

———. 1993. *Bodies That Matter: On the Discursive Limits of "Sex."* New York: Routledge.

———. 1995. "Contingent Foundations." In *Feminist Contentions: A Philosophical Exchange*. New York: Routledge.

———. 1997. *Excitable Speech: A Politics of the Performative*. New York: Routledge.

———. 1998. *The Psychic Life of Power: Theories in Subjection*. Stanford: Stanford University Press.

———. 2004. *Undoing Gender*. New York: Routledge.

Campbell, Annily. 1999. *Childfree and Sterilized: Women's Decisions and Medical Responses*. London: Cassell.

Castel, Robert. 1991. "From Dangerousness to Risk." In *The Foucault Effect: Studies in Governmentality*, edited by Graham Burchell, Colin Gordon, and Peter Miller. Chicago: University of Chicago Press.

Christman, John. 2004. "Relational Autonomy, Liberal Individualism, and the Social Constitution of Selves." *Philosophical Studies* 117 (1) (January 10): 143–64.

Clarke, Adele E. 1998. *Disciplining Reproduction: Modernity, American Life Sciences, and the Problems of Sex*. Berkeley: University of California Press.

Clarke, Adele E., Laura Mamo, Jennifer Ruth Fosket, Jennifer R. Fishman, and Janet K. Shim, eds. 2010. *Biomedicalization: Technoscience, Health, and Illness in the U.S.* Durham: Duke University Press.

Coombe, Rosemary J. 1989. "Room for Manoeuver: Toward a Theory of Practice in Critical Studies." *Law and Social Inquiry* 14: 69–121.

Cornell, Drucilla. 1995. *The Imaginary Domain: Abortion, Pornography and Sexual Harassment*. New York: Routledge.

———. 1998. *At the Heart of Freedom*. Princeton: Princeton University Press.

Cornell, Drucilla, and Stephen D. Seely. 2014. "There's Nothing Revolutionary about a Blowjob." *Social Text 119* 32 (2): 1–23.

Crenshaw, Kimberlé. 1989. "Demarginalizing the Intersection of Race and Sex: A Black Feminist Critique of Antidiscrimination Doctrine, Feminist Theory and Antiracist Politics." *University of Chicago Legal Forum* 139: 139–67.

———. 1991. "Mapping the Margins: Intersectionality, Identity Politics and Violence against Women of Color." *Stanford Law Review* 43 (6): 1241–99.

Cruikshank, Barbara. 1999. *The Will to Empower: Democratic Citizens and Other Subjects*. Ithaca: Cornell University Press.

D'Adamo, Amadeo F., and Elaine Hoffman Baruch. 1986. "Whither the Womb? Myths, Machines, and Mothers." *Frontiers: A Journal of Women's Studies* 9 (1): 72–79.

Davey, Monica. 2006. "National Battle over Abortion Focuses on South Dakota Vote." *New York Times*, November 1.

Davidson, Arnold. 2007. Introduction to *Security, Territory, Population: Lectures at the Collège de France, 1977—1978*, by Michel Foucault. New York: Palgrave Macmillan.

———. 2011. "In Praise of Counter-conduct." *History of the Human Sciences* 24 (4): 25–41.

Davis, Angela. 1983. *Women, Race, and Class*. 1st Vintage Books ed. New York: Vintage.

Davis, Kathy. 1997. "Embody-ing Theory: Beyond Modernist and Postmodernist Readings of the Body." In *Embodied Practices: Feminist Perspectives on the Body*, edited by Kathy Davis. London: Sage.

Day, Suzanne. 2007. "Fitness, Fertility and Femininity: Making Meaning in the Tying of Tubes; A Feminist Discourse Analysis of Women's Sterilization." Master's thesis, Queen's University, Kingston, Ontario, Canada. https://qspace.library.queensu.ca/bitstream/1974/450/1/Day_Suzanne_L_200707_MA.pdf.

Dean, Jodi. 2009. *Democracy and Other Neoliberal Fantasies: Communicative Capitalism and Left Politics*. Durham: Duke University Press.

Deutscher, Penelope. 2008. "The Inversion of Exceptionality: Foucault, Agamben, and 'Reproductive Rights.'" *South Atlantic Quarterly* 107 (1): 55–70.

Duden, Barbara. 1993. *Disembodying Women: Perspectives on Pregnancy and the Unborn*. Cambridge: Harvard University Press.

Duff, Brian. 2011. *The Parent as Citizen: A Democratic Dilemma*. Minneapolis: University of Minnesota Press.

Duggan, Lisa. 2003. *The Twilight of Equality? Neoliberalism, Cultural Politics, and the Attack on Democracy*. Boston: Beacon.

Dworkin, Gerald. 1982. "Is More Choice Better Than Less?" *Midwest Studies in Philosophy* 7: 47–61.

———. 1988. *The Theory and Practice of Autonomy*. New York: Cambridge University Press.

Edelman, Lee. 2004. *No Future: Queer Theory and the Death Drive*. Durham: Duke University Press.

Elliot Institute. 2010. "The Unchoice Campaign." *Abortion Is the Unchoice* (blog). http://www.unfairchoice.info/display.htm.

Elwan, Ann. 1999. "Poverty and Disability: A Survey of the Literature." Working Paper 21315, Social Protection Discussion Paper, World Bank. http://documents.world-bank.org/curated/en/1999/12/717470/poverty-disability-survey-literature. Accessed July 21, 2014.

Ewald, François. 1990. "Norms, Discipline, and the Law." *Representations* (30) (April 1): 138–61.

Eze, Emmanuel Chukwudi, ed. 1997. *Race and the Enlightenment: A Reader*. Malden, MA: Wiley-Blackwell.

Feinberg, Joel. 1989. "Autonomy." In *The Inner Citadel: Essays on Individual Autonomy*, edited by John Christman. Oxford: Oxford University Press.

Ferguson, Susan J., and Carla Parry. 1998. "Rewriting Menopause: Challenging the Medical Paradigm to Reflect Menopausal Women's Experiences." *Frontiers: A Journal of Women's Studies* 19 (1): 20–41.

Finger, Anne. 1984. "Claiming All of Our Bodies." In *Test Tube Women: What Future for Motherhood?*, edited by Rita Arditti, Renate Duelli-Klein, and Shelley Minden. London: Pandora.

Fisher, Sue. 1988. *In the Patient's Best Interest: Women and the Politics of Medical Decisions*. New Brunswick: Rutgers University Press.

Flavin, Jeanne. 2009. *Our Bodies, Our Crimes: The Policing of Women's Reproduction in America*. New York: New York University Press.

Fletcher, John C., and Mark I. Evans. 1983. "Maternal Bonding in Early Fetal Ultrasound Examinations." *New England Journal of Medicine* 308: 392–93.

Foucault, Michel. 1971. "A Conversation with Michel Foucault." *Partisan Review* 38 (2): 192–201.

———. 1977. *Discipline and Punish: The Birth of the Prison*. New York: Pantheon.

———. 1978. *The History of Sexuality*. Vol. 1, *An Introduction*. New York: Vintage.

———. 1980. *Power/Knowledge: Selected Interviews and Other Writings, 1972–1977*. Edited by Colin Gordon. New York: Pantheon.

———. 1982. "The Subject and Power." *Critical Inquiry* 8 (4): 777–95.

———. 1984. "What Is Enlightenment?" In *The Foucault Reader*, edited by Paul Rabinow. New York: Pantheon.

———. 1988. *The History of Sexuality*. Vol. 3, *The Care of the Self*. Translated by Robert Hurley. New York: Vintage.

———. 1990. "Practicing Criticism." In *Politics, Philosophy, Culture: Interviews and Other Writings, 1977–1984*, edited by Lawrence Kritzman. New York: Routledge.

———. 1996. "What Is Critique." In *What Is Enlightenment? Eighteenth-Century Answers and Twentieth-Century Questions*, edited by James Schmidt. Berkeley: University of California Press.

———. 1998. *Ethics: Subjectivity and Truth*. Vol. 1 of *Essential Works of Foucault, 1954–1984*. Edited by Paul Rabinow. New York: New Press.

———. 2003. *"Society Must Be Defended": Lectures at the Collège de France, 1975–1976*. Translated by David Macey. New York: Picador.

———. 2010. *The Birth of Biopolitics: Lectures at the Collège de France, 1978–1979*. New York: Picador.

Franke, Katherine M. 2001. "Theorizing Yes: An Essay on Feminism, Law and Desire." *Columbia Law Review* 101: 181–208.

Frankfurt, Harry G. 1971. "Freedom of the Will and the Concept of a Person." *Journal of Philosophy* 68 (1): 5–20.

Franklin, Sarah. 1991. "Fetal Fascinations: New Dimensions to the Medical-Scientific Construction of Fetal Personhood." *Off-Centre: Feminism and Cultural Studies*, 190–205.

———. 1997. *Embodied Progress: A Cultural Account of Assisted Conception*. New York: Routledge.

Franklin, Sarah, and Helena Ragoné, eds. 1998. *Reproducing Reproduction: Kinship, Power, and Technological Innovation*. Philadelphia: University of Pennsylvania Press.

Fraser, Nancy. 1995. "False Antitheses." In *Feminist Contentions: A Philosophical Exchange*. New York: Routledge.

Friedman, Marilyn. 2003. *Autonomy, Gender, Politics*. New York: Oxford University Press.

Frost, Jennifer, and Anne K. Driscoll. 2006. "Sexual and Reproductive Health of U.S. Latinas: A Literature Review." Occasional Report 19, Allan Guttmacher Institute, New York. http://www.alanguttmacherinstitute.com/pubs/2006/02/07/or19.pdf. Accessed July 21, 2014.

Gaylord, Scott W., and Thomas J. Molony. 2013. "*Casey* and a Woman's Right to Know: Ultrasounds, Informed Consent, and the First Amendment." *Connecticut Law Review* 45 (2): 595–652.

Gill, Rosalind. 2008. "Culture and Subjectivity in Neoliberal and Postfeminist Times." *Subjectivity* 25 (1) (December): 432–45.

Gillespie, Rosemary. 2003. "Childfree and Feminine: Understanding the Gender Identity of Voluntarily Childless Women." *Gender and Society* 17 (1) (February 1): 122–36.

Gilligan, Carol. 1982. *In a Different Voice: Psychological Theory and Women's Development*. Cambridge: Harvard University Press.

Ginsburg, Faye D., and Rayna Rapp. 1995. *Conceiving the New World Order: The Global Politics of Reproduction*. Berkeley: University of California Press.

Godecker, Amy L., Elizabeth Thomson, and Larry L. Bumpass. 2001. "Union Status, Marital History and Female Contraceptive Sterilization in the United States." *Family Planning Perspectives* 33 (1) (January): 35–41.

Gold, Rachel Benson, and Elizabeth Nash. 2007. "State Abortion Counseling Policies and the Fundamental Principles of Informed Consent." *Guttmacher Policy Review* 10 (4): 6–13.

Goodman, Madeleine. 1980. "Toward a Biology of Menopause." *Signs: Journal of Women in Culture and Society* 5 (4): 739–53.

Gordon, Linda. 1990. *Woman's Body, Woman's Right: Birth Control in America*. New York: Penguin.

——. 2007. *The Moral Property of Women: A History of Birth Control Politics in America*. Urbana: University of Illinois Press.

Gould, Stephen Jay. 1985. "Carrie Buck's Daughter." *Natural History* 93 (July): 14–18.

Grewal, Inderpal. 2006. "'Security Moms' in the Early Twentieth-Century United States: The Gender of Security in Neoliberalism." *Women's Studies Quarterly* 34 (1–2): 25–39.

Grimshaw, Jean. 1993. "Practices of Freedom." In *Up against Foucault: Explorations of Some Tensions between Foucault and Feminism*, edited by Caroline Ramazanoglu. New York: Routledge.

Grosz, Elizabeth. 2005. *Time Travels: Feminism, Nature, Power*. Durham: Duke University Press.

Guenther, Lisa. 2012. "The Most Dangerous Place: Pro-Life Politics and the Rhetoric of Slavery." *Postmodern Culture* 22 (2). http://muse.jhu.edu.une.idm.oclc.org/journals/postmodern_culture/v022/22.2.guenther.html. Accessed July 21, 2014.

Guttmacher Institute. 1999. "Women Who Are Sterilized at Age 30 or Younger Have Increased Odds of Regret." *International Family Planning Perspectives* 31 (6): 6–13.

——. 2008. "Laws Affecting Reproductive Health and Rights: State Policy Review for 2008." http://www.guttmacher.org/statecenter/updates/2008/statetrends42008.html. Accessed July 21, 2014.

——. 2013. "State Policies in Brief." http://www.guttmacher.org/statecenter/spibs/index.html. Accessed November 15, 2013.

Guyer, Paul. 2000. *Kant on Freedom, Law, and Happiness*. Cambridge: Cambridge University Press.

Halberstam, J. Jack. 2012. *Gaga Feminism: Sex, Gender, and the End of Normal*. Boston: Beacon.

Haraway, Donna. 1991. "A Cyborg Manifesto." In *Simians, Cyborgs, and Women: The Reinvention of Nature*. New York: Routledge.

——. 1996. "Donna Haraway Interview Transcript (Interview with Hari Kunzru for Wired)." http://harikunzru.com/archive/donna-haraway-interview-transcript-1996. Accessed July 21, 2014.

——. 2004. *The Haraway Reader*. New York: Routledge.

Harding, Kate. 2010. "Is Forced Sterilization Ever OK?" *Salon*, January 5. http://www.salon.com/mwt/broadsheet/feature/2010/01/05/forced_sterilization/index.html. Accessed July 21, 2014.

Harris, Angela P. 1990. "Race and Essentialism in Feminist Legal Theory." *Stanford Law Review* 42 (3) (February): 581–616.

Harrison, D. D., and C. W. Cooke. 1988. "An Elucidation of Factors Influencing Physicians' Willingness to Perform Elective Female Sterilization." *Obstetrics and Gynecology* 72 (4) (October): 565–70.

Hartouni, Valerie. 1997. *Cultural Conceptions: On Reproductive Technologies and the Remaking of Life*. Minneapolis: University of Minnesota Press.

Hecht, Jeff. 1999. *City of Light: The Story of Fiber Optics*. New York: Oxford University Press.

Hendrix, N. W., S. P. Chauhan, and J. C. Morrison. 1999. "Sterilization and Its Conse-quences." *Obstetrical and Gynecological Survey* 54 (12): 766–77.

Henshaw, Stanley K., and Lawrence B. Finer. 2003. "The Accessibility of Abortion Services in the United States, 2001." *Perspectives on Sexual and Reproductive Health* 35 (1) (February): 16–24.

Hird, Myra J. 2002. "Re(pro)ducing Sexual Difference." *Parallax* 8 (4) (October): 94–107.

———. 2003. "Vacant Wombs: Feminist Challenges to Psychoanalytic Theories of Childless Women." *Feminist Review* 75: 5–19.

Hirschmann, Nancy J. 2003. *The Subject of Liberty: Toward a Feminist Theory of Free-dom*. Princeton: Princeton University Press.

Ikemoto, Lisa C. 1996. "The In/Fertile, the Too Fertile, and the Dysfertile." *Hastings Law Journal* 47: 1007–52.

Jaggar, Alison M. 1988. *Feminist Politics and Human Nature*. Totowa, NJ: Rowman and Littlefield.

Jesudason, Sujatha, and Susannah Baruch. 2011. "Race and Sex in Abortion Debates: The Legislation and the Billboards." Generations Ahead, Oakland, CA.

Jones, R. K., M. R. Zolna, S. K. Henshaw, and L. B. Finer. 2008. "Abortion in the United States: Incidence and Access to Services, 2005." *Perspectives on Sexual and Repro-ductive Health* 40 (1): 6–16.

Justice Now. 2012. "Budget Testimony Submitted to Loni Hancock and Budget Sub-committee 5." March 13. Justice Now, Oakland, CA. http://jnow.org/downloads/JusticeNow.3.15.BudgetTestimony.FemaleOff.pdf. Accessed July 21, 2014.

Kant, Immanuel. 1991a. *Kant: The Metaphysics of Morals*. Edited by Mary Gregor. Cam-bridge: Cambridge University Press.

———. 1991b. "On the Common Saying: 'This May Be True in Theory, but It Does Not Apply in Practice.'" In *Kant: Political Writings*. 2nd ed. Edited by H. S. Reiss. Cam-bridge: Cambridge University Press.

———. 1997. "On Natural Characteristics" and *Physical Geography*. In *Race and the Enlightenment: A Reader*, edited by Emmanuel Chukwudi Eze. Malden, MA: Wiley-Blackwell.

———. 1998. *Groundwork of the Metaphysics of Morals*. Edited by Mary J. Gregor. Cam-bridge: Cambridge University Press.

Kaplan, Deborah. 1989. "Disability Rights Perspective." In *Reproductive Laws for the 1990s*, edited by Sherrill Cohen and Nadine Taub. Clifton, NJ: Humana Press.

Kaplan, E. Ann, and Susan Merrill Squier, eds. 1999. *Playing Dolly: Technocultural For-mations, Fantasies, and Fictions of Assisted Reproduction*. New Brunswick: Rutgers University Press.

King, Leslie, and Madonna Harrington Meyer. 1997. "The Politics of Reproductive Ben-efits: U.S. Insurance Coverage of Contraceptive and Infertility Treatments." *Gender and Society* 11 (1) (February): 8–30.

Klein, Ezra. 2012. "Mitt Romney Flashback: Stay-at-Home Moms Need to Learn 'Dig-nity of Work.'" *Washington Post Blog*, April 15. http://www.washingtonpost.com/

blogs/ezra-klein/post/mitt-romney-flashback-stay-at-home-moms-need-to-learn-dignity-of-work/2012/04/15/gIQAhmbZJT_blog.html. Accessed July 21, 2014.

Kluchin, Rebecca M. 2009. *Fit to Be Tied: Sterilization and Reproductive Rights in America, 1950–1980*. New Brunswick: Rutgers University Press.

Kuhn, Thomas. 1970. *The Structure of Scientific Revolutions*. Chicago: University of Chicago Press.

———. 1991. "The Essential Tension." In *The Philosophy of Science*, edited by Richard Boyd. Cambridge: MIT Press.

Kurjak, A., T. Hafner, M. Kos, S. Kupesic, and M. Stanojevic. 2000. "Three-Dimensional Sonography in Prenatal Diagnosis: A Luxury or a Necessity?" *Journal of Perinatal Medicine* 28 (3): 194–209.

Laqueur, Thomas. 1990. *Making Sex: Body and Gender from the Greeks to Freud*. Cambridge: Harvard University Press.

Laughlin, Harry Hamilton. 1922. *Eugenical Sterilization in the United States*. Chicago: Psychopathic Laboratory of the Municipal Court of Chicago. http://www.people.fas.harvard.edu/~wellerst/laughlin/.

LaVaque-Manty, Mika. 2006. "Kant's Children." *Social Theory and Practice* 32 (3): 365–88.

Law, Sylvia A. 1984. "Rethinking Sex and the Constitution." *University of Pennsylvania Law Review* 132: 955–1040.

Lawrence, R. E., K. A. Rasinski, J. D. Yoon, and F. A. Curlin. 2011. "Factors Influencing Physicians' Advice about Female Sterilization in USA: A National Survey." *Human Reproduction* 26 (1) (January): 106–11.

Lee, Alex, Robin Levi, and Chivy Sok. 2008. "Human Rights Violations against Women of Color in the United States: A Report on U.S. Government Compliance with the United Nations International Convention on the Elimination of All Forms of Racial Discrimination (CERD)." WILD for Human Rights, Justice Now, and the Transgender, Gender Variant and Intersex Justice Project. http://ourhumanrights.files.wordpress.com/2008/02/cerd-shadow-report_final_3dec2007-_sent-to-richie-and-crooms_-1-1.pdf. Accessed July 21, 2014.

Lemke, Thomas. 2001. "'The Birth of Bio-Politics': Michel Foucault's Lecture at the Collège de France on Neo-liberal Governmentality." *Economy and Society* 30 (2): 190–207.

Levi, Robin. 2006. "Doing What Is Medically Necessary." *Off Our Backs* 36 (4): 77–81.

Littlewood, Thomas B. 1977. *The Politics of Population Control*. Notre Dame: University of Notre Dame Press. http://www.getcited.org/pub/101693694.

Ludlow, Jeannie. 2008. "The Things We Cannot Say: Witnessing the Trauma-tization of Abortion in the United States." *Women's Studies Quarterly* 36 (1–2): 28–41.

Luker, Kristin. 1985. *Abortion and the Politics of Motherhood*. Berkeley: University of California Press.

———. 1997. *Dubious Conceptions: The Politics of Teenage Pregnancy*. Cambridge: Harvard University Press.

Luna, Zakiya. 2009. "From Rights to Justice: Women of Color Changing the Face of U.S. Reproductive Rights Organizing." *Societies without Borders* 4 (3) (October 1): 343–65.

Lupton, Deborah. 1997. "Foucault and the Medicalisation Critique." In *Foucault, Health and Medicine*, edited by Robin Bunton and Alan Petersen. London: Routledge.

Mackenzie, Catriona, and Natalie Stoljar. 2000. Introduction to *Relational Autonomy: Feminist Perspectives on Autonomy, Agency, and the Social Self*, edited by Catriona Mackenzie and Natalie Stoljar. New York: Oxford University Press.

MacKinnon, Catharine. 1989. *Toward a Feminist Theory of the State*. Cambridge: Harvard University Press.

———. 2005. *Women's Lives, Men's Laws*. Cambridge, MA: Belknap.

Macleod, Catriona, and Kevin Durrheim. 2002. "Foucauldian Feminism: The Implications of Governmentality." *Journal for the Theory of Social Behaviour* 32 (1): 41–60.

Maher, JaneMaree. 2002. "Visibly Pregnant: Toward a Placental Body." *Feminist Review* 72 (1): 95–107.

Mahmood, Saba. 2005. *Politics of Piety: The Islamic Revival and the Feminist Subject*. Princeton: Princeton University Press.

Martin, Julia. 1996. "On Healing Self/Nature." In *Between Monsters, Goddesses, and Cyborgs: Feminist Confrontations with Science, Medicine, and Cyberspace*, edited by Nina Lykke and Rosi Braidotti. London: Zed Books.

May, Elaine T. 1997. *Barren in the Promised Land: Childless Americans and the Pursuit of Happiness*. Cambridge: Harvard University Press.

McClain, Linda. 1996. "'Irresponsible' Reproduction." *Hastings Law Journal* 47 (2): 339–454.

McDonagh, Eileen L. 1996. *Breaking the Abortion Deadlock: From Choice to Consent*. New York: Oxford University Press.

McNay, Lois. 2000. *Gender and Agency: Reconfiguring the Subject in Feminist and Social Theory*. Cambridge, MA: Polity.

———. 2008. *Against Recognition*. Cambridge, MA: Polity.

McRobbie, Angela. 2008. *The Aftermath of Feminism: Gender, Culture and Social Change*. London: Sage.

Mehaffy, Marilyn Maness. 2000. "Fetal Attractions: The Limit of Cyborg Theory." *Women's Studies* 29 (2): 177–94.

Menon, Nivedita. 2004. *Recovering Subversion: Feminist Politics beyond the Law*. Urbana: University of Illinois Press.

Meyers, Diana. 1989. *Self, Society, and Personal Choice*. New York: Columbia University Press.

———. 1999. "Intersectional Identity and the Authentic Self? Opposites Attract!" In *Relational Autonomy: Feminist Perspectives on Autonomy, Agency, and the Social Self*, edited by Catriona Mackenzie and Natalie Stoljar, 151–80. New York: Oxford University Press.

———. 2001. "The Rush to Motherhood: Pronatalist Discourse and Women's Autonomy." *Signs: Journal of Women in Culture and Society* 26 (3): 735–73.

Mill, John Stuart. 1998. *On Liberty and Other Essays*. New York: Oxford University Press.

Miller, W. B., R. N. Shain, and D. J. Pasta. 1991. "The Pre-and Poststerilization Predictors of Poststerilization Regret in Husbands and Wives." *Journal of Nervous and Mental Disease* 179 (10): 602–3.

———. 1993. "A Model of Pre-sterilization Ambivalence and Post-sterilization Regret in Married Couples." *Advances in Population: Psychosocial Perspectives* 1: 173–206.

Moore, Lori. 2012. "Rep. Todd Akin: 'Legitimate Rape' Statement and Reaction." *New York Times*, August 20, sec. U.S./Politics. http://www.nytimes.com/2012/08/21/us/politics/rep-todd-akin-legitimate-rape-statement-and-reaction.html. Accessed July 21, 2014.

Morell, Carolyn Mackelcan. 1994. *Unwomanly Conduct: The Challenges of Intentional Childlessness*. New York: Routledge.

Mosher, William D., and Christine A. Bachrach. 1996. "Understanding U.S. Fertility: Continuity and Change in the National Survey of Family Growth, 1988–1995." *Family Planning Perspectives* 28 (1) (January): 4.

Mosher, William D., and Jo Jones. 2010. "Use of Contraception in the United States: 1982–2008." *Vital and Health Statistics. Series 23, Data from the National Survey of Family Growth* (29) (August): 1–44.

Muñoz, José Esteban. 2009. *Cruising Utopia: The Then and There of Queer Futurity*. New York: New York University Press.

Munro, Vanessa E., and Jane Scoular. 2012. "Abusing Vulnerability? Contemporary Law and Policy Responses to Sex Work in the UK." *Feminist Legal Studies* 20 (3) (November 1): 189–206.

Myers, Ella. 2008. "Resisting Foucauldian Ethics: Associative Politics and the Limits of the Care of the Self." *Contemporary Political Theory* 7 (2) (May): 125–46.

———. 2013. *Worldly Ethics: Democratic Politics and Care for the World*. Durham: Duke University Press.

Nedelsky, Jennifer. 1989. "Reconceiving Autonomy: Sources, Thoughts and Possibilities." *Yale Journal of Law and Feminism* 1: 7–36.

———. 2011. *Law's Relations: A Relational Theory of Self, Autonomy, and Law*. New York: Oxford University Press.

Okin, Susan Moller. 1989. *Justice, Gender, and the Family*. New York: Basic Books.

Oshana, Marina. 2006. *Personal Autonomy in Society*. Aldershot, UK: Ashgate.

Oudshoorn, Nelly. 1996. "The Decline of the One-Size-Fits-All Paradigm, or, How Reproductive Scientists Try to Cope with Postmodernity." In *Between Monsters, Goddesses, and Cyborgs: Feminist Confrontations with Science, Medicine, and Cyberspace*, edited by Nina Lykke and Rosi Braidotti. London: Zed Books.

Palmer, Julie. 2009. "The Placental Body in 4D: Everyday Practices of Non-diagnostic Sonography." *Feminist Review* 93 (1) (November): 64–80.

Pateman, Carole. 1988. *The Sexual Contract*. Stanford: Stanford University Press.

Paul, Pamela. 2012. "Just How Hard Can It Be to Avoid Getting Pregnant?" *Vogue*, August.

Petchesky, Rosalind. 1981. "Reproductive Choice in the Contemporary United States: A Social Analysis of Female Sterilization." In *And the Poor Get Children: Radical Per-*

spectives on Population Dynamics, edited by Karen Michaelson. New York: Monthly Review Press.

———. 1987. "Fetal Images: The Power of Visual Culture in the Politics of Reproduction." *Feminist Studies* 13 (2) (July 1): 263–92.

Phillips, Macon. 2009. "Responsible Fatherhood: The White House." *White House Blog*, June 21. http://www.whitehouse.gov/blog/Responsible-Fatherhood/. Accessed July 21, 2014.

Pitney, Nico. 2008. "McCain's Birth Control Problem." *Huffington Post*, July 18. http://www.huffingtonpost.com/2008/07/10/mccains-birth-control-pro_n_112048.html.

Poovey, Mary. 1992. "The Abortion Question and the Death of Man." In *Feminists Theorize the Political*, edited by Judith Butler and Joan Wallach Scott. New York: Routledge.

Post, Robert. 2007. "Informed Consent to Abortion: A First Amendment Analysis of Compelled Physician Speech." Faculty Scholarship Series, Paper 170, Yale Law School, New Haven, CT, January 1. http://digitalcommons.law.yale.edu/fss_papers/170. Accessed July 21, 2014.

Post-tubal Coalition. 2006. "Post Tubal Ligation Syndrome (PTLS)." http://tubal.org/VGHPTS.htm. Accessed July 21, 2014.

Price, Kimala. 2010. "What Is Reproductive Justice? How Women of Color Activists Are Redefining the Pro-Choice Paradigm." *Meridians: Feminism, Race, Transnationalism* 10 (2): 42–65.

Ranji, Usha. 2009. "State Medicaid Coverage of Family Planning Services: Summary of State Survey Findings." Publication of the Kaiser Family Foundation and the George Washington University Medical Center, Henry J. Kaiser Family Foundation.

Rapp, Rayna. 2000. *Testing Women, Testing the Fetus: The Social Impact of Amniocentesis in America*. New York: Routledge.

Rasmussen, Claire E. 2011. *The Autonomous Animal: Self-Governance and the Modern Subject*. Minneapolis: University of Minnesota Press.

Reardon, David C. 1996. *Making Abortion Rare: A Healing Strategy for a Divided Nation*. Springfield, IL: Acorn Books.

Roberts, Dorothy. 1991. "Punishing Drug Addicts Who Have Babies: Women of Color, Equality, and the Right of Privacy." *Harvard Law Review* 104 (7) (May): 1419–82.

———. 1998. *Killing the Black Body: Race, Reproduction, and the Meaning of Liberty*. New York: Vintage.

Rose, Nikolas. 1990. *Governing the Soul: The Shaping of the Private Self*. New York: Routledge.

———. 1998. *Inventing Our Selves: Psychology, Power, and Personhood*. New York: Cambridge University Press.

Ross, Loretta. 2006. "Understanding Reproductive Justice." Trust Black Women, November. http://www.trustblackwomen.org/our-work/what-is-reproductive-justice/9-what-is-reproductive-justice. Accessed July 21, 2014.

———. 2008. "Re-enslaving African American Women." *On the Issues*, fall. http://www.ontheissuesmagazine.com/2008fall/cafe2/article/22. Accessed July 21, 2014.

Roth, Rachel. 2003. *Making Women Pay: The Hidden Costs of Fetal Rights*. Ithaca: Cornell University Press.

———. 2004. "'No New Babies?' Gender Inequality and Reproductive Control in the Criminal Justice and Prisons System." *Journal of Gender, Social Policy and the Law* 12 (3): 391–425.

Rousseau, Jean-Jacques. 1964. *The First and Second Discourses*. Edited by Roger D. Masters. Translated by Roger D. Masters and Judith R. Masters. New York: St. Martin's.

———. 1968. *The Social Contract*. Translated by Maurice Cranston. London: Penguin.

———. 1979. *Emile, or On Education*. Translated by Allan Bloom. New York: Basic Books.

Rowland, Robyn. 1987. "Technology and Motherhood: Reproductive Choice Reconsidered." *Signs: Journal of Women in Culture and Society* 12 (3): 512–28.

Rubin, Gayle. 1984. "Thinking Sex: Notes for a Radical Theory of the Politics of Sexuality." In *Pleasure and Danger: Exploring Female Sexuality*, edited by Carole S. Vance, 267–319. London: Routledge.

Rungby, J. A., H. B. Dahl, J. Krogh, and E. Kvist. 1994. "Vasectomy: Who Regrets It and Why?" *Ugeskrift for Laeger* 156 (16) (April 18): 2377–80.

Saletan, William. 2004. *Bearing Right: How Conservatives Won the Abortion War*. Berkeley: University of California Press.

Sandel, Michael. 1998. *Liberalism and the Limits of Justice*. New York: Cambridge University Press.

Sandelowski, Margarete. 1990. "Failures of Volition: Female Agency and Infertility in Historical Perspective." *Signs: Journal of Women in Culture and Society* 15 (3): 475–99.

———. 1994. "Separate, but Less Unequal: Fetal Ultrasonography and the Transformation of Expectant Mother/Fatherhood." *Gender and Society* 8 (2) (June 1): 230–45.

Sanger, Carol. 2008. "Seeing and Believing: Mandatory Ultrasound and the Path to a Protected Choice." *UCLA Law Review* 56 (November 26): 351–408.

Sawicki, Jana. 1991. *Disciplining Foucault: Feminism, Power, and the Body*. London: Routledge.

Saxton, Marsha. 1984. "Born and Unborn." In *Test Tube Women: What Future for Motherhood?*, edited by Rita Arditti, Renate Duelli Klein, and Shelley Minden. London: Pandora.

Schilt, K., and L. Westbrook. 2009. "Doing Gender, Doing Heteronormativity: 'Gender Normals,' Transgender People, and the Social Maintenance of Heterosexuality." *Gender and Society* 23 (4) (July 16): 440–64.

Schmidt, Johannes E., Susan D. Hillis, Polly A. Marchbanks, Gargy Jeng, and Herbert B. Peterson. 2000. "Requesting Information about and Obtaining Reversal after Tubal Sterilization: Findings from the U.S. Collaborative Review of Sterilization." *Fertility and Sterility* 74 (5) (November): 892–98.

Schneider, Anne, and Helen Ingram. 1993. "Social Construction of Target Populations: Implications for Politics and Policy." *American Political Science Review* 87 (2): 334–47.

Schoen, Johanna. 2005. *Choice and Coercion: Birth Control, Sterilization, and Abortion in Public Health and Welfare*. Chapel Hill: University of North Carolina Press.

Schultz, Vicki. 1989. "Room to Maneuver (f)or a Room of One's Own? Practice Theory and Feminist Practice." *Law and Social Inquiry* 14 (1): 123–46.

Scott, Elizabeth S. 2002. "Sterilization of Mentally Retarded Persons: Reproductive Rights and Family Privacy." In *Legal and Ethical Issues in Human Reproduction*, edited by Bonnie Steinbock. Burlington, VT: Ashgate.

Scott, Joan W. 1991. "The Evidence of Experience." *Critical Inquiry* 17 (4): 773–97.

Scoular, Jane. 2010. "What's Law Got to Do with It? How and Why Law Matters in the Regulation of Sex Work." *Journal of Law and Society* 37 (1): 12–39.

Scoular, Jane, and Maggie O'Neill. 2007. "Regulating Prostitution: Social Inclusion, Responsibilization and the Politics of Prostitution Reform." *British Journal of Criminology* 47 (5) (September 1): 764–78.

Scraton, Phil, and Jude McCulloch. 2008. *The Violence of Incarceration*. New York: Taylor and Francis.

Shapiro, Thomas. 1985. *Population Control Politics: Women, Sterilization, and Reproductive Choice*. Philadelphia: Temple University Press.

Shear, Michael D., and Susan Saulny. 2012. "Hilary Rosen's Comments Spark Campaign Debate." *New York Times*, April 12, sec. U.S./Politics. http://www.nytimes.com/2012/04/13/us/politics/hilary-rosens-ann-romney-comments-spark-campaign-debate.html.

Shen, Evelyn. 2006. "Reproductive Justice: Towards a Comprehensive Movement." *Collective Voices* 1 (4): 1–3.

Showden, Carisa R. 2011. *Choices Women Make: Agency in Domestic Violence, Assisted Reproduction, and Sex Work*. Minneapolis: University of Minnesota Press.

Shultz, Marjorie Maguire. 1990. "Reproductive Technology and Intent-Based Parenthood: An Opportunity for Gender Neutrality." *Wisconsin Law Review* 1990: 297–398.

Siegel, Reva. 1992. "Reasoning from the Body: A Historical Perspective on Abortion Regulation and Questions of Equal Protection." *Stanford Law Review* 44 (2) (January): 261–381.

———. 2007. "The New Politics of Abortion: An Equality Analysis of Woman-Protective Abortion Restrictions." *University of Illinois Law Review*, no. 3, 991–1054.

———. 2008. "The Right's Reasons: Constitutional Conflict and the Spread of Woman-Protective Antiabortion Argument." *Duke Law Journal* 57: 1641.

Silliman, Jael, Marlene Gerber Fried, Loretta Ross, and Elena Gutierrez. 2004. *Undivided Rights: Women of Color Organizing for Reproductive Justice*. Cambridge: South End Press.

Silver, Michael G. 2004. "Eugenics and Compulsory Sterilization Laws: Providing Redress for the Victims of a Shameful Era in United States History." *George Washington Law Review* 72: 862–92.

Smith, Anna Marie. 2007. *Welfare Reform and Sexual Regulation*. New York: Cambridge University Press.

Smith, Carole. 2000. "The Sovereign State v. Foucault: Law and Disciplinary Power." *Sociological Review* 48 (2): 283–306.

Snitow, Ann. 1992. "Feminism and Motherhood: An American Reading." *Feminist Review* 40: 32–51.

Solinger, Rickie. 2001. *Beggars and Choosers: How the Politics of Choice Shapes Adoption, Abortion, and Welfare in the United States*. New York: Hill and Wang.

Solomon, Akiba. 2011. "Latinos Fall Prey to the Danger-Womb Epidemic!" *Colorlines*, June 10. http://colorlines.com/archives/2011/06/danger_womb_billboards_now_have.html. Accessed July 21, 2014.

Sourbut, Elizabeth. 1996. "Gynogenesis: A Lesbian Appropriation of Reproductive Technologies." In *Between Monsters, Goddesses, and Cyborgs: Feminist Confrontations with Science, Medicine, and Cyberspace*, edited by Nina Lykke and Rosi Braidotti. London: Zed Books.

South Dakota State Legislature. 2005. "Report of the South Dakota Task Force to Study Abortion." http://www.dakotavoice.com/200601/20060114_1.html. Accessed July 21, 2014.

Spade, Dean. 2006. "Mutilating Gender." In *The Transgender Studies Reader*, edited by Susan Stryker and Stephen Whittle, 315–32. New York: Routledge.

——. 2011. *Normal Life: Administrative Violence, Critical Trans Politics, and the Limits of Law*. New York: South End Press.

Stabile, Carol A. 1992. "Shooting the Mother: Fetal Photography and the Politics of Disappearance." *Camera Obscura* 10 (1 28): 178–205.

——. 1994. *Feminism and the Technological Fix*. Manchester: Manchester University Press.

Stanworth, Michelle. 1987. *Reproductive Technologies: Gender, Motherhood, and Medicine*. Minneapolis: University of Minnesota Press.

Stoljar, Natalie. 2000. "Autonomy and the Feminist Intuition." In *Relational Autonomy: Feminist Perspectives on Autonomy, Agency, and the Social Self*, edited by Catriona Mackenzie and Natalie Stoljar. New York: Oxford University Press.

Stone, Sandy. 2006. "The Empire Strikes Back: A Posttranssexual Manifesto." In *The Transgender Studies Reader*, edited by Susan Stryker and Stephen Whittle. New York: Routledge.

Subramaniam, Vanitha. 1999. "The Impact of Globalization on Women's Reproductive Health and Rights: A Regional Perspective." *Development* 42 (4): 145–49.

Suk, Jeannie. 2010. "The Trajectory of Trauma: Bodies and Minds of Abortion Discourse." *Columbia Law Review* 110 (5): 1193–1252.

Taylor, Janelle. 1998. "Image of Contradiction: Obstetrical Ultrasound in American Culture." In *Reproducing Reproduction: Kinship, Power, and Technological Innovation*, edited by Sarah Franklin and Helena Ragoné. Philadelphia: University of Pennsylvania Press.

Thompson, Charis. 2005. *Making Parents: The Ontological Choreography of Reproductive Technologies*. Cambridge: MIT Press.

Thornton, Margaret. 2006. "Feminism and the Changing State." *Australian Feminist Studies* 21 (50): 151–72.

Velleman, J. David. 2007. "Against the Right to Die." http://www.academia.edu/2048245/Against_the_Right_to_Die. Accessed July 21, 2014.

Volz, Vanessa. 2006. "A Matter of Choice: Women with Disabilities, Sterilization, and Reproductive Autonomy in the Twenty-First Century." *Women's Rights Law Reporter* 27 (3): 203–16.

West, Robin. 1988. "Jurisprudence and Gender." *University of Chicago Law Review* 55 (1): 1–72.

Williams, Joan. 1991. "Gender Wars: Selfless Women in the Republic of Choice." *New York University Law Review* 66: 1559–1634.

Williams, Patricia. 1991. *The Alchemy of Race and Rights: Diary of a Law Professor.* Cambridge: Harvard University Press.

Woods, Nancy Fugate. 1998. "Menopause: Models, Medicine, and Midlife." *Frontiers: A Journal of Women's Studies* 19 (1): 5–19.

Young, Iris Marion. 1995. "Mothers, Citizenship, and Independence: A Critique of Pure Family Values." *Ethics* 105 (3) (April): 535–56.

Zurawin, Robert K. 2009. "Tubal Sterilization." Medscape, October 5. http://emedicine.medscape.com/article/266799-overview. Accessed July 21, 2014.

Zylbergold, Bonnie. 2007. "Are You Kidding?" National Sexuality Resource Center, San Francisco, July 18. http://nsrc.sfsu.edu/article/tubal_ligation_denied. Accessed May 15, 2010.

INDEX

abortion: as an alternative to punishment for some women, 84; association with queerness, 16; and autonomy, 92–93; construction of, 122–124; as counter-conduct, 20, 63–64, 66, 68, 80, 89; as genocide, 86–87, 144, 178; impediments to, 85; importance to sense of self, 58; legal discourse of, 61–68; as marked by injury, 20, 66, 77, 80–81, 107; moral evaluation of, 3, 82, 105, 178; providers, 85, 98, 113, 114, 117; as a public concern, 17, 178

abortion restrictions, 1, 15, 72, 97, 102; in Alabama, 97; in Arizona, 86–87, 103; and autonomy, 86–90, 99, 106, 191; and the Equal Protection Clause, 73–81; and expertise, 121, 123; in Idaho, 113; justification of using feminist arguments, 107, 116; in Ohio, 110; in Oklahoma, 113; rape and incest exceptions, 92, 114; in South Dakota, 98–100, 112–113, 116–118, 120–121, 123; subversive potential of, 57–58; in Texas, 99–100, 103, 114; and the woman/mother link, 64, 74, 87, 100–101, 126, 173, 184; in Virginia, 97, 138. See also *Gonzales v. Carhart*; informed consent laws; *Minnesota v. Rounds* (2011) *(Rounds I)*; *Minnesota v. Rounds* (2012) *(Rounds II)*; Partial Birth Abortion Act; *Planned Parenthood v. Casey*; *Roe v. Wade*; suicide advisories; *Texas Medical Providers v. Lakey*; ultrasound mandates; woman-protective antiabor-

tion arguments; Woman's Right to Know Act (Texas)

abortion rights, 86–88, 116, 118, 125; as enabling of increased governance of women, 61–62, 81, 86, 106, 111; framed as a woman's interest in privacy, 116; transformative potential of, 19–20, 63–66, 68–69, 72, 75, 79–80, 89–90, 94–96, 184, 188; undermined by informed consent laws, 99. See also antidiscrimination argument; antisubordination argument

Affordable Care Act, 103, 133

agency, 7–9, 43–44, 47, 54–55; relation to social construction of the subject, 19, 28, 48

Aid to Families with Dependent Children with Temporary Assistance for Needy Families, 104

Allen, Amy, 5, 44, 47

American Civil Liberties Union, 167

anti-coercion provisions, 98, 100, 113, 117, 120; co-optation of feminist ideas by, 106

antidiscrimination argument, 65–66, 73, 75, 88–89, 96, 125, 184–185

antisubordination argument, 73–75; depoliticization of abortion by, 20, 65–66, 79, 184–185; faults of, 75–80, 89, 91, 125–126

Asian Communities for Reproductive Justice, 181

Association for Voluntary Sterilization, 166

ABOUT THE AUTHOR

Jennifer M. Denbow is Assistant Professor of Political Science at California Polytechnic State University in San Luis Obispo.